1992–2006

PURPLE ANTHOLOGY

Aballea, Martine
25
Acconci, Vito
204
Ackermann, Rita
45, 114, 153, 179, 204,
225, 234, 235, 244, 265
Ackermann, Haider
260
Aitken, Doug
102, 103, 131
Antich, Alex
122, 170, 182
Argento, Asia
221
Armleder, John
224
Auermann, Nadja
214
Aurell, Annette
221, 233
Bag, Alex
67, 68, 69
Bailly, Pierre
215
Baldessari, John
242
Bambou
161
Beckwith, Patterson
116, 117, 122
Beecroft, Vanessa
40, 41, 53, 82, 106
Belhaj Kacem, Mehdi
179, 182, 196

Benat, Leatitia
73, 114, 173, 179, 182,
188, 196, 212, 213, 219,
245, 263
Benderson, Bruce
134
Berman, David
87, 179
Bernadette Corporation
84, 98, 122
Bertoli, Giasco
148, 149, 151
Bickerton, Ashley
233
Bidault-Waddington, Camille
92, 167, 268
Bogawa, Roddy
16, 41
Bond, Henry
24
Borthwick, Mark
66, 72, 73, 75, 82, 88, 99,
125, 140, 141, 150, 178,
186, 187, 221, 222, 223,
224
Bosé, Eleonora
151
Bougatsos, Lizzi
122, 196, 218, 244, 263
Browstone, Catherine
26, 27
Brunnquell, Christophe
197, 211, 233, 261
Calderon, Miguel
180, 181

Cattelan, Maurizio
26, 27, 73, 107, 179, 186,
187, 189, 204, 218
Caven, Ingrid
255
Cennotoglu, Banu
89, 114, 182
Christensen, Helena
268
Christie, Donald
257
Cianciolo, Susan
83, 103, 108, 114, 120,
145, 224
Closky, Claude
110
Cole, Todd
260
Comme des Garçons
88, 109, 111, 150, 161
Dalle, Béatrice
233
Day, Corinne
178
De La Barra, Pablo Leon
260
Decter, Joshua
142
Deland, Colin
115, 170
Deneuve, Catherine
154, 167
Diekgerdes, Horst
92, 268
D'Orazio, Sante
244

Dubosc, Anna
219
Dunning, Jeanne
16
Duras, Marguerite
214, 232
Edstrom, Anders
66, 67, 74, 81, 87, 92,
109, 120, 127, 170, 172,
179, 211
Eggleston, William
130
Einarsson, Gardar Eide
257
Eldridge, Susan
210, 214, 215
Elkan, Judy
114, 182
Elson, Karen
161, 164, 165
Eri
189
Even, Pierre
233
Fassbinder, Rainer Werner
211, 235, 255
Fillieres, Helene
66
Fleiss, Elein
68, 69, 103, 114, 115,
145, 184, 185, 188
Gallo, Vincent
264, 265, 266
General Idea
16, 144, 147
Genzken, Isa
190

Ghesquière, Nicolas
151, 169, 189, 222, 223
Gibson, William
58, 59
Gokita, Tomoo
183
Goldberg, Natanael
80, 109, 115
Goldfarb, Seth
215
Goldwyn, Liz
120
Gonzales, Mark
134
Gonzalez-Foerster,
Dominique
28
Gonzalez-Torres, Felix
28
Gordon, Kim
12, 13, 93, 170, 224
Graham, Dan
115, 160
Griffin, Tim
142
Guillen, Mauricio
82
Hall, John S.
25, 38, 39
Hearn, Pat
170
Homma, Takashi
82, 108, 188, 203, 204
Huyghe, Pierre
57
Jacobs, Marc
168, 226, 227, 243, 269

Johnston, Daniel
204
Joisten, Bernard
27, 37, 58, 59
Kern, Richard
47, 110, 202
Kerrigan, Lodge
145
Knes, Heinz Peter
270, 271
Koether, Jutta
12, 13, 57, 123, 127
Kokosalaki, Sophia
167
Korine, Harmony
71, 87, 132, 133
Krasilcic, Marcelo
86, 92, 106, 125, 135,
145
Lalique, René
212, 213
Lang, Helmut
93, 115, 128, 129, 145,
152
Leblon, Serge
191
Lebon, Jasmine
256
Leccia, Ange
72, 103, 134
Leguillon, Pierre
142
Leonard, Zoe
107
Leveque, Claude
92, 115, 190

Lindell, John
103, 142
Lindvall, Angela
88, 220, 221
Lonsdale, Michael
214
Lum, Ken
58, 59
Lutz
66, 151, 161
Maeda, Yukinori
173, 253
Manetas, Miltos
45, 81, 82
Manzon, Serge
211
Margiela, Martin
26, 29, 32, 33, 82, 89,
114, 150, 170, 252
Marshall, Chan
150, 155
Mastroianni, Chiara
166, 167
McCracken, John
104
McGinley, Ryan
188
McMenamy, Kristen
227, 243
Messager, Annette
115
Messe, Jonathan
233
Miss, Kittin
182
Moisdon, Stéphanie
224

Moor, Chris
170, 202
Mori, Mariko
56
Moss, Kate
161, 162, 163, 168, 232
Nagashima, Yurie
60, 61
Nakahira, Takuma
204, 218
Newton, Helmut
255
Nickas, Bob
142
Nicky
86, 92
O'Brien, Glenn
255, 268
ODB
234
Oldham, Will
202
Opie, Catherine
242
O'Rourke, Jim
204
Owen, Kirsten
202
Owens, Rick
242
Peckinpah, Sam
198, 199
Peyton, Elizabeth
63, 221
Phillips, Bijou
232

Pierson, Jack
37, 100, 101, 128, 129, 189

Pilati, Stefano
257

Pitt, Brad
129

Pop, Iggy
131

Prince, Richard
112, 113, 115, 123, 136, 137, 152, 158, 159, 171, 230, 244, 257

Rahlwes, Katja
104, 153, 167, 172, 211, 214, 216, 217, 256

Rampling, Charlotte
182

Ranaldo, Lee
54

Rayder, Frankie
215

Rian, Jeff
68, 69, 142, 244

Ribeiro, Vava
232, 242

Richardson, Terry
90, 91, 94, 95, 104, 121, 125, 132, 133, 143, 151, 154, 155, 161, 164, 165, 166, 167, 168, 169, 171, 189, 196, 204, 206, 207, 210, 214, 215, 220, 224, 230, 231, 238, 239, 240, 241, 255, 256, 257, 261, 264, 265, 268

Richardson, Bob
143, 261

Robbins, David
37

Roitfeld, Carine
248, 254

Rourke, Mickey
238, 239

Roversi, Paolo
215

Roy, Henri
174, 175, 182, 191, 218, 262

Sagnier, Ludivine
174, 175

Sanai, Masafumi
126, 173

Sassen, Viviane
124, 125

Saville, Peter
196, 257

Sevigny, Chloë
71, 140, 141, 169, 221, 222, 223, 230, 231, 258, 259

Seymour, Stephanie
238, 239, 240, 241

Seyrig, Delphine
214

Sherman, Cindy
31

Shields, Brooke
244

Slimane, Hedi
233, 238

Snow, Dash
257

Sobieski, Leelee
268

Sorrenti, Mario
76, 77

Sorrenti, Vanina
151

Spencer, John
121

St Hill, Tara
178

Star, Zora
99, 215

Stegner, Julia
216, 217

Subkoff, Tara
233

Suzuki, Chikashi
189, 204

Swinton, Tilda
260

Takahashi, Kyoji
178

Tatsuno, Koji
80

Teller, Juergen
127, 161, 162, 163, 172,
220, 221, 226, 227, 243,
255, 269

Thompson, Anna
191, 204

Tillmans, Wolfgang
20, 21, 36, 42, 43, 48, 49,
57, 71, 83, 143, 173, 182,
188, 190, 192, 193, 196,
200, 201

Tremblay, John
142

Van Lamsweerde, Inez
52, 54

Van Lamsweerde, Inez
& Matadin, Vinoodh
84, 232, 248, 254, 258,
259, 268

Viktor & Rolf
31, 47, 94, 95, 108, 111

Vilmouth, Jean Luc
25

Vivier, Camille
99

Vojnovic, Natasa
167

Vydia & Jean Michel
44, 46, 57, 70, 81

Walzac, Antek
173

Watanabe, Junya
82

Waters, John
202

Wawrzyniak, Martynka
202, 232

Wesson, Amy
151

Wool, Christopher
268, 269

Wyn Evans, Cerith
173, 201

Zahm, Olivier
18, 28, 32, 33, 46, 54,
73, 87, 103, 255, 266

Zittel, Andrea
17, 83

An alternative magazine is a poetic and political response. We launched *Purple Prose* in the early 1990s without any means, and without any experience, because we wanted to make a magazine that was radically different. We wanted to support the artists around us no one else supported, who were much less talked about. We wanted nothing to do with the demands of advertising or advertisers. Writing exhibition reviews based on press releases was out of the question. We didn't want to publish theory or criticism; we thought that most of the time it was irrelevant in art magazines. We wanted to make a magazine that reflected the way we were, and the way we wanted to live. A magazine that was the direct and spontaneous expression of the vision of the artists we invited to write for, photograph for, and participate in, *Purple Prose*. In 1992, faced with the crumbling of social utopias and artistic avant-gardes–the result of the Postmodernism of the 1980s, and of the triumph of capitalist simulation (Jean Baudrillard) over every other suggestion of desire–the only possible path for us seemed to be an independent label. This took shape at the beginning of the 1990s, in a global alternative movement in music, film, and art galleries such as American Fine Art and Air de Paris. But it was no longer "underground," in the political sense of the word widely used in the 1970s. Counterculture was disappearing; the new movement started as a commercial simulation (think back to Kate Moss in Calvin Klein ads by David Sims, or Madonna's book, *Sex*, shot by Steven Meisel). Our idea at *Purple* was to try and activate subtle subversion from within the system, not from outside of it, as the purity of the underground's ethic had always demanded. Certainly we were against the hyper-capitalistic evolution of all systems of art and fashion. But we'd lost any kind of naïve fantasies of rebellion, dreams of revolution, or Punk visions of destruction and chaos. The times were far more complex. And far more interesting. We had to invent a different way of expressing a true and radical opposition that was light and delicate. One that was political but not militant, esthetic but not pretentious, sexual but not pornographic. One that was filled with love but not sentimentality, generous and lucid, non-philosophical in the vein of Gilles Deleuze, Jacques Lacan, and later, Alain Badiou, and open to abstract forms. It would be a form of opposition of our own, different from the critical jargon of the generation of 1968. A generation, incidentally, that

took power and blocked every other vision of the time, including that of the contemporary art media. A generation from which, nevertheless, we descended.

We understood one thing: A single negation was no longer relevant. A double negation was absolutely necessary. Let me try to explain. The magazine we envisioned was not going to express the first conventional alternative, that of the negation of the underground, but the alternative to the alternative, the double negation. However abstract this may seem, it's really only an instinctive attitude, one that continues to be relevant in 2008. Double negation isn't a simple position; it involves reacting to all the complexity of contemporary situations. It's a position open to poetic blur, double play, intimate withdrawal, generosity, multiple identities, mystery, abstraction, and conceptual fluidity. It's a simulation of simulations, but also of dissimulations. We curated an exhibition called *L'Hiver de l'Amour* at the Musée d'Art Moderne de la Ville de Paris (which we later mounted at P.S.1 in Queens as *Winter of Love*) that transposed this position. From the start, *Purple*'s conceptual territory has been chiaroscuro, double-edged, ambiguous, on the verge of abstraction. It refuses to explain itself or offer apology. It's an artistic position still largely unexplored.

For many years the magazine was associated with a realist esthetic, that of the new photography of the early 1990s–of photographers like Juergen Teller, Terry Richardson, Wolfgang Tillmans, and Mario Sorrenti. From a visual standpoint, we represented the break from '80s imagery (like Richard Avedon's photography for Versace, for example). From an artistic standpoint, the artists from the early 1990s were rising up against art as capitalist fetish; they were aligning themselves with the artistic social and political practices of the 1970s–those of performance, video art, Fluxus, and the conceptual and minimalist avant-garde. Our magazine was an integral part of this burgeoning context, which included the deconstruction of fashion by Martin Margiela and Comme des Garçons; the return of subtle political art, with that of Felix Gonzalez-Torres, Maurizio Cattelan, and Philippe Parreno, among others; the photography of Juergen Teller and Terry Richardson; and Harmony Korine's and Larry Clark's independent filmmaking. *Purple* emerged directly out of this artistic context, and our esthetics, like our editorial decisions, were, and still are, directly connected to it, and that which results from it. We continue to depend on this context, but *Purple*'s "realism" is not only an esthetic matter: it also involves a paradoxical relationship with Guy Debord's *Society of the Spectacle*, and includes fashion, art, and magazines. We thought it was entirely possible to fight against the ugliness, standardization, violence, and vulgarity that marked the triumph of industrial culture over the avant-garde. This meant we had to reconsider everything: Which texts should be published? What images interested us? Which designers? Which sexuality? Which forms of art? Which desires? Fifteen years later, we're still asking ourselves the same questions, but in a context that has changed radically: Debord's "integrated spectacle" has become global virtual reality. But there is still the same political need and relevance. This is why it still makes sense to put out a magazine like *Purple* today—it has its raison d'être in the age of the Internet, in the age of generalized cultural consumption and virtual amnesia.

A magazine is a dream—to quote the artist Robert Filiou, "a butterfly's dream, but which one?" Seemingly light, with an extreme economic fragility, and a lifespan lasting only a few weeks, a magazine is capable of action that deeply affects the propagation of ideas, beauty, and their explosive power. It's the dream of a group of people who share, and experiment with, a singular vision and a desire for change and escape—without necessarily knowing how to articulate it. All in a time when everyone feels change is impossible, a lost cause. A magazine is not exactly media, in the sense of information; it is a visual, textual space that can shape a generation. In its pages, a generation invents itself, finds itself, and deceives itself. In saying that *Purple* is the portrait of a generation, I mean a portrait of those who embody their times. At the same time, it's a portrait of myself and Elein Fleiss, our ideas, our lives, and our esthetic. If a magazine doesn't reflect its creators, it has no real reason to exist—it's just more press, a vehicle for information transmitted through images and articles that has no real quality. All the magazines that inspired us, like *Interview, Ray Gun, Nova,* and *File* by General Idea or *Helmut Newton's Illustrated*, have this personal touch. In our magazine we wanted to resurrect the old utopian ideals that narrow the gap between art and life. And we wanted, and continue

to want, our lives to be the grounds of possibility. Ambitious? Perhaps. But, there was, and is, nothing else interesting enough for us to attempt to achieve.

Purple was, and continues to be today, something worth holding on to, at all costs, even while up against the overwhelming laws of business and the virtual dimension of cultural consumption. What is *Purple*'s dream? To escape the syndromes of depression, by celebrating art as the only true antidote to cultural consumption. Art as creation is superior to cultural consumption. This has been *Purple*'s credo from the beginning, a credo that connects us to the reality of our lives, and strengthens our desire to change our way of life. *Purple* asserts that art is the reality point that you should never let go of, and that we have access to it through the magazine itself. We declare loud and clear, with all the means of the virtual world if necessary, that art as creation is superior to culture as consumption, no matter how hip and contemporary that culture may be. In this sense, the magazine's realism is not only a question of photographic or artistic esthetics. The magazine itself is a reality point, an exception to the commercial rules of other magazines, as well as to the anti-commercial stance of the underground. From this point of view, *Purple*'s independence is an editorial position that continuously strives for liberation by piercing through the artificial and downward spiraling bubble of capitalist virtuality. This may be impossible to achieve and end in failure. But this is our position, and we hold it not with a sense of arrogance or snobbery, but with an instinct for survival. The alternative to the alternative was, and remains, open territory, a place where *Purple* has been an antecedent. And while *Purple* has been copied widely—or has at least inspired many other magazines—it is less because of its esthetic, which has been called "realist" and anti-fashion, than because it cleared a path: the alternative to the alternative. This path does not live by the laws of business or media marketing that lead to the domination of commercial criteria. Nor does it live by the purist discretion of an underground cult magazine that clings to its righteousness as it falls and fails, devoting itself only to depression and the metaphysics of The End, as it details the world's rush to ruin. *Purple* is a dream that keeps the desire alive.

interview
Jutta Koether

We are Kitten
and we're better than you...

Jens Jorgensen & Jim Spring

Kim Gordon and Julie Cafritz

Kitten *is a band with just two guitar players:*
Kim Gordon from Sonic Youth and Julie Cafritz, who played in the first line-up of Pussy Galore
and in several other bands like SPT, Action Swingers and even once with the Velvet Monkeys.
Kim also has an artists' approach, she studied art, abandoned it for music and is responsible
for the making of the covers of Sonic Youth. Their shows last 25 minutes and deal with thin asses,
violence and being shopping victims. They are full of in-jokes ("Thurston Moore - what a bore"
- Thurston Moore from Sonic Youth usually does the live-mix for Kitten). Their music blends
aggressiveness with tenderness, as both qualities are found in the music they're listening to: Punk,
Hardcore, Rap plus the music they used to play in their several other bands.
They wear kitten-necklaces, Ski-caps or baseball-caps with cannabis leaves. They include all kinds
of female issues in their performance; from style to the latest pro-choice demonstration in
Washington. Kim's favourite phrase "Women are anarchists". Every possible use of the guitar
is allowed and used during their performance. Their last song is always a question/answer-play
that refers to the situation, in which they perform: the venue, the group they are opening for,
and so on. This caused trouble from time to time, when the next group felt attacked or ridiculed.
But their latest problem as feminist anarchists might even force them to change their name,
before they are going to release their first record (in September): a woman confronted them after

ether: *The last line of your set is always:*
Kitten and we're better than you…"

that's the punk-rock-thing, that when you attack
or something, you triumphed already.

e it's more a rap thing. In punk-rock bands were
, but they were'nt talking that much about it,
o-groups are boasting about, who is better.

that point very little in the song is scripted,

e idea, to do something free outside of the
gs you're doing ?

plays in a very structured band. But in all thor
were in, we were not alone, we were for example
m section. I was expected to stay even when the
d me were going off in jam, he has a considerable
freedom.

o be a future of this punk attitude:
to it, with a very deliberate move to
eestyle.

n lot of free music there she is playing the guitar
ng bass in Sonic Youth, and we both chang
tuning and I maybe masked my guitar playing.
n conventional and
play the lead guitar, but I don't like the lead gu
o listen to it. I can see that they are more f
an to listen to it. And I'm not vaguely more
by lead-guitarrists.

though I still think they should not be doing this
ressed that they can do it. But I wish they

ut the performing aspect? I mean, you do
ings on stage. You also do a lot in Sonic
t this expressiveness… Like rolling around
sting…

e not doing it…

sting for… like Kim is the straight man and I'm
questions that I have set up, basically; so she is
man and I am the goofy one. But then she just
olls around the floor.

did that come about? Did it just happen?
k.

)

nted to do all the clichés, like playing the strings
th.

Thurston usually goes off into his own
world and Lee reacts to it. And Lee is
very positive towards Thurston.
But what I do stop when she stops
mostly I stop before her…
K: That's another thing. Boys usually
don't see the benefit in not everyone
playing at once, in stopping and
letting the other person play…

I STOLE
MY SISTER'S
BOYFRIEND.
IT WAS ALL
WHIRLWIND,
HEAT, AND
FLASH. WITH-
IN A WEEK
WE KILLED
MY PARENTS
AND HIT THE
ROAD.

GED 24297
DGCD 24297

Cover by Raymond Pettibon

J: They don't listen. Well, one reason is
that they play their instruments longer
and so, within a song they don't have
to listen and to keep track with what
the others are doing. Because they
know it. I always had to be painfully
aware of the others.

It began in Paris at the end of 1989, when a man and a woman–Olivier Zahm and myself–met. I was twenty-one. He was twenty-six. From day one, it was love.
In the months that followed we travelled–to New York, to Cologne. We went to galleries, and spent our time with French, American, Italian, and German artists.
We watched the work of filmmakers like David Lynch and Jean-Luc Godard. Our lives were light and carefree. Olivier lived in the third district, near the Centre Pompidou. I lived in the sixth, on Rue des Saints-Pères. He wrote about art. I collected it, and had just organized my first exhibition.

At the time, people were getting their first computers. We all communicated by fax. Cell phones and the Internet didn't exist. There were still smoking cars on trains.

One day in 1992, while Olivier and I were walking down the staircase of my building, I had an idea. Why not start a magazine? A few months before, a new contemporary art magazine was launched in France, but it didn't speak to us. We needed to share our viewpoints and intuitions. Olivier had envisioned projects with other people, but they never got off the ground. For me, though, it was all new. We weren't afraid of problems or obstacles because we didn't imagine they existed. We had no experience with publishing, graphic design, printing, advertising, or distribution. All we had was boundless enthusiasm.

The magazine we wanted to make would know no boundaries–not of geography, or of genre. It would be a venue to create and experiment. It would represent our desires, and describe our encounters. Artists would help with the concept–it would be not only a magazine about artists, but a kind of artist's notebook. We were wary of dogmatic criticism, stifling theory, and pretentious discourse. We were also circumspect of London and "English Art." The Paris–New York connection was a key one for us, as a Paris–Tokyo one would be a bit later. Contemporary art would be the launching pad from which we could access music, film, fashion, and dance. We would interact with the people around us, people we met, whether they were French or not. The texts we published would be in French and English, without translations.

We thought about a name for weeks. I wanted to use the name of a color, something in line with the work of Dominique Gonzalez-Foerster, like her "color rooms." She was our friend, and helped us with the concept of the magazine. I liked purple–the color and the word. Dike Blair, a New York artist and a great friend who collaborated on the magazine from the start, suggested "Purple Prose." The name, which is practically impossible for any French person to pronounce, stuck.

One evening at dinner in a Paris brasserie, the artist Claude Closky expressed to us his concern about our lack of publishing experience. He earned his living as a graphic designer and offered his help in making a mock-up of *Purple Prose*. My little computer wasn't up to the task, but Jennifer Flay, whose gallery exhibited artists we were close to, invited us to come work on her computer after-hours. Closky and I would arrive at seven p.m. The first nights we worked until midnight. Soon it was three a.m., then daybreak, then when Jennifer and her assistants arrived to open up at ten. Time to go! Every night we worked I made Earl Grey tea for Closky and myself, and we'd drink cup after cup. No alcohol. Closky has a very unique sense of humor, and we were often bursting with laughter. I learned the profession of graphic design from watching him putting *Purple Prose* together those nights on end.

On October 21, 1992, the same day Madonna's book, *Sex*, came out, we launched *Purple Prose*, *Issue One* at the bookstore in the Musée d'Art Moderne in Paris.

Previous spread: We are Kitten and We're Better Than You, Julie Cafritz and Kim Gordon interviewed by Jutta Koether, photograph by Jens Jorgensen and Jim Spring, Purple Prose #1

Elein Fleiss

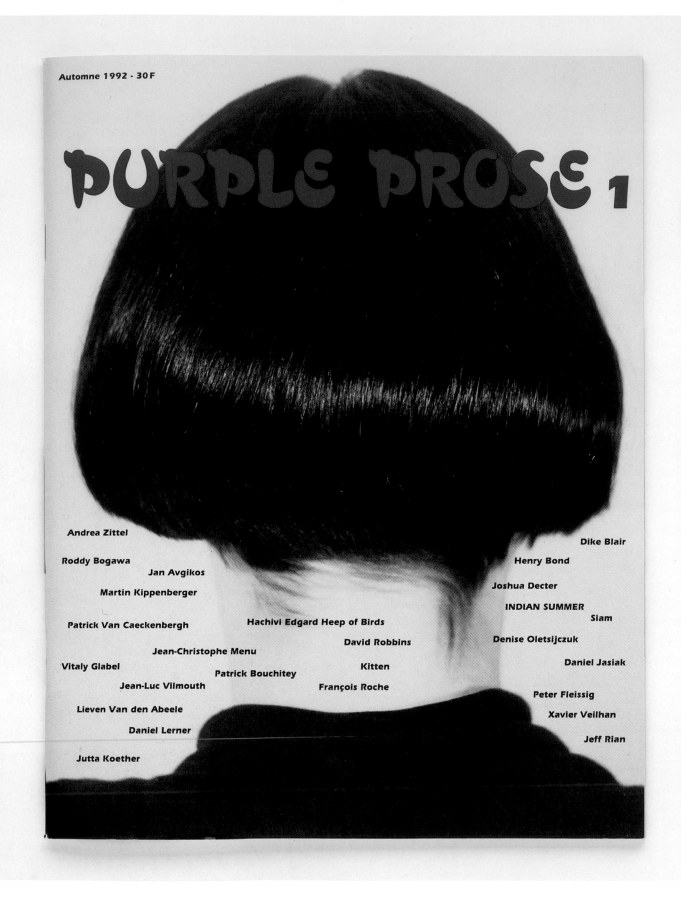

Cover, Head 2, photograph by Jeanne Dunning, Purple Prose #1

Areas of Investigation, Andrea Zittel interviewed by Benjamin Weil, Purple Prose #1

The Maine Thing, text by Daniel Lerner, photographs by Daniel Lerner, Purple Prose #1
The World's a Mess, It's in My Kiss, text by Roddy Bogawa, photograph by Roddy Bogawa, Purple Prose #1

Une civilisation s'élève toujours sur la destruction de la précédente. Avec le laminage des civilisations amérindiennes, l'Amérique n'a pas fait exception, d'autant qu'elle n'a jamais su vraiment maquiller le crime originel. Dans les westerns des années 50-60 peut-être, mais certainement pas dans les pubs Malboro, ni dans la figure récente du

DANSE
AVEC
LES ARTISTES

Olivier Zahm

Serial Killer, dernier avatar de cette violence fondatrice.

Car l'Amérique est la seule civilisation contemporaine à faire de la violence son sens ultime. Non seulement violence des rapports sociaux, des relations éthniques et inter-culturelles, mais de tous les rapports. Violence de tous les instants, fonctionnalisée, plus ou moins canalisée, faite valeurs et monnaie courante. Ce qui s'échange aux Etats-Unis, et ce qui fait sens, fait violence.

Mais ce n'est pas seulement contre cette loi, c'est-à-dire contre l'oppression des minorités amérindiennes (Native Americans) par la culture dominante, que s'élève l'oeuvre de Hachivi Edgar Heap of Birds. Pas plus qu'il ne faut lire ses mots d'ordre, sorte de "Truisms" (Jenny Holzer) emportés par le vent mauvais de la plaine amérindienne, comme une simple revendication

Politically Correct ou Politically Cheyenne.

Comme chez tous les vrais artistes de ce continent, Heap of Birds est lui aussi du côté de la Violence originelle, c'est-à-dire du côté de l'Amérique réelle, non de son Rêve. Ce qui veut dire pour lui, en tant que "Native American", prendre le parti de la Nature américaine, non de sa Culture (le cinéma, l'image). La violence US n'est pas selon lui qu'une machine culturelle à broyer les minorités (les lettres d'HOLLYWOOD), mais une force naturelle (la COLLINE du même nom). S'il s'insurge contre la violence, ce n'est pas tant contre celle qui extermina ses "ancêtres", mais contre son maquillage dans des fictions matérielles (l'image américaine). Alors que la vraie violence, celle du continent américain, est d'abord géologique, minérale et végétale.

Les mots-vents, les mots-saisons, les mots-continent de Heap of Birds sont le langage d'une violence américaine originelle, celle d'avant la mort de sa culture amérindienne, celle de l'événement géologique d'un continent : cataclysmes naturels, immensité des déserts et montagnes, brutalité des paysages vierges, blocs minéraux de violence à l'échelle cosmique, avec lesquels les "Native Américans" avaient appris à danser et vivre ("LOVE EARTH"), sans chercher à les domestiquer (parc naturel et réserves).

Une langue de la terre, du sol et de l'herbe circule dans les slogans de Heap of Birds, non pas une langue politique (de la cité). Une langue qui fait de la violence US une géologie, une minéralogie, une étendue inhumaine et climatique : "NO TIME JUST SEASON".

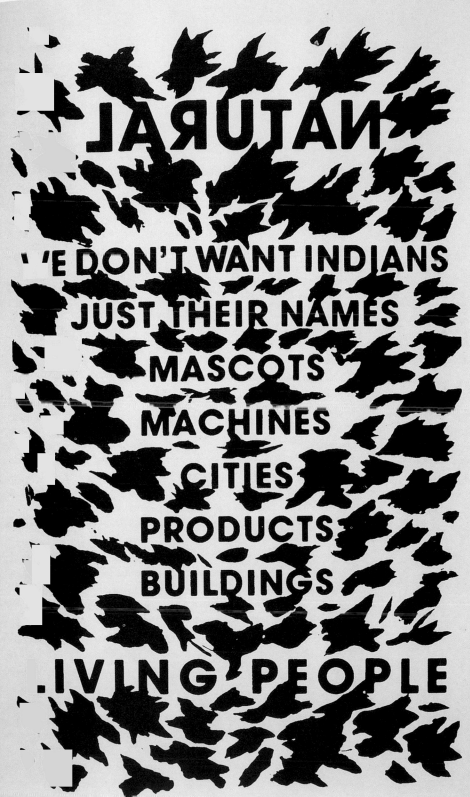

NATURAL

'E DON'T WANT INDIANS

JUST THEIR NAMES

MASCOTS

MACHINES

CITIES

PRODUCTS

BUILDINGS

.IVING PEOPLE

Hachivi Edgar Heap of Birds "Telling Many Magpies, Telling Black Wolf, Telling Hachivi", 1989

Danse avec les artistes, text by Olivier Zahm, drawing by Hachivi Edgar Heap of Birds, Purple Prose #1

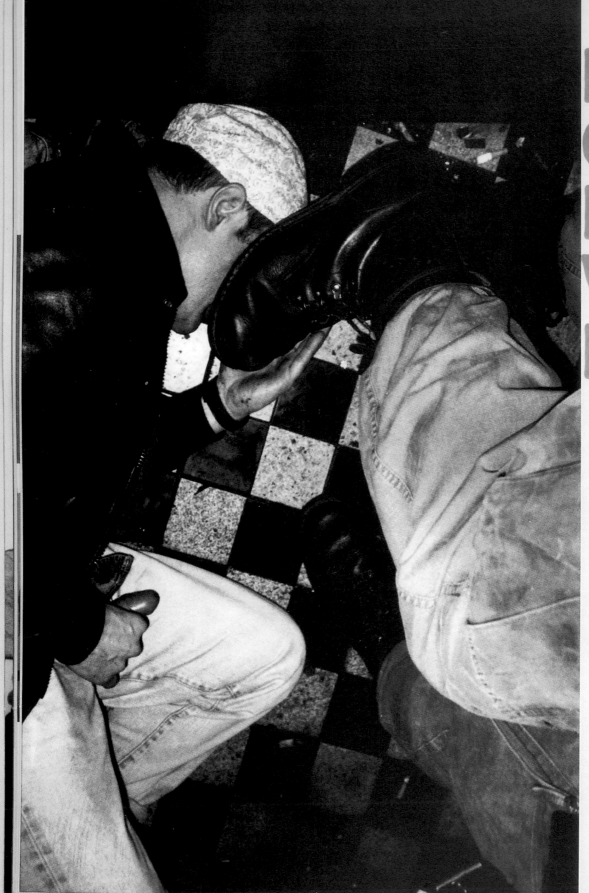

PEA-CE MO-VE-MENT

WOLFGANG
TILLMANS

SM role play,
Stiefelknecht,
Cologne, 1993

antifascist
short-haired
punk,
Berlin, 1992

I spent most of 1993 in New York City. After wandering between the worlds of Cologne and New York for a few years, I decided to stay in New York, and for the next 14 years I did. Total Transition. Although, at first it didn't feel like it.

The art-scene was definitely located in SoHo back then. There were a lot of experimental galleries, and temporary motions. People were talking about things, rare things, almost unthinkable things.

I remember it being a somewhat torturous time, but it was exciting, and I was exposed to quite a few new perspectives. I attended the Whitney program in 92–93, finishing up in May '93. I re-read Walter Benjamin in English, which was difficult for me.

I started to get interested in the idea of affects and how they determine and shape artistic production. I made big colorful paintings, developing and indexing affects/ expressions. In paint, in conceptual moves, and in social structures.

I remember hanging out in the studio on Lafayette Street a lot. Part of the night crew. One of my studio neighbors was Mariko Mori. Others included Lyle Ashton Harris, Johan, Lynn Yamamoto, and Michael Richards, who died in the events of 9-11. I also had a temporary studio situation at the then quite decrepit PS1 building. Being almost alone in there at night was very lonely, and very creepy. There was a lot of subway riding that year. Lots of lugging stuff from one place to another. Lots of trips to Pearl Paints.

My first New York solo show was mounted at the Pat Hearn Gallery. Title: *Affective Imports (Antibodies I-V!)* All big paintings. Not the most popular medium of artistic discourse at the time, but maybe that was a good thing.

I remember hanging out on the stoops at 39 Wooster Street a lot. I was heavily into red-green contrasts, biting colors, and extreme but non-authentic directness. Heavy, yet exploding with content. It was also the time people began making funky photo-shopped flyers. I made paintings based on the compositional structures of flyers for raves like the "Disco 2000" events at Limelight, which were decadent, colorful, ugly, and druggy. I liked to go there totally sober, and get assaulted by everything, and then use that sensory overload as a parameter to make a painting.

Other memories: Pat Hearn, Colin de Land, and their scenes. Lots of get-togethers and parties. Having tea with Mary Heilmann or Renee Green. Seeing a lot of bands every week, and writing about music on a regular basis. I didn't listen to anything old in 1993, only contemporary music. I saw lots of music shows, and often went to "The Cooler" club in the meat market area of (pre-gentrified) Chelsea.

Kim Gordon and Daisy Cafritz put on their X-girl fashion open-air runway shows on the same block on Wooster Street, and I was one of their non-model models. I still have the clothes I modeled. They're my work clothes when I go back to Europe in the summers.

Nineteen ninety-three marked the beginning of my living more seriously in NYC. I had high hopes, and there were blissful events. But there were struggles too, and extreme creepiness. I did things I would not do today. I went to Princeton on my birthday to hang out at the Record Exchange and some bookshops. While I was there the first reports from Waco came in over the radio. Nineteen ninety-three was also the year of the first World Trade Center bombing, as well as the Bombay Stock Exchange bombing. The media focused in on terrorism. The first wave of terrorism. Or some wave of terrorism, which has not stopped rolling around. I guess it was the beginning of what became known as Global Terrorism and marked the debut of the new century for everybody.

Death all around. In 1993 there was a bad Neo-Nazi incident in Solingen, Germany. Five Turkish women were killed. Mayhem guitarist Euronymus was stabbed to death by his sort-of-former-buddy Count Grishnack. Frank Zappa died of cancer. So did Mick Ronson. GG Allin overdosed. Leo Ferrer passed away. And Sun Ra…well, I don't think he really died, he just moved into a sphere somewhere that had always been his real world.

Then there was the extremely sticky-all-over hit by Whitney Houston, "I Will Always Love You," that tried to grab a hold on us. Of course, it wasn't real. Well, then again, maybe it was. But the idea of reality had already taken a big turn.

We all started getting sucked into the virtual world. The transition from the analogue world to the digital one was starting….Some music that was defiant of it all: *Houdini* by The Melvins, *In Utero* by Nirvana, *Where You Been* by Dinosaur Jr., *4-Track Demos* by PJ Harvey, and, of course, Free Kitten's music at their live shows. I also remember the ugly, numbing-all-over hits by Pearl Jam, and Aerosmith's *Get A Grip*.

Prince announced that he was changing his name to a symbol.

Somehow, things that were so self-assuredly posed began falling apart. But new forms emerged, forms that continue to be built and modified, such as alternative rock, which peaked with Nirvana's *In Utero* and then integrated progressive influences and new technology, as in the music of Radiohead and Tool.

I think 1993 was the year I learned how to use a gun.

Yet, all this did not stop the beginning of some kind of abyss. The opening up. The total unrest of Becoming.

There were the first so-called free elections in the former Soviet Union. The question of what is, who is, and what functions as a democracy was debated in a new way. This was true for Americans as well; the first Iraq war was over, but in the U.S. a nagging feeling still lingered.

There was a huge blizzard in New York. Really huge. Never saw anything like it. Then, for a moment, it was so quiet. So extreme in its softness.

Since then, well, the affects were imported, and they're still active and acting up with, and against, the surrounding forces, events, people, and massive webs of desires.

In 1993, I was massively shaken up. I accepted New York, accepted to be part of it and its defining and (cruel) conditions, for the chance to think about art anew, to experiment with painting as a new form.

Cover, Health and Beauty, photograph by Henry Bond, Purple Prose #2

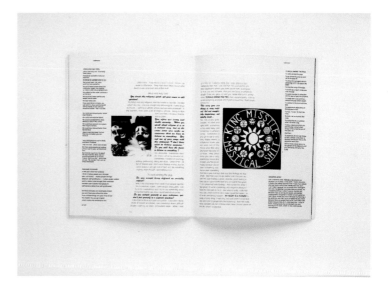

La botanique des sensations, Martine Aballéa interviewed by Elein Fleiss, Purple Prose #2
La vie d'un acarien, Dermatophagoïdes Pteronyssissus interviewed by Jean-Luc Vilmouth, photographs by Regis Gleva & Michaël Crotto, Purple Prose #2

Apprehended: Julia Scher, Occupation: Artist, Julia Scher interviewed by Barbara Osborn, Purple Prose #2
A Sensitive Singer, John S. Hall of King Missile interviewed by Elein Fleiss and Olivier Zham, Purple Prose #2

Cover, Catherine Bret-Brownstone, Purple Prose #3
Noir et blanc, collage by Martin Margiela, Purple Prose #3

In Italy There is No Sport as Popular as Football, Maurizio Cattelan interviewed
by Tommaso Corvi Mora, Purple Prose #3

In Italy There is No Sport as Popular as Football, Maurizio Cattelan interviewed by Tommaso Corvi Mora, Purple Prose #3
Cover, Catherine Bret-Brownstone, Purple Prose #3

Ambiance origami de néon fluide, text by Bernard Joisten, Purple Prose #3

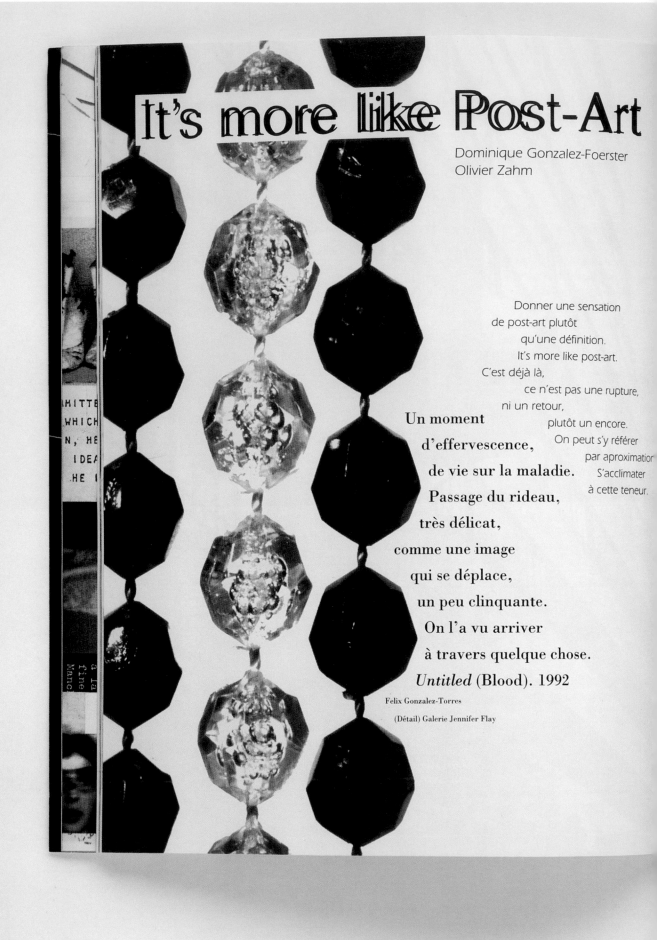

It's more like Post-Art

Dominique Gonzalez-Foerster
Olivier Zahm

Donner une sensation
de post-art plutôt
  qu'une définition.
It's more like post-art.
C'est déjà là,
    ce n'est pas une rupture,
  ni un retour,
      plutôt un encore.

Un moment
        On peut s'y référer
d'effervescence,
      par aproximation
de vie sur la maladie.
        S'acclimater
Passage du rideau,
      à cette teneur.
très délicat,

comme une image

qui se déplace,

un peu clinquante.

On l'a vu arriver

à travers quelque chose.

Untitled (Blood). 1992

Felix Gonzalez-Torres

(Détail) Galerie Jennifer Flay

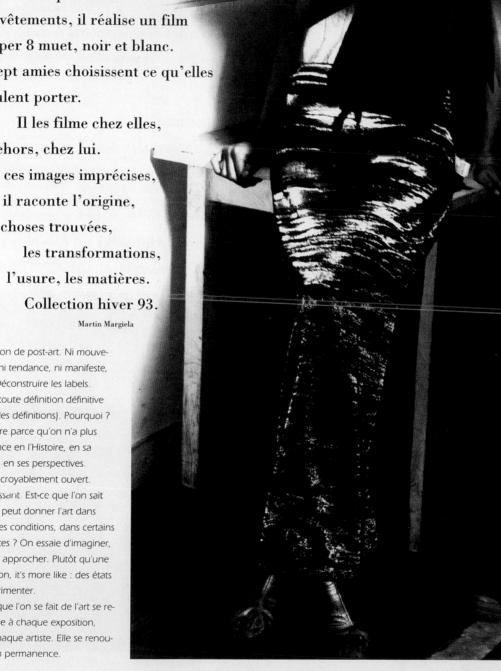

Pour présenter
ses vêtements, il réalise un film
super 8 muet, noir et blanc.
Sept amies choisissent ce qu'elles
veulent porter.
Il les filme chez elles,
dehors, chez lui.
Sur ces images imprécises,
il raconte l'origine,
les choses trouvées,
les transformations,
l'usure, les matières.
Collection hiver 93.

Martin Margiela

Sensation de post-art. Ni mouvement, ni tendance, ni manifeste,
etc... Déconstruire les labels.
Défier toute définition définitive
(après les définitions). Pourquoi ?
Peut-être parce qu'on n'a plus
confiance en l'Histoire, en sa
finalité, en ses perspectives.
C'est incroyablement ouvert.
Envahissant. Est-ce que l'on sait
ce que peut donner l'art dans
certaines conditions, dans certains
contextes ? On essaie d'imaginer,
de s'en approcher. Plutôt qu'une
définition, it's more like : des états
à expérimenter.
L'idée que l'on se fait de l'art se re-
distribue à chaque exposition,
avec chaque artiste. Elle se renou-
velle en permanence.

It's More Like Post-Art, text by Dominique Gonzalez-Foerster and Olivier Zahm,
Purple Prose #3

**It's More Like Post-Art, text by Dominique Gonzalez-Foerster and Olivier Zahm,
Purple Prose #3**

Cover, photograph by Rolf Snoeren, Purple Prose #4
Collection No.1: Detachement, clothes by Viktor & Rolf, Purple Prose #4

Faces of Eve and Ego of Adam, text by Laura Cottingham,
photograph by Cindy Sherman, Purple Prose #4

Olivier Zahm

Quand en 1988 se découvre l'univers de Margiela, maritime, industrieux, portuaire, traversé d'affinités chaotiques avec les femmes et les hommes de Genet, de Fassbinder ou de Conrad, c'est l'apogée des années 80, le retour du glamour, de l'hyper-sexy et des fantasmes sublimés de Mugler, Montana, Alaia. Paris revient à l'avant-scène sous forme d'un défilé de clichés couture avec entre autres événements l'arrivée de Christian Lacroix, l'anniversaire des Quarante ans du New Look et le déclin des créateurs Japonais dont le minimalisme épuré a dominé le début de la décennie.

Dans ce contexte parisien, les vêtements défaits, dépecés, récuperés de Margiela passent d'emblée pour une provocation post-punk, immédiatement indexée sur le registre du spectaculaire anti-mode. On ne comprend pas d'où viennent et où vont ces mannequins aux longues silhouettes, aux visages genres lunaires, filant à travers la foule vers on ne sait quelle forme d'élégance a vif, faite de superpositions et récuperations chaotiques. Mécompréhension relayée ensuite par l'association de Margiela avec le mouvement grunge dont il sera désigné comme le fer de lance "récup" et porté a l'avant-garde de ce soit-disant "paupérisme destroy" venu du Nord (Anvers), qui menace de dévaster le séculaire Faubourg St-Honoré. "Une mode de crise" dit-on alors, qui devrait en toute logique disparaitre avec son temps ou s'auto-détruire.

Margiela occupe dans l'imaginaire de ce début des années 90 la position futuriste, mais desormais inversée, d'un Courrege. Celle d'un futur sans illusion, d'un futur invaginé sur son propre passé, dans la dépression des apparences, articulant désillusion, violence et mémoire. Pour beaucoup, l'élégance définitive de Margiela flirte avec l'auto-destruction suicidaire. On y voit une mode en lambeaux, une mode désafectée, en haillons, dépeuplée, dévastée. La plupart des lectures de son travail se sont faites sur le registre négatif de l'avant-garde suicidaire et de l'anti-mode, souvent doublées d'attaques sur le prix (le theme des frippes de luxe). *"Je ne comprend pas l'idée de destruction que l'on rattache souvent à mon style"*, disait-il à Laurence Benaim. *"Mon approche n'est pas destroy. Quand je découpe mes vêtements, anciens ou nouveaux, pour les transformer, je ne pense pas les détruire. C'est au contraire une façon de les faire renaitre sous une autre forme".*[1]

Margiela c'est au contraire la renaissance de la mode. D'autant plus inattendue qu'elle survient au moment ou la mode perdait toute raison d'etre. Depassee par l'imagination de la rue recyclant en tous genres frippes, vetements de sport ou habits de travail. Tandis que dans les salons de St-Laurent à Lagerferd (aujourd'hui définitivement transformés en parasols publicitaires par Kookai), on saccage sans complexe son héritage. En fait, celui que l'on voyait comme une impasse esthétique, va renouveler de fond en comble la mode. Son archéologie de derniere minute renoue avec ce rituel en passe de disparaitre. Elle en rassemble les fragments epars, recompose en longues silhouettes d'une grande pureté, ce que le vent mauvais de l'époque disperse.

Cette étiquette grunge, "récup", "destroy" va accompagner son succes grandissant. D'autant que délaissant les chapelles consacrées et autre cour carrée, Margiela va entretenir le malentendu anti-mode en multipliant les défilés-campements installés en périphérie de l'économie mondaine (post-fashion). Une saison en banlieue avec des enfants courant entre les jambes des mannequins avec fond de terrain vague, une autre fois dans un garage bas de plafond, puis au milieu du bric-à-brac des meubles de l'Armée du Salut, dans une station de métro, dans un supermarche vide... Par ailleurs, d'un naturel discret, Martin Margiela évite de se montrer, de se faire photographier et de trop parler de lui. Il feint d'annuler sa signature derriere un bout de tissu blanc, bout de pansement accroché au vetement. Et il renvoie avec courtoisie la presse mode à l'observation attentive de ses vetements (ce qui d'ailleurs ne semble plus du tout se faire). Ainsi qu'à l'observation de son art de la coupe, de son sens des compositions (matieres, couleurs), de son traitement tactile des surfaces et textures (peintes, froissées, pliées, chiffonnées, froissées)...

Il faudra comprendre pourquoi son succes nous revient surtout des USA, du Japon, et de Londres (le magazine ID), alors que Paris, là meme ou il a décidé de s'installer, fait encore mine de ne pas tres bien comprendre ce qui s'est passé avec lui (hier au Métro Strasbourg Saint-Denis, aujourd'hui dans ces locaux derriere la Gare du Nord).

This was the best year and the worst year. Coco Hayley Gordon Moore was born on 7/1/94. But a few months before, on April 5th, Kurt Cobain died. Before Coco was born and Kurt died, I had dreams about Frances Bean. Someone was asking me to take care of her and I was feeling like I wasn't ready to do that. Coco wasn't born yet, and I felt unprepared to take care of an actual little person. I remember lying on the bed at Daisy von Furth's apartment, six months pregnant. We were getting ready for our X-Girl gorilla style sidewalk fashion show that was going to happen in a few days. It was being held right after Marc Jacob's show, his first after leaving Perry Ellis. I forget exactly what was going on. Fittings? Planning the logistics of everything? Photo shoot? I was feeling rather uncomfortable and out of it. Then the phone rang, and it was Thurston. He told me that Bob Whittiger, a good friend of Mudhoney's, called and said he had bad news. I immediately thought that something had happened to Mark Arm, because he was having drug problems back then. We were actually much closer to Mark and Mudhoney than to Nirvana. He told me about Kurt. I somehow wasn't surprised that he was dead, but I was shocked by the violence and finality of it all. Like Nirvana's music, there was no in between about it. No overdose/maybe suicide question mark lingering in the air. Only the feeling of one's heart being pulled out and thrown against a concrete wall. I can still barely listen to a Nirvana song, especially in public. I had basically written Kurt off in my mind as a goner a couple years previously, as soon as he became involved with Courtney Love. For the next year I saw one bad Kurt Cobain T-shirt after another. Plus all the celebrity bohemian's versions of how affected they were by "the boy's" death. We were sitting around talking to William Burroughs, while we were on tour with R.E.M., and he turned to Michael Stipe and asked him about Kurt. Michael was a little embarrassed, and told him he should ask us. The truth is no one knew Kurt, but everyone had their own experiences with him. Because he was a public figure, the communal mourning was a T-shirt, no matter how exploitative it seemed. The difference, though, is that if you knew the person, then their death is not cool, it's not a cool stance. It's not a cool T-shirt. Like the way childbirth is not cool: it's gruesome, exhausting and exhilarating. In fact, it kind of eliminates the idea of coolness from your reference point. Although "bump watch" in the gossip weeklies would make it seem like pregnancy and child rearing are a walk in the park. Oozing fluids out of your breast and vagina? Sore and bleeding nipples? Leaking breast pads? I actually didn't have the agonizing pain of childbirth. Coco was born by Caesarean section in an operating room overlooking the East River. Yes, I can romanticize it. But, in fact, I was so scared as I was wheeled in that I had to imagine I was in a TV medical show. Afterwards, it was painful. But, as I looked at Coco, with her incredible creamy skin, beautiful rosebud lips, perfect eyes, and long lanky body, it made me even sadder about Kurt, about what he left behind, and how much pain he must of felt to leave Frances.

Kim Gordon

Rubriques Textes Interviews - Hiver 1996 30 F

Shugi Aryioshi
Olivier Badot
Olivier Blanckart
Greg Bordowitz
Tommaso Corvi Mora

PURPLE PROSE 5

Andrew Cross
Liz Dalton
Joshua Decter
André Durandeau
Atom Egoyan
Danielle Flaumenbaum
Peter Fleissig
Valentine de Ganay
Ami Garmon
John S. Hall
Markus Hansen
Carsten Höller
Stephen Joannon
Ginette Le Maître
Claude Lévêque
Loïs E. Nesbitt
Guillaume Nez
Bob Nickas
POST SEXE
David Robbins
François Roche
Alberto Sorbelli
Therapy?
Wolfgang Tillmans
Francisco J. Varela
Vydia
Benjamin Weil

Cover, photograph by Wolfgang Tillmans, Purple Prose #5

Tilt, text by Bernard Joisten, Purple Prose #5
Going to Heaven, Markus Hansen interviewed by Andrew Cross, Purple Prose #5
Post-Sexe, text by Olivier Zahm, photographs by Jack Pierson, Purple Prose #5

Correspondence from The Institute for Advanced Comedic Behavior,
text by David Robbins; Squirts, text by Dike Blair, Purple Prose #5
Going to Heaven, Markus Hansen interviewed by Andrew Cross, Purple Prose #5
Post Sexe, photographs by Wolfgang Tillmans, Purple Prose #5

song
John S. Hall

D E-TA-CHA-BLE

I woke up this morning with a bad hang-over
And my penis was missing again
This happens all of the time,
It's detachable
This comes in handy a lot of the time.
I can leave it home when I think it's gonna get me in trouble
Or I can rent it out when I don't need it
But now and then, I go to a party, get drunk, and
I can't for the life of me remember what I did with it
First I looked around my apartment and I couldn't find it,
So I called the place where the party was, they hadn't seen it either
I asked them to check the medicine cabinet, cause for some reason,
I leave it there sometimes
But not this time
So I told them if it pops up to let me know,
I called a few people who were at the party,
But they were no help either
I was starting to get desperate,
I really don't like being without my penis for too long
It makes me feel like less of a man and
I really hate having to sit down every time I take a leak
After a few hours of searching the house,
Calling everyone I could think of,
I was starting to get very depressed
So I went to the Kiev and ate breakfast
Then, as I walked down 2nd Avenue toward St. Marks Place,
Where all those people sell used books and other junk on the street,
I saw my penis lying on a blanket next to a broken toaster oven.
Some guy was selling it
I had to buy it of him.
He wanted 22 bucks, but I talked him down under 17
I took it home, washed it off and put it back on
I was happy again
Complete
People sometimes tell me I should get it permanently attached
But I don't know,
Even though sometimes it's a pain in the ass,
I like having a detachable penis
Detachable penis...
Copyright 1992 Atlantic Record / King Missile

POST SEXE

48

De-ta-cha-ble Penis, song by John S. Hall of King Missile, Purple Prose #5

Cover, **JANE Bleibt JANE** by Vanessa Beecroft,
photograph by Armin Linke, **Purple Prose #6**

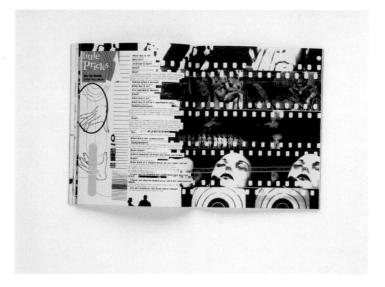

Cowboys and Girls de Danse, text by Ami Garmon, Purple Prose #6
Beautiful Decade, Jon Moritsugu interviewed by Elein Fleiss, Purple Prose #6
The (Process) Art of Filmmaking, text by Roddy Bogawa, Purple Prose #6

Bustes, text by Vanessa Beecroft, photograph by Vanessa Beecroft,
Purple Prose #6
Little Pricks, text by Lee Ronaldo, photographs by Leah Singer, Purple Prose #6

The problem with youth-culture and the media today is, that young people are given the impression that they actually are doing something, when in fact they are only needed as participants in a staged marketing event. Take for example MTV's environmental and political messages, all they are is feel-good-messages which leave the viewer with a comforting feeling of "something is being done about the shit in the world". The same goes for the style-magazines' interest in 'real issues' and the change in taste and fashion. Have the much talked about nineties really happened, or did we just believe they happened? As soon as 1990 approached suddenly everyone knew what the nineties would be like. The nineties sensibility was called more caring, softer and more true and real. But being almost halfway through this decade, the realness we were looking for turned out to be not much more than Kate Moss on a Calvin Klein poster. People really do believe that there has been change. We want things to be caring, aware and real, as long as we can carry on with our business the way we are. As no one is prepared to question power involved, anybody telling us that we actually are is highly welcome. The feeling of guilt about the eighties fuels the talk of the nineties, with all its ambitious statements turning out to be wishful thinking. Because when in a couple of years, or as we are already today, we will start to look for the new climate and the new words that will ease our hang-over from the nineties, we will realize that the nineties never really happened. They were just a change of taste, a change of form, with everything else underneath still intact and probably reinforced. Therefore all talk of future suggests that progress is being achieved. To be really futuristic we should maybe try and act out the promises of the nineties to their very last extent to their very last minute...

Lumière de mon coeur, ne laisse pas mes ténèbres me parler ! J'ai dérivé vers les choses d'ici-bas et je suis devenu obscurité; mais de là, même de là, je t'ai profondément aimée. J'ai erré et je me suis souvenu de toi. J'ai entendu ta voix derrière moi me disant de revenir, mais j'ai mal . entendu dans le tumulte des contestations. Et maintenant voici que je reviens tout brûlant et haletant vers ta source. Que nul ne m'en écarte! Que j'y boive et en vive. Que moi je ne sois pas ma vie.

Saint Augustin

Wir kriechen den Faschisten in ihr dreckiges, braunes Arschloch

Hanna Wolf SPD

LES ANNÉES DIX ?

THE NINETIES HAVEN'T HAPPENED YET !

Wolfgang Tillmans

Les Années Dix? The Nineties Haven't Happened Yet!, text by Wolfgang Tillmans,
photographs Wolfgang Tillmans, Purple Prose #6

Cover, photograph by Vidya & Jean-Michel, Purple Prose #7

Instincts d'architecture, text by Jean-Michel Fradkin, Purple Prose #7
Bustes, with Butthole Surfers, Rita Ackermann, Guillaume Laidain
and Frederic Drappier, Purple Prose #7
Violet Violence, photographs by Vidya & Jean-Michel, Purple Prose #7

Bustes, text by Miltos Manetas, photograph by Armin Linke, Purple Prose #7
This Wonderful Life, text by Jeff Rian, photographs by Stephen Shames,
Purple Prose #7

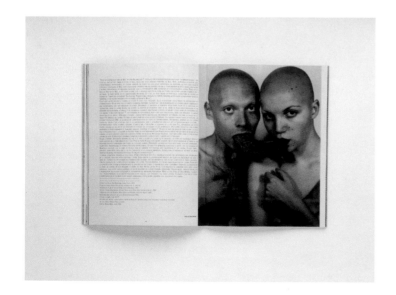

Rape Me, My Friend, text by Olivier Zahm, photogrphs by Charles Ray, Alix Lambert and Bob Flanagan, Purple Prose #7
Rape Me, My Friend, text by Olivier Zahm, photograph by Vidya & Jean-Michel, Purple Prose #7

Shoot and Kiss, Richard Kern interviewed by Olivier Zahm, stills by Richard Kern, Purple Prose #7
Un scénario des filles des heures, text by Dominique Gonzalez-Foerster, Purple Prose #7
Passive Violent Clothes, Viktor & Rolf interviewed by Elein Fleiss, Purple Prose #7

Shoot and Kiss, Richard Kern interviewed by Olivier Zahm, stills by Richard Kern, Purple Prose #7
Passive Violent Clothes, Viktor & Rolf interviewed by Elein Fleiss, Purple Prose #7
Measured in Desire, Sarah Schwartz interviewed by Elein Fleiss & Jeff Rian, Purple Prose #7

First thought of the morning: why do I have six different ideas at the same time about what I'm going to do when I finish what I'm doing? Followed by: what if this book isn't any good after I've spent three years on it? Then: I don't have that much time left. Then: I'll never write that play about Doris Duke. I know it. Then: In fifteen years I'll be sixty. Then: if I'm lucky. Then: unless I'm lucky.

I hate myself when I feel a twinge of envy.

One feels flattened by the superior energy of hateful, obsessed people.

Argentina, Chile, Peru, Bolivia, Paraguay, Uruguay, Brazil: three months in these countries, and except for the occasional weird fuck, I don't think I spoke to a single soul, aside from Luisa Valenzuela and some other friends in Buenos Aires. A day here, a week there, the high or low point of which, depending on how I look at it, was getting gang-banged by ten sailors in Valparaiso. Machu Picchu was also a thrill, of course. So were Lake Titicaca, which is shrinking away to the size of a golf pond, and the water falls at Iguazu.

Neil Bartlett gave me his really desolate council flat in Limehouse while I was working with him on the Genet play. I couldn't get myself to work. If you left the flat in the morning, you left the flat for the day, and for the evening too, because Limehouse is way east of nowhere. I continually wondered something I've wondered all my life, especially when I'm in South America: "Do I exist as a subject if I'm alone?" I mean, does my subject have a personality? A value? Am I here? It was especially weird for me in London, where my work is known and taken seriously, to have conversations with people "as if" I existed. Existed in some literary continuum, and in other people's mental associations. Weird to have that kind of existence there and not here, where I live.

The last line here from Pierre, "dabbling in the vomit of his own identity," instantly reminded me of watching *The Manchurian Candidate* with Barbara K. years ago. Specifically, the scene in which Sinatra and Harvey get drunk on Christmas Eve, and the radio's playing "The Twelve Days of Christmas," Harvey says something like, "Twelve days of Christmas! One day of Christmas is repulsive enough." Barbara said, "You realize you would never hear that line in a Hollywood movie today."

Had a meeting with my editor last Thursday. He was surprised that I actually knew what I was doing. For example, when I mentioned Plutarch's book on Sparta as something the "Martinez" father would've read. And when I spoke of Justinian's Lex Aquilia as being a source of modern tort litigation. I also talked about Tolstoy's and Victor Hugo's writings on capital punishment, and the history of the guillotine. He was surprised in a pleased kind of way, but obviously confounded that I might actually have some moral reason for writing my book, some intellectual issues to resolve, and because the book is so negative and depressing.

SUMMER DOLDRUMS

I was sad to hear that Terry Southern died. He was a real madman, one of the good ones. I phoned him about a year ago to tell him somebody at *The New Yorker* had plagiarized one of his stories. Not to upset him, but to let him know someone remembered his story. I couldn't get through, so phoned Victor Bockris and asked him to tell Terry. I wonder if he did.

I'm editing my book of essays. Now that I have the galley proofs, I discover that I really hate the essays. Everything was written on deadlines, so it's not exactly what I would have wished to say. It was the worst miscalculation I ever made. It was twelve or thirteen years of writing with the wrong tone, as far as I can tell.

About the Rabin assassination: an Italian woman I know who runs a restaurant in the West Village told me, disgustedly, that she tried to talk to some of her customers about it, and they all said, "Oh, it's terrible, what's the special tonight?" As if it had happened on another planet, and was no concern of theirs.

Last night, I dreamed I was driving in a car with Orson Welles in Los Angeles. We were on our way to lunch. In the dream I thought, "Everyone will see I'm having lunch with Orson Welles, even though he's dead."

Someone told me a story about Mark Leyner, a writer whose work I haven't read. He met a producer who encouraged him to write screenplays, and told him, "Nobody reads books." Leyner asked, "Why are you telling me this?" he answered, "Because I like you."

I met the actor who played Hannibal Lecter in *Manhunter* the other night. We got into a wrangle over *Macbeth*. I shouldn't have opened my mouth. I said that *Macbeth* isn't a tragedy, and neither is *Richard III*. He pointed out that the actual title is *The Tragedy of Richard III*. I said surely in Shakespeare's time it was received as a comedy, and *Macbeth* received as a melodrama. A completely malignant personality who does nothing but kill people so he can be King isn't a tragic figure like Lear, who could've changed his mind about dividing the kingdom before going blind and crazy. Lear could have said, "Cordelia's right, and my other daughters are shitty gold diggers." Richard is incapable of doing anything other than what he actually does. Macbeth is a mediocrity dominated by his wife. If Shakespeare had called it "The Tragedy of Lady Macbeth," then maybe I'd buy it. But as Mary McCarthy pointed out, *Macbeth* features a rather tiresome general who enters the play talking about the weather. I always thought tragedy was about two people who are equally right but diametrically at odds with each other. Or, you can have, say, an individual in conflict with the state, as in *Antigone*, or even in conflict with himself, as in *Hamlet*.

CHILLY SCENES OF WINTER
About *I Shot Andy Warhol*: Lynne said it disturbed her, as it naturally would, seeing a piece of history she experienced re-interpreted by someone who wasn't there and doesn't know what it was really like. Disturbing that a history has to be reinvented.

We're on *Tornado Watch* in New York City tonight. I refuse to believe it's anything more than a promotional stunt for *Twister*. I'm torn between stupidly going out and stupidly staying in.

In this week's *US Magazine*, someone asked Matt LeBlanc what's going to happen on *Friends* next season. He said "I'm going to fuck Chandler in the ass."

Too bad that Newt Gingrich is such a creep. The night he was on *Larry King* with those zoo animals he showed a side of himself I would never have expected. People ridiculed him for that show. That's the trouble with politics. Kluge told me that Franz-Josef Strauss said he—Strauss—would have been a good history teacher if he hadn't gone into politics. If Gingrich wasn't a politician, he'd make one of the better zookeepers.

Baltimore for Christmas: I never stay with the family. I check into the Tremont Plaza with Lily, and then walk down the street to look in the bodegas that sell handguns and brass knuckles. I visit John Waters. I visit Sue Lowe. Then I have my niece drive me out to the compound. I told her, "You know, Beth, I love your Mom and Dad, but I can't stand being around them longer than three hours." Luckily, she can't either.

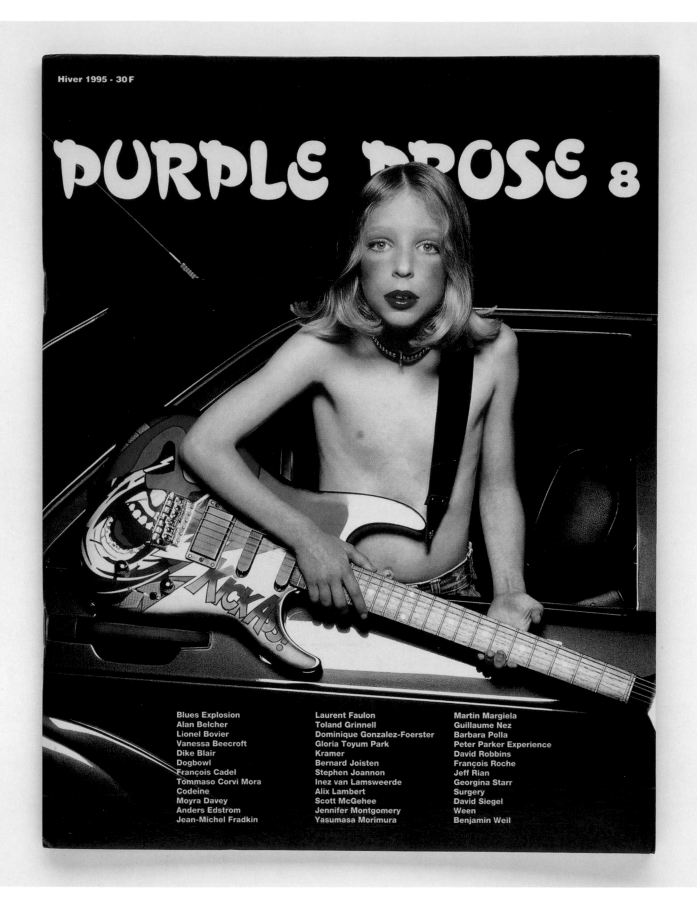

Hiver 1995 - 30 F

PURPLE PROSE 8

Blues Explosion
Alan Belcher
Lionel Bovier
Vanessa Beecroft
Dike Blair
Dogbowl
François Cadel
Tommaso Corvi Mora
Codeine
Moyra Davey
Anders Edstrom
Jean-Michel Fradkin

Laurent Faulon
Toland Grinnell
Dominique Gonzalez-Foerster
Gloria Toyum Park
Kramer
Bernard Joisten
Stephen Joannon
Inez van Lamsweerde
Alix Lambert
Scott McGehee
Jennifer Montgomery
Yasumasa Morimura

Martin Margiela
Guillaume Nez
Barbara Polla
Peter Parker Experience
David Robbins
François Roche
Jeff Rian
Georgina Starr
Surgery
David Siegel
Ween
Benjamin Weil

Cover, Floortje, style by Vinoodh Matadin, photograph by Inez van Lamsweerde,
Purple Prose #8

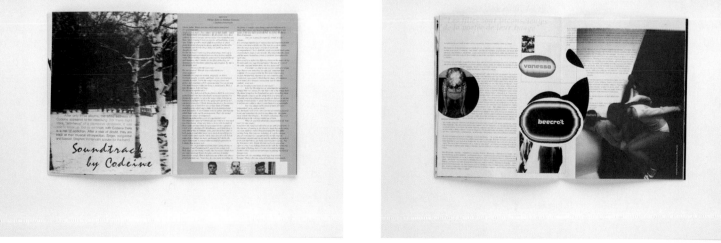

Table of Contents, Purple Prose #8
Soundtrack by Codeine, Matthew Connors and Stephen Immerwahr interviewed
by Olivier Zham, Purple Prose #8

Vanessa Beecroft, text by Barbara Polla, Purple Prose #8

Glamour 7.0, text by Olivier Zahm, photographs by Inez van Lamsweerde,
Purple Prose #8
Glamour 7.0, text by Olivier Zahm, Rebecca 1993, style by Vinoodh Matadin,
photograph by Inez van Lamsweerde; Lucy 1990, photograph by Inez van
Lamsweerde; Jessica, style by Vinoodh Matadin, photograph by Inez van Lamsweerde,
Purple Prose #8

Glamour 7.0, text by Olivier Zahm, Joan 1993, photograph by Inez van Lamsweerde;
Friduwitt 1994, style by Vinoodh Matadin, photograph by Inez van Lamsweerde,
Purple Prose #8

Kill Me, Alan Belcher interviewed by Elein Fleiss, Purple Prose #8
From the Movie, text by Lee Ranaldo, Purple Fiction #1

Cover, Collage by Christophe Brunnquell, Purple Fiction #1

Cover, photograph by Mariko Mori, Purple Prose #9
We've Got Twenty-Five Years, Mariko Mori interviewed by Dike Blair,
Purple Prose #9

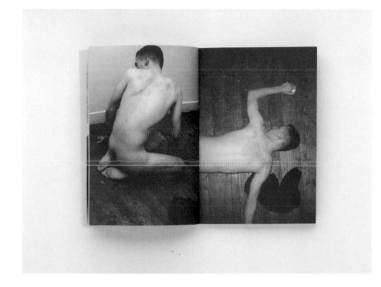

Vidya & Jean-Michel, Serge & Christophe, text by Olivier Zahm, drawings by Vidya & Jean-Michel, Purple Prose #9
How Much, photographs by Wolfgang Tillmans, Purple Prose #9
Sporting Dreams, text by Jutta Koether, Purple Prose #9

How Much, photographs by Wolfgang Tillmans, Purple Prose #9
L'etat de chantier, Pierre Huyghe interviewed by Dominique Gonzalez-Foerster, Purple Prose #9

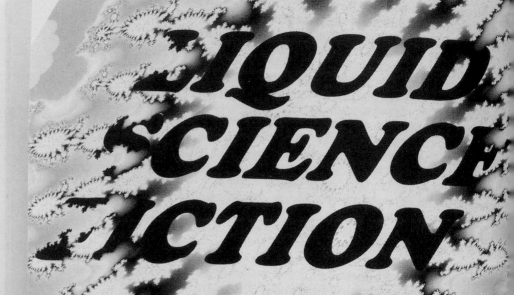

LIQUID SCIENCE FICTION

Interview : 10 pages
  Questions : Bernard Joisten.
artist, lives in Paris.
"unplugged" European city.
  Ken Lum : Canadian artist.
lives in Paris and Vancouver
    Answers : William Gibson. writer.
lives in Vancouver.
« a postmodern Pacific Rim info-node.
swarming with Hong Kong venture
capital and Japanese tourists. »
Date of interview : April 1995
  Introduction : Dike Blair

William Gibson is known to the culture-at-large for his coinage of the term «cyberspace,» but it was his cyberspace trilogy (*Neuromancer, Count Zero, Mona Lisa Overdrive*) that actually changed the culture. By putting grace and style into science fiction prose–something that concerned few serious writers in the early 80's–he changed the face of science fiction and was responsible, at least in part, for designing the template of content and style called cyberpunk. He injected SF with invigorating doses of extrapolated rock'n'roll, fashion, art, and architecture, and in doing so took the nerdiness out of the genre. His terse descriptive phrases capture the moods which surround technologies, rather than their engineering. Although it is the noir side of Gibson's vision that is most often noted, behind every wall of Black Ice (deadly anti-viral programs) he offers a fleeting glimpse of the possibility of transcendence–either in the quasi-religious moment of a human finding selflessness or of a machine finding self. Like Raymond Chandler, John D. MacDonald, or P. K. Dick, Gibson took a genre and instilled it with enough art and imagination to make us reexamine it. He wrote «road» novels about the Infobahn while its entrance ramps were still under construction.

Coming to the screen this summer is Robert Longo's film (see interview in this issue) version of Gibson's short story «Johnny Mnemonic» (from *Burning Chrome*) for which Gibson wrote the screenplay. The French translation of his last American novel, *Virtual Light*, is now available from J'ai Lu.

**Liquid Science Fiction, William Gibson interviewed by Bernard Joisten,
Purple Prose #9**

I'm not really interested in the obsession Japanese male photographers have with taking pictures of teenagers girls and their panties. It seems to me they don't know what's really exciting. Some of my self-portraits look similar, but they're completely different. Theirs are about sexual appetite, while mine are about my delusions.

People in Tokyo Call Me a Photographer, Yurie Nagashima interviewed by Elein Fleiss, photographs by Yurie Nagashima, Purple Prose #9

1996: The richest man in the world is Bill Gates, worth an estimated 18.5 billion dollars. Ten years later, he'll be worth 56 billion dollars. Gates perpetually holds the number one spot on the *Forbes* list of the world's richest people. Number two, in 1996, is Warren Buffett, with 15 billion dollars. Ten years later, Buffett, now with 52 billion dollars, also ranks second on the *Forbes* list. In this unchanging ranking, there is both a diagnostic and a prognostic, both uncontestable.

1996: There are no cell phones. There are less than 50 million Internet users worldwide. Google does not yet exist.

1996: Leigh Bowery has been dead for two years. Bernard Buffet has only three years to live.

1996: I know I want to be a curator when Andy Warhol dies. His works are worth almost nothing. The art world is still obsessed with Marcel Duchamp. I write in the magazine *Documents sur l'art* about "the artistic options at the close of the century, which prefers to glorify Duchamp and ignore Warhol, choosing the silence of Duchamp over the noise of Warhol, even though his noise is so much more meaningful indeed…" In 1989, I entitled my first exhibit *A Talk Show*, as if I already knew that television would end up being a much more fascinating medium to me than the exhibition.

1996: Twenty years ago, Steve Rubell and Ian Schrager opened Studio 54 in a former CBS television studio at 254 W. 54th Street in New York City.

1996: On January 1, one of the most extraordinary projects of the end of the twentieth century comes to an end when its sponsor, the Texan billionaire Edward Bass (*Forbes'* 369th richest person in 2007, with 2.5 billion dollars), decides to stop renting the site of Biosphere II

(which Bass invented), to Columbia University. Between 1991 and 1993, five men and three women lived in the glass dome, an artificially closed ecological system located in the Arizona desert. The experiment was not in vain: it, along with Orwell's *1984*, would inspire Dutchman John de Mol (*Forbes'* 432nd richest person in 2007, with 2.2 billion dollars) to create the reality show *Big Brother*, his genius art project, thereby ringing in the twenty-first century and putting an end to avant-garde art.

1996: I think that a certain kind of enthusiasm, the kind that led me to create the magazine *Documents sur l'art* in 1992 (the same year *Purple* was launched), is waning. Art isn't the socialite twaddle in service of commerce that it will quickly become. But, something has changed, especially in artists of my generation. They understand that, from now on, art will be an easy conduit into another social class. It's no longer about changing art, it's about having a career. At the beginning of the decade, with the Young British Artists, a new category has emerged: "Young Artists." Later to become "Emerging Artists." (There weren't any before: Dan Graham was never a "Young Artist.")

1996: François Mitterrand dies at the beginning of the year, Félix González-Torres before its end. It would be another six years before I meet Debbie Harry.

2007: I'm in the south of France, with my friend Trisha Donnelly. I ask her, "What were you doing in 1996?" She answers, "Cocktail waitressing. I had been fired from KooKooRoo, a chicken restaurant. I finally graduated from UCLA, a year late. I was working with transgenders in retail, as a floater. That was 1996."

1996: I read *Cool Memories III* by Baudrillard ("Telecom snobbery: to receive calls everywhere—in the street, on the train, at friends—on a direct portable line. An instrument

Previous Spread: Gillian Haratani and Elizabeth Peyton, style by Bernadette Corporation, photographs by Wolfgang Tillmans, Purple Fashion #1

PURPLE FASHION 1, PURPLE PROSE 10, 11, PURPLE FICTION 2

64

worthy of the *Précieuses Ridicules*, and their kind. You have
to outdo, out-snob, be even more sociable: from now on,
instead of having my maid come to my house, I'll go to
hers.") and *Zombies* by Bret Easton Ellis. Since that day in
1986, when Rosemary, a friend from college, lent me *Less
Than Zero*, I've been crazed with impatience, waiting for
Bret Easton Ellis' next book. And every time I finish one,
I hope that I'll be alive when the next one comes out.
In 1996, I meet Bret Easton Ellis backstage at a literature
television program. After the show, he's there, eating a
few nuts from dishes on a table covered with a paper
cloth, looking very weary.

1996: I work on an exhibition, one of the three that
would keep me busy for the next ten years. It's entitled
Dramatically Different, and opens the following year at the
Centre National d'Art Contemporain in Grenoble.
Then comes *Weather Everything* at the Leipzig museum
in 1998, and *Coollustre* at the Avignon museum in 2003.
Then, as an epilogue, *Superdefense*, at the Grand Palais in
Paris, 2006. I thought of something very exciting that
year: rather than mount shows with artists, I'd mount
them only with their works. Exhibitions without artists.
I'd do it by manipulating their sold, collected works.
By drawing them out from their possible destinations–in
a museum, over a couch, in storage. Little by little, artists
have become fairly ordinary people. But great works have
escaped the sad fate of becoming common. Sometimes
exhibiting works in a somewhat bold way–in unexpected
proximities, for example–can make them better still.
But, in the end, isn't this true for all consumer goods, all
accessories?

1996: In less than a year, the IBM computer Deep Blue
will beat the chess champion Garry Kasparov at his own
game.

Cover, photograph by Anders Edström, Purple Fashion #1
Clothes by Lutz Huelle, photographs by Anders Edström, Purple Fashion #1
Clothes by Marcel Verheijen, photographs by Mark Borthwick, Purple Fashion #1

Clothes by Bernadette Corporation, photographs by Wolfgang Tillmans,
Purple Fashion #1
Clothes by Lutz Huelle, photographs by Anders Edström, Purple Fashion #1
Clothes by Marcel Verheijen, photographs by Mark Borthwick, Purple Fashion #1

Cover, still by Alex Bag, Purple Prose #10
Swedish Erotic Sequences, photographs by Anders Edström, Purple Prose #10

Swedish Erotic Sequences, photographs by Anders Edström, Purple Prose #10
Sonic Stoll by Georges Stoll, text by Charles Arthur Boyer,
photographs by Georges Stoll, Purple Prose #10

Alex Bag's Girl World

Get Back TV

Interview
Questions Elein Fleiss & Jeff Rian
Answers Alex Bag, artist, lives in NYC
Images from Alex Bag's Fall '95 videos

Alex Bag's Girl World, Alex Bag interviewed by Elein Fleiss & Jeff Rian,
stills by Alex Bag, Purple Prose #10

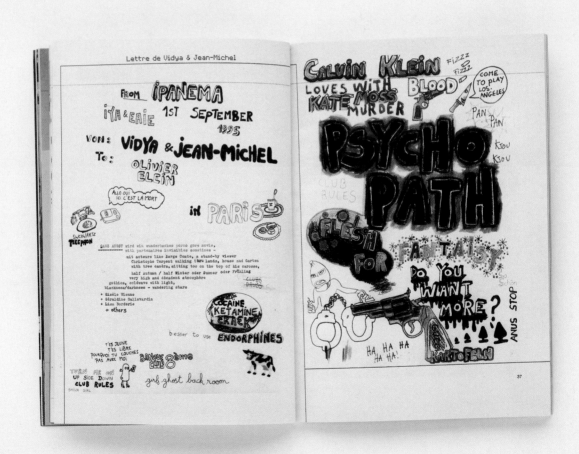

**Letter from Vidya & Jean-Michel, drawings by Vidya & Jean-Michel,
Purple Prose #10**

**Letter from Vidya & Jean-Michel, drawings by Vidya & Jean-Michel,
Purple Prose #10**

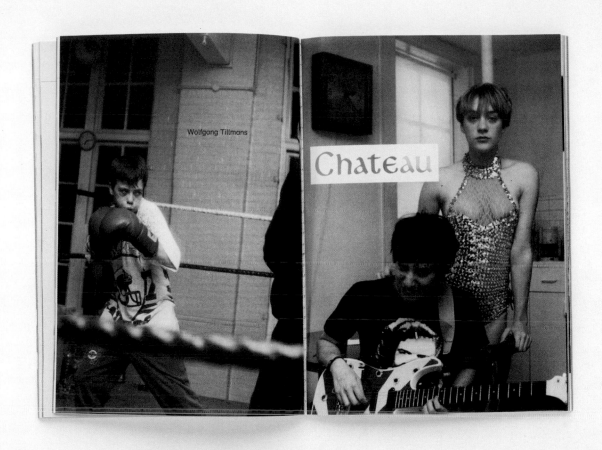

Chateau, photographs by Wolfgang Tillmans, Purple Prose #10

Photographs by Ange Leccia, Purple Prose #10
Autodidact Michael Banicki interviewed by David Robbins,
photographs by Michael Banicki, Purple Prose #10
Cover, photograph by Camille Vivier, Purple Fiction #2

Autodidact Michael Banicki interviewed by David Robbins,
photographs by Michael Banicki, Purple Prose #10
1978, photographs by Mark Borthwick, Purple Fiction #2

Cover, photograph by Laetitia Benat, Purple Prose #11
World Tour, text by Olivier Zahm, Purple Prose #11
Proposals for an Anti-Erotic Year, text by Jeff Rian, photographs by Mark Borthwick,
Purple Prose #11

World Tour, text by Olivier Zahm, Purple Prose #11
Meanderings on the Age of Blur and Blah, Blah, Blah, text by Dike Blair,
Purple Prose #11

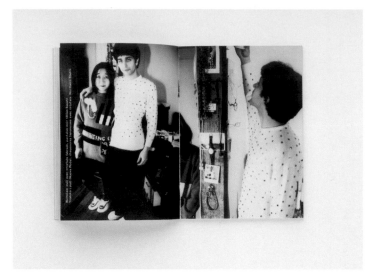

Racing Cup models, photographs by Anders Edström, Purple Prose #11

Proposals for an Anti-Erotic Year, text by Jeff Rian, photographs by Mark Borthwick,
Purple Prose #11

Memory and the ability to access it–both the short and long term versions–are certainly crucial to intelligence. Both versions of my memory are lousy, so it's to Wikipedia I go to jolt my 1997 neurons back to life. The Heaven's Gate cultists commit mass suicide; Deep Blue defeats Garry Kasparov; Mother Teresa, Martin Kippenberger, Princess Di, and Robert Mitchum die. There are plenty of atrocities and disasters, both natural and manmade–a major earthquake in Iran and continuing massacres in Algeria. However, I do recall the year being one of the better ones in terms of the generalized global disposition. While the Doomsday Clock is not the only gauge of such matters, I note that it was set at fourteen minutes to midnight back in '97, but it's crept up, and today…only five minutes left to Armageddon.

To reassess the state of *Purple* one decade ago, up the ladder to my higher bookshelves I go…somewhat less nimbly than I would have ten years ago. I find *Purple Fashion #2* and *#3*, *Purple Fiction #3*, and *Purple Prose #12*. I'm sure it's been noted elsewhere that *Purple Prose* fractured into thematic sub-zines in 1995.

Purple Fiction #3 includes fiction, of course, but also poetry and photography. Its contributors, like Vito Acconci, Jutta Koether, and Dominique Gonzalez-Foerster, tend to have at least one foot firmly planted in the art world. *#3*'s cover photo, by Chikashi Suzuki, is of a Japanese woman seated in a subway car wearing traditional garb; that choice certainly reflected Elein Fleiss's ongoing fascination with *la esthétique Japonaise*.

Purple Fashion #3 has a distinctly different and more substantial feel than *#2* and its sibling zines–it has big-name advertising, and that's what ultimately distinguishes a magazine from a zine. So, in 1997 it became clear that *Fashion* would be The Purple Institute's moneymaker, and a big part of its image. Mark Borthwick's great cover photo of a model in Comme des Garçons clothing was probably the choice of both Elein and Olivier Zahm. The inside of the issue is almost entirely dedicated to pictures, and contains very little text. The photographers, like Frenchwoman Laetia Benat, Turkish-born Banu Cennetoglu, and Mexican Mauricio Guillen, were essential to *Fashion's* look and success. Terry Richardson is here, too, probably at Olivier's invitation, and his cool raunchiness will become a big part of *Fashion's* future. All the photographers' work is some combination of the casual-edgy, the soft-sublime, and the everyday-erotic; their contributions to *Fashion* became part of a redefinition of what fashion photography could be and would become. And of course, there's the fashion itself, with perennial *Purple* (especially Elein) favorites Martin Margiela and Susan Cianciolo, as well as the cool–and, in 1997, obscure–contributions by the likes of Owen Gastor and Yab-Yum.

I was only tangentially involved with *Purple*, other than *Purple Prose*, for which I did some writing, editing, and legwork. *Prose* was conceived as a new kind of art magazine, with artist contributors, and a very open approach to content. For me the very best aspect of writing for *Prose* was the almost-total editorial freedom the writers were given. However, to keep *Prose* from being a total mess, each issue had a theme, and *#12*'s was "Inc." We were somewhat enthralled with the real international style: corporate style. There was certainly an aspect of it being a cultural critique of things corporate, but I think there was a shared sense that the poetic and aesthetic possibilities of corporate and institutional style were being under-appreciated and under-utilized. The cover image of *#12*, a cute blond touching herself, shot by the Brazilian photographer Marcelo Krasilcic, is sweetly salacious, and was probably Olivier's choice. Inside Olivier wrote a text, a kind of channeled update of D&G (ironically referring to Gilles Deleuze and Felix Guattari, not the fashion folk) on the perverse seductions of corporate design. Jeff Rian (who's the semi-anonymous hand in editing the texts in all the magazines) constructed a relationship between the religious Word and the corporate Icon. Bernard Joisten wrote on Hollywood special effects. Anders Edstrom contributed lovely, strange, and banal photos of Tokyo office workers to the Style section. Andreas Angelidakis wrote about Celebration, the city Disney built in Florida, and Joshua Decter wrote about Tommy Hilfiger. I interviewed the entertainment and corporate architect, Karen Daroff, Elein had the idea for her and I to co-interview a Nike designer for the "Inc." issue. Gordon Thompson, Nike's vice president of research, design, and development, and co-designer of Niketown New York, agreed to talk with us. Niketown was a week away from opening, but the IBM atrium, which is adjacent to Niketown, provided an appropriate venue for the interview. I remember formulating the interview questions with Elein—she went right to the central issues of design and politics, and I handled the fluff, the stuff about putting computer chips in shoes. Thompson was brilliant and slick; the interview came out well and has been republished in a number of places.

Certainly our enchantment with the corporate aesthetic played out later in other Purple projects. Jacques Tati's *Playtime*, and German modernist designer Lilli Reich's trade fair architecture (Dominique Gonzalez-Foerster introduced me to her work) served as design inspirations for *Elysian Fields*, Purple's exhibition at the Pompidou, several years later. I think the umbrella moniker, The Purple Institute, came into to usage for all Purple projects, and the actual offices of the magazines, around this time.

Purple has moved on. A decade later, Elein helms her *Journal* and Olivier commands *Fashion*. Both are great magazines, definitely more mature, with more sophisticated content, contributed by ever more professional photographers and writers. Both magazines still share masthead contributors, like long-time *Purple* designer, Christophe Brunnquell, who was always crucial to the look of the magazines. But when I look at the 1997 issues, I'm reminded of the unusual valance between Elein and Olivier that makes *Purple* so beautiful and so influential. Both are deeply intelligent and have a passion for fashion and the visual arts. Elein's critical eye is sharp, while her personal aesthetic is soft, a pale-gray-and-beige. She's a photographer of subtle sensibility and a critic of great acumen. Olivier knows his theory, his advertising, and his media. He's intellectual hip, he's charm and sex… a kind of Gainsbourg of the glossies. Together, certainly with pleasure, and surely not without tension, they've created an aesthetic that continues to influence both the international art and fashion worlds, and the relationship between those worlds.

In a piece I wrote for *Purple* a few years ago (1992: *My Year in Paris, Purple #14*, Winter 03) I expressed, somewhat obliquely, my gratitude to Elein and Olivier for including me in their endeavors. This is a good opportunity to be more explicit about that gratitude. Their support of me, from our first meeting in 1991 until the present, has enhanced my life immeasurably. Through them I've met great artists, many of whom are now friends. Because of them, I had writing and photos published that certainly wouldn't have found a home elsewhere (or at least not so stylish a one). They've included me in exhibitions and in the planning of them. They expanded my world. Mostly I'm grateful for their friendship, and the pleasure of their company, which I wish was more frequent. I think of them often. They occupy a big chunk of my long-term memory, which, when it comes to them, I find isn't so lousy after all.

purple fashion
number 2
1997
40 f - $10

Cover, photograph by Nathaniel Goldebrg, Purple Fashion #2

Snow White, concept by Miltos Manetas, photographs by Armin Linke,
Purple Fashion #2
Chinese Ladies, photographs by Anders Edström, Purple Fashion #2
Le chic gauchiste, photographs by Vidya & Jean-Michel, Purple Fahion #2

Chinese Ladies, photographs by Anders Edström, Purple Fashion #2
Le chic gauchiste, photographs by Vidya & Jean-Michel, Purple Fahion #2

Junya Watanabe, photographs by Takashi Homma, Purple Fashion #2
Horses, Horses comin' in in all directions, white, silver...,
photographs by Mark Borthwick, Purple Fashion #2
Martin Margiela inevitably here and now, photographs by Marina Faust,
Purple Fashion #2

Pause, photographs by Armin Linke, Purple Fashion #2
Horses, Horses comin' in in all directions, white, silver...,
photographs by Mark Borthwick, Purple Fashion #2
Carla's Choice, photographs by Mauricio Guillen, Purple Fashion #2

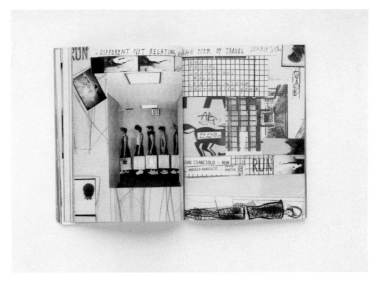

Susan Cianciolo, Run, photographs by Marcelo Krasilcic, Purple Fashion #2
Andrea Zittel by Andrea Zittel, photographs by Peter Muscato, Purple Fashion #2
Faridi, photographs by Wolfgang Tillmans, Purple Fashion #2

Susan Cianciolo, Run, photographs by Marcelo Krasilcic, Purple Fashion #2
Andrea Zittel by Andrea Zittel, photographs by Peter Muscato, Purple Fashion #2
Faridi, photographs by Wolfgang Tillmans, Purple Fashion #2

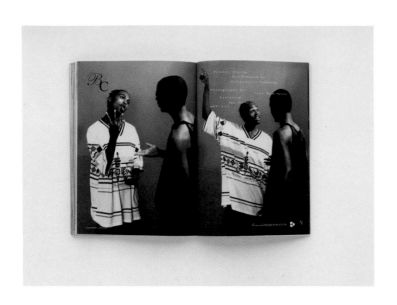

Concept and style by Bernadette Corporation, photographs by John Wayne Nguyen,
Purple Fashion #2
Keyboard Standard, photographs by Inez van Lamsweerde & Vinoodh Matadin,
Purple Fashion #2

purple fiction
number 3
1997
40f . $10

writing & photography

Cover, photograph by Chikashi Suzuki, Purple Fiction #3

Cover, photograph by Marcelo Krasilcic, Purple Prose #12

Iris-In, Iris-Out, text by Jeff Rian, Purple Prose #12
Nostalgia and Prophesy, David Berman of Silver Jews interviewed
by Bennett Simpson, Purple Prose #12
Style, photographs by Anders Edström, Purple Prose #12

Highway to Hell, Harmony Korine interviewed by Laetitia Benat and Camille Vivier,
Purple Prose #12
Style, photographs by Anders Edström, Purple Prose #12
D&G Corporate Song, text by Olivier Zahm, Purple Prose #12

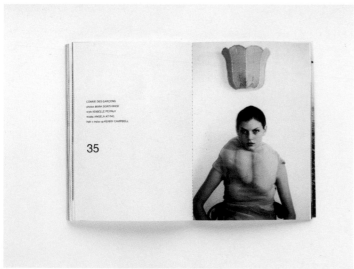

Cover, Angela Lindvall, photograph by Mark Borthwick, Purple Fashion #3
Photographs by Mark Borthwick, Purple Fashion #3

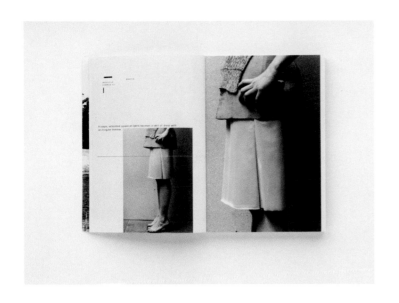

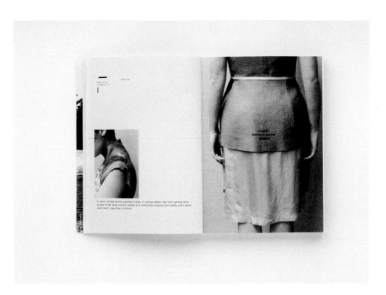

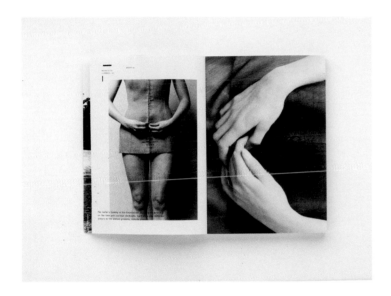

**Summer 1997 Martin Margiela, concept by Olivier Zahm,
photographs by Anders Edström, Purple Fashion #3
Run #2, photographs by Banu Cennetoglu, Purple Fashion #3**

**Summer 1997 Martin Margiela, concept by Olivier Zahm,
photographs by Anders Edström, Purple Fashion #3
Run #2, photographs by Banu Cennetoglu, Purple Fashion #3**

**Whooshh..., style by Eric Damon, photographs by Terry Richardson,
Purple Fashion #3**

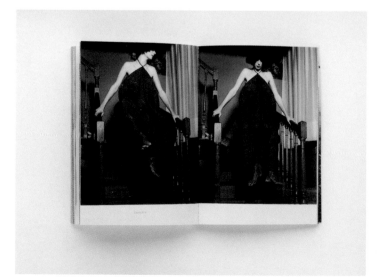

Sportswear, concept by Elein Fleiss, photographs by Anders Edström,
Purple Fashion #3
The Periodic Table, style by Gabriel Feliciano, photographs by Marcelo Krasilcic,
Purple Fashion #3
Nevers 79, photographs by Claude Lévêque, Purple Fashion #3

The Periodic Table, style by Gabriel Feliciano, photographs by Marcelo Krasilcic,
Purple Fashion #3
Nevers 79, photographs by Claude Lévêque, Purple Fashion #3
Clothes by Marie-Ange Guilleminot, photographs by Horst Diekgerdes,
Purple Fashion #3

Kim Gordon, photographs by Mark Borthwick, Purple Fashion #3

MORE CONFETTI◆

◆◆◆◆◆

STRAPLESS, BLACK-SILK POLKA-DOT DRESS

I slept on the floor, on the tiles. A Russian woman was sleeping in my bed. To get to the bathroom, she had to straddle over me, like a bridge over a stream.

In January, I was sitting in a train, facing a man. We were going to the same place. Not only the same city, the same address. He said he wanted to see me again. Yet he had already looked at me quite a bit.

For all of 1998, I thought about love. It was a year that only lasted nine months, because love changes the duration of years. Who knows why, but love accelerates and slows down reality. Love has special lighting, and a soundtrack: it's a movie. I saw *The Big Lebowski* with a friend from New York. Nine years later, in Jerusalem, I slept with a man in someone's bed. On the wall above us was the movie's poster.

In March, the man I was obsessed with met me in the Jardin des Tuileries, and he became obsessed with me too. It was blue out, pale blue. The twilight man took my frozen hands, pink in his giant hands, and warmed them. We walked through the empty alleys, alongside the bare trees. With a kiss, we became lovers at twilight. Since then, everyday I look forward to nightfall.

I cried in a telephone booth in front of Café de Flore. I saw eyes staring at me. My tears gave me the unpleasant feeling I was a star.

I received pornographic mail. A woman sent it to me.

I smuggled some cheese into New York.

I noticed time passed slower outside in the sun than inside in the dark.

The French soccer team won the World Cup. On this occasion, I was congratulated. An Austrian friend called me from Vienna. We never spoke again after that. I still don't understand.

I went to Walter Benjamin's grave in Portbou with a man. We crossed the border into Spain like escapees. But the situation held no suspense.

In August, walking across Paris, I had a metallic taste in my mouth.

For a few days during the summer, I camped on a cliff with two children, who have since disappeared. They're adults now.

I went to a wedding for the first time. I felt like I was witnessing the most indiscreet ceremony possible.

I didn't have a cell phone, and at home the phone line was often cut.

A man recited a well-known poem by Victor Hugo to me, holding my hand, and I cried. "Tomorrow at dawn, when the countryside grows white, I shall set off." The man continued, "I cannot dwell apart from you any longer." Actually, I don't think the man was holding my hand, and I think he made the words he recited his own. After that, I wrote a novel in the first person so that everyone could make my words their own. In any case, they're not really mine.

A petition was going around that year, but I didn't sign it. It was a petition in support of writer's rights. Property is sometimes stolen, including intellectual property.

That year, there were two very different winters, January's and December's. It was very cold in January, at least in Paris. I saw a Woody Allen film twice, not because I didn't understand it the first time, but because I liked it, and so I could laugh again, with people I didn't know. In a movie theater I always feel I'm in a mute relationship with the crowd—sometimes a silent crowd, on the brink of tears, or annoyed; sometimes a tiny crowd, laughing, a crowd of silhouettes. Inevitably, one silhouette always flashes by, like a bird through the sky, dashing to the candy stand, or the bathroom. The title of the movie was *Deconstructing Harry*.

No one talks in the theater, or if they do, it's to tell other people to be quiet. Would you ever ask that of someone you weren't intimate with?

In New York, a man I was in a theater with got into a fight with a silhouette. They fought over a comment made about a line of the movie's dialogue.

Previous spread: Fashion, Amsterdam, Viktor & Rolf Haute Couture, Winter 1999, concept and style by Olivier Zahm, photographs by Terry Richardson, Purple #2

PURPLE PROSE 13, PURPLE 1, 2, PURPLE FICTION 4, PURPLE FASHION 4, PURPLE SEXE 1, 3

It was cold that second winter of 1998, between January and March. I was obsessed not only with love, but also with massacre.

In Algeria, on the thirteenth day of Ramadan, during the first winter of the year 1998, certain men, shortly after breaking their fast, came down from the mountains into a town. There were many of them, maybe a hundred.

It was nighttime. Those who saw them first quickly went home and locked themselves in. In a hall, teenagers were watching a movie. They heard a loud noise, like an explosion. A silhouette jumped up. Then all the silhouettes panicked. They were gunned down.

The men who had entered the town were Muslim extremists.

They burned down homes. Children running away were caught not by their mothers, but by the Muslim extremists who slaughtered them with axes. They also killed the women, killed them with axes and shovels. A man and his two sons were able to defend themselves with three AK-47s. He later recounted how his cousin had put up a fight until the very end, but when his bullets ran out the Muslim extremists entered his home and killed him. They cut off his hands. Once they had accomplished their mission, the Muslim extremists left. Dawn came in their wake. The village of Sidi Hamed, in Algeria, was nothing but the charred remains of houses, puddles of blood, bodies, and wounded men and women on the ground.

I thought I would like it if for once the sun did not rise, if it was dark for all of one day, and not a single bird sang. Just to scare the men who did this.

Cover, photograph by Chikashi Suzuki, Purple Fashion #4
Hell on Earth, Fall/Winter 1997, photographs by John Minh Nguyen
and Bernadette Corporation, Purple Fashion #4

Hell on Earth, Fall/Winter 1997, photographs by John Minh Nguyen
and Bernadette Corporation, Purple Fashion #4

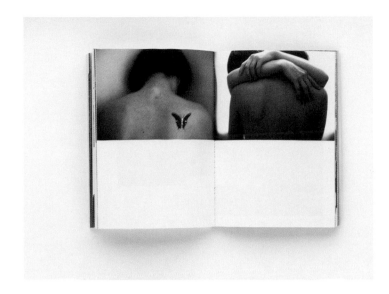

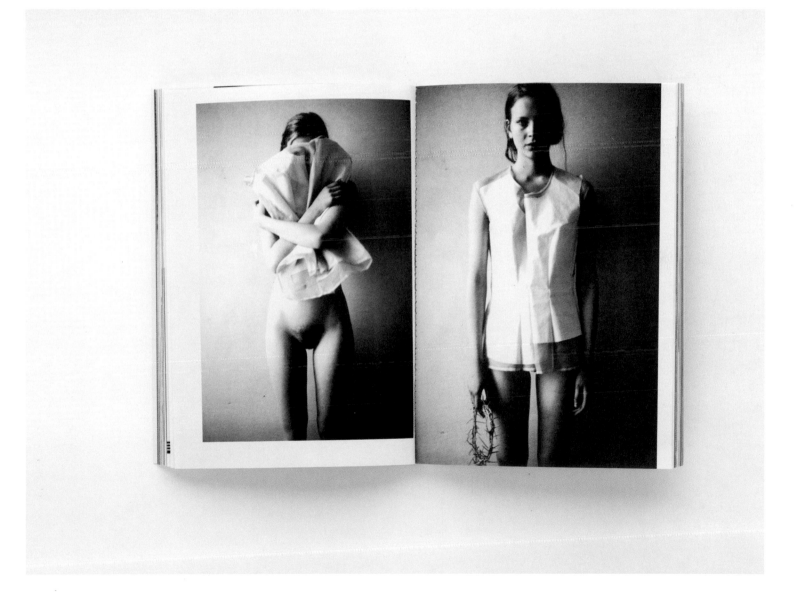

A Minor Mode, photographs by Camille Vivier, Purple Fashion #4
Comme des Garçons Fall/Winter 1997/1998, style by Jane Howe,
photographs by Mark Borthwick, Purple Fashion #4

Comme des Garçons Fall/Winter 1997/1998, style by Jane Howe,
photographs by Mark Borthwick, Purple Fashion #4

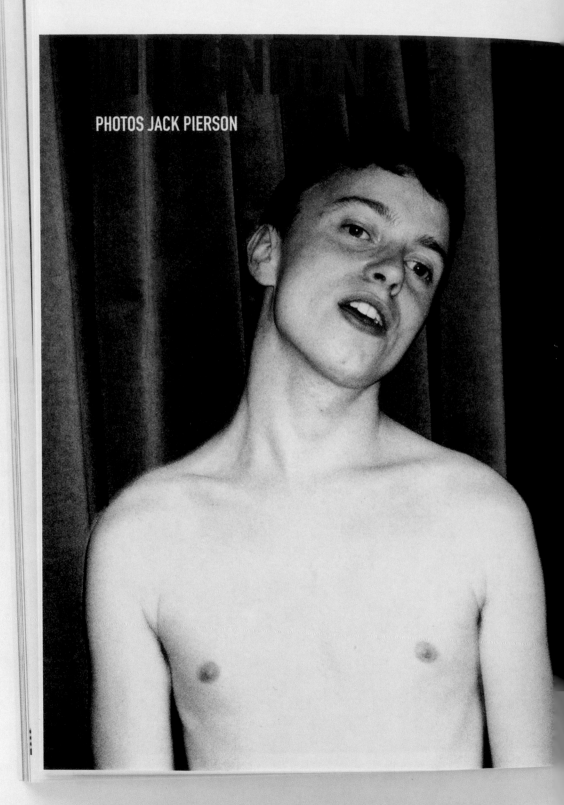

PHOTOS JACK PIERSON

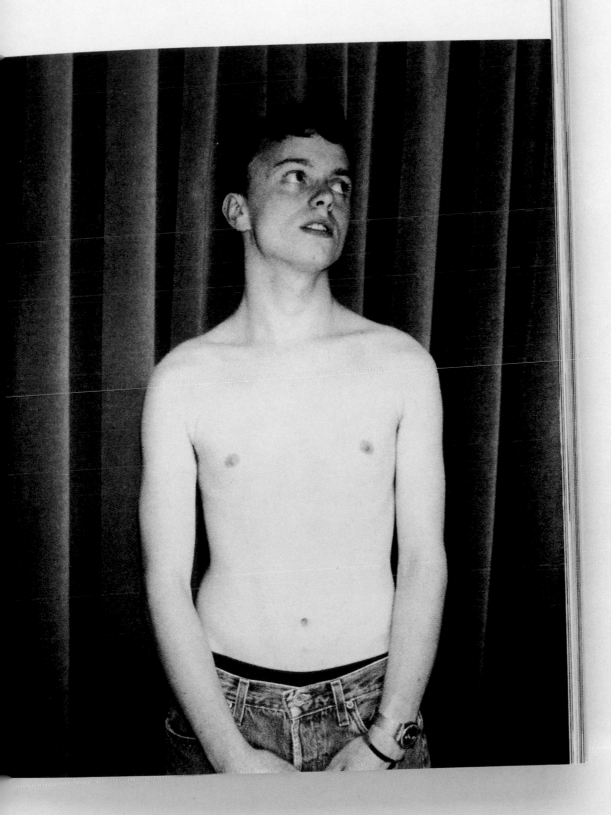

London, photographs by Jack Pierson, Purple Fashion #4

Purple Prose

13

WINTER 1998
$10 - 40 F
THE ABSTRACT ISSUE
ISBN 2-912684-02-1

Cover, Searchers: Salton Sea, photograph by Doug Aitken, Purple Prose #13

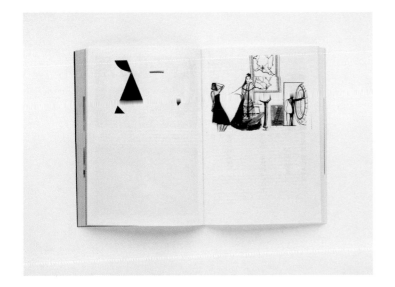

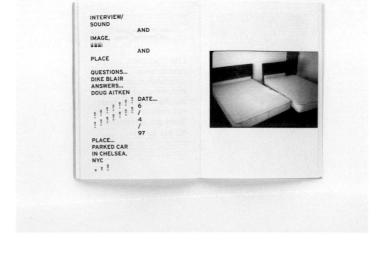

Ange Leccia: Face to Face, text by Olivier Zahm and Elein Fleiss, Purple Prose #13
Abstraction, photographs by John Lindell, Purple Prose #13
Run Abstraction, photograph by Ari Marcopoulos, Purple Prose #13

Run Abstraction, photograph by Ari Marcopoulos, Purple Prose #13
Sound and Image, Self and Place, Doug Aitken interviewed by Dike Blair, Purple Prose #13

GUARDIAN, 1995; PHOTOGRAPHED NEAR MCCRACKEN'S STUDIO IN NEW MEXICO

**Otherworldly, John McCracken interviewed by Dike Blair, Purple Prose #13
Cover, photograph by Mauricio Guillen, Purple Fiction #4**

Tropicide, photographs by Katja Rahlwes, Purple Fiction #4

Cover, photograph by Terry Richardson, Purple Sexe #1
The Dynamic Duo, photographs by Terry Richardson, Purple Sexe #1

Stretch, photographs by Marcelo Krasilcic, Purple Sexe #1
Blond-age, photographs by Armin Linke, Purple Sexe #1

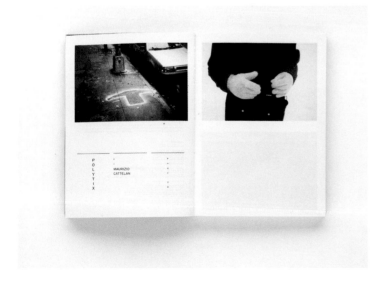

Cover, photograph by Takashi Noguchi, Purple #1
Polytix, photographs by Maurizio Cattelan, Purple #1

Polytix, photographs by Zoe Leonard, Purple #1

Fashion, Viktor & Rolf by Viktor & Rolf, photographs by Anuschka Blommers, Purple #1
Fashion, Susan Cianciolo Summer 1998, style by Nakako Hayashi, photographs by Takashi Homma, Purple #1

Fashion, Susan Cianciolo Summer 1998, style by Nakako Hayashi, photographs by Takashi Homma, Purple #1
Fashion, Owen Gaster Summer 1998, style by Stephen Da Silva, photographs by Johnny Gembitsky, Purple #1

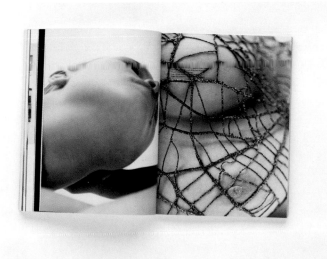

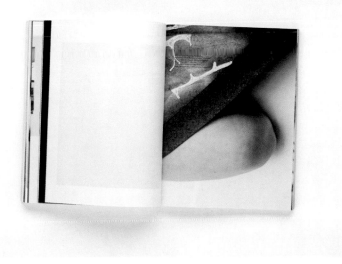

Fashion, Comme des Garçons Summer 1998, concept by Olivier Zahm,
photographs by Anette Aurell, Purple #1
Dimanche, concept by Elein Fleiss, photographs by Anders Edström, Purple #1
Purple Fashion, Koji Tatsuno Summer 1998, style by Isabelle Peyrut,
photographs by Nathaniel Goldberg, Purple #1

Dimanche, concept Elein Fleiss photographs by Anders Edström, Purple #1
Fashion, Koji Tatsuno Summer 1998, style by Isabelle Peyrut,
photographs by Nathaniel Goldberg, Purple #1

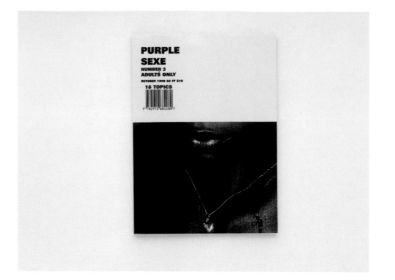

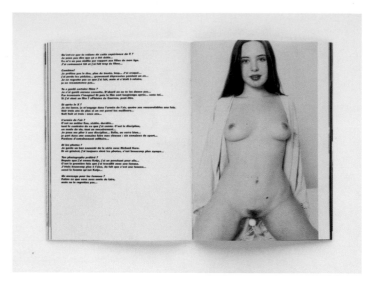

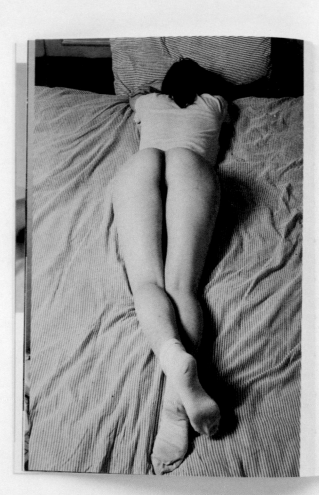

Cover, photograph by Terry Richardson, Purple Sexe #3
Lucy, Glasgow Ireland, photograph by Richard Kern, Purple Sexe #3
Singles, text by Claude Closky, Purple Sexe #3

The Purple Girl, photographs by Katja Rahlwes, Purple Sexe #3

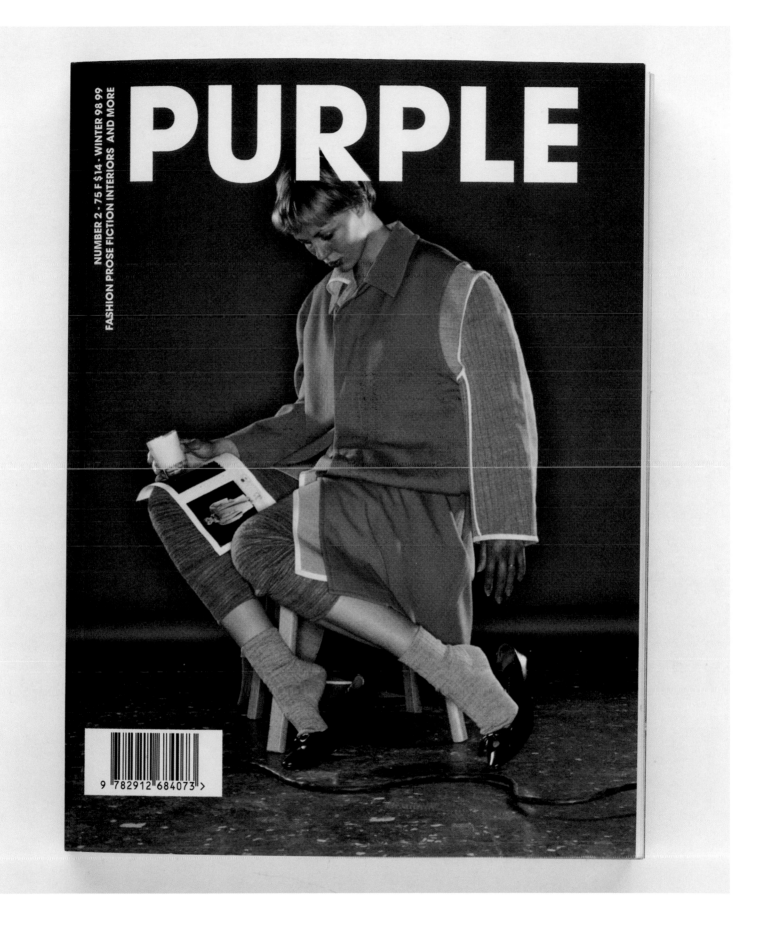

Cover, photograph by Anushka Blommers, Purple #2

Fashion, New York, Helmut Lang, concept by Olivier Zahm,
style by Melanie Ward, photographs Richard Prince, Purple #2

Fashion, Paris, Martin Margiela Winter 1998/1999, style by Susan Cianciolo,
photographs by Banu Cennetoglu, Purple #2
Fashion, New York, Susan Cianciolo Winter 1998/1999,
photographs by Laetitia Benat, Purple #2
Beauty, concept by Chiaki Tamura, photographs by Kenshu Shintsubo, Purple #2

Fashion, Paris, Martin Margiela Winter 1998/1999, style by Susan Cianciolo,
photographs by Banu Cennetoglu, Purple #2
Fashion, New York, Susan Cianciolo Winter 1998/1999,
photographs by Laetitia Benat, Purple #2
Beauty, concept by Chiaki Tamura, photographs by Kenshu Shintsubo, Purple #2

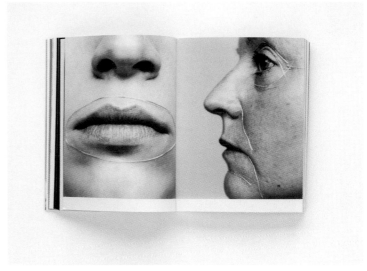

Fiction, Tracks, photographs by Claude Lévêque, Purple #2
Looks, Colin De Land, Dan Graham, David Karlin and Debra Kinery,
concept by Elein Fleiss, photographs by Marcelo Krasilcic, Purple #2
Purple Fashion, New York, Helmut Lang, concept by Olivier Zahm, style
by Melanie Ward, photographs Richard Prince, Purple #2

Beauty, concept Elein Fleiss, photographs Nathaniel Goldberg, Purple #2
Looks, Colin De Land, Dan Graham, David Karlin and Debra Kinery,
concept by Elein Fleiss, photographs by Marcelo Krasilcic, Purple #2
Purple Fashion, New York, Helmut Lang, concept by Olivier Zahm,
style by Melanie Ward, photographs Richard Prince, Purple #2

I am in the capital
of the Capitalism, New York
by Patterson Beckwith

Patterson Beckwith is an artist living in New York City.

01.   What is your sex?
Male.

02.   Where are you now?
I am in the capital of the Capitalism, New York City. The big fucking ap
busy.

03.   What's your favorite year since 1968?
2000 is my favorite year.

04.   Do you think the 90's ever existed, and what did you offer?
I can't prove it, but I think it's real. The late 90's arc the new mid-80's.

05.   Is your definition of "free time" uncommitted space to fill up? If so, what does that say about the idea that artists are never on vacation? And what does that say about the connections between leisure, boredom, and guilt?

I think "free time" is whenever you're awake and not working; it's what the Spectacle is supposed to occupy—the purpose of which is to make people into spectators rather than participants. I guess that artists are in a better position than most to avoid getting screwed out of "participating," because if they are working on their own stuff, that's unalienated labor.

06.   Can you describe the reasons you make art and how those reasons have changed, if they have, over time?

I make art for other people and the gratification that comes from my audience or the feedback I get from other artists. I am also habituated to the satisfactions that result from seeing my ideas realized; the way creation makes me feel is the opposite of depression.

07.   How do you decide when a project is worth realizing?

I ask Alex [Bag] to help me decide if something is worth doing. I think her criteria have to do with humor-entertainment value, clear communication of ideas, and visual pleasure.

08.   In the West, we seem to have developed a conception of culture which positions it as something used by children to form themselves. Children absorb music, movies, TV, etc., to create identities. One use which adults have for culture is to sell it to children, and thereby, in effect, to live off children. Other than these commercial transactions, what is it that adults use culture for?

I think culture is a portrait of the oppression and exploitation, and adults use it to delimit the spectrum of permissible behavior and politics.

09.   An artist, writer, filmmaker, or musician that particularly inspires you at the moment?

Colin de Land, Bernadette, Todd Solondz, Harmony Korine, Bill Owens, Missy Elliot.

10.   What is the image that counts the most for you? (Please describe it or send one.)

It's a picture of my dog, because she is my muse.

11.   When you wake up in the middle of the night, how do you occupy time and space?

I like to watch TV. I have cable!

12.   Should you? When?

Maybe sometimes, if it seems appropriate.

13.   Have you ever experienced the madness of the unexpected?

I don't think I have ever experienced the madness of the unexpected, man.

14.   What would you do if you inherited a million dollars?

I think it would be enough money that I could try to make sure I never have to work another day in my life. I think most artists, when they get money, invest very conservatively.
They buy real estate.

15.   One of your favorite hotels?

The Four Seasons. It was designed by I. M. Pei. Michael Jackson stays there when he's in town (because it's close to the Sony building), and the bathtubs fill in 30 seconds.
It's too expensive to actually stay there, but they'll show you a room for free.
Ask to see one with a balcony.
57 E.57th St. Tel 758-5700.

I'm under the rooftops of Paris. The date is December 26. It's nighttime. I know perfectly well what's happening out there—it's a devastating storm. But in here, where I am, what I hear is the most magnificent sound. Is the roof going to be torn off? I think back to the total eclipse of August 11, its light, and contradictory darkness, and I think back to the most beautiful girl in the world. She's smiling at me, with love. We're on the Place des Pyramides of the Louvre, in view of the equestrian statue of Louis XIV, which they say can be seen differently from eight sides at a time….

My favorite albums of the year: *Nigga Please* by ODB, *Eureka* by Jim O'Rourke, the *POLA X* soundtrack, *SYR 4: Goodbye 20th Century* by Sonic Youth, *Juxtapose* by Tricky, and *2007* by Alan Vega.

Mariah Carey is singing live on Argentinian television. The television studio has a decor inspired by Mondrian's geometric compositions. The singer's silhouette is outlined by three distinct elements. At the top left, there's a red rectangle—the star's head covers a corner of it. At the bottom right, standing on the floor, there's a reproduction of Mona Lisa against a white background in a simple black frame. Then there's a yellow rectangle that fills most of the background, over which all the other elements are layered. Mariah Carey performs "Against All Odds," the popular love song by Phil Collins: "How can I just let you walk away/Just let you leave without a trace/When I stand here taking every breath with you/OOH." With her eyes closed, she sings, "You're the only one who really knew me at all." Her right hand releases her microphone. She shakes her hand in a low-to-high movement that lasts almost four seconds, a movement that includes a discrete gesture in which she points her index finger towards her ear. We have a problem: Mariah Carey can't hear the music in her earphones well enough.

Facing the TV screen, the Peronist banker cries. Over and over, a very crazy thought goes through his head: "Just increasing the discount rates simply won't do."

Yes, indeed, this is the year of *Matrix* effects, the "Bullet time" one and the "flowing green characters" one.

Bill Clinton says, "For the first time in three decades, the budget is balanced. From a deficit of $290 billion in 1992, we had a surplus of $70 billion last year, and now we are on course for budget surpluses for the next 25 years. With the number of elderly Americans set to double by 2030, the baby boom will become a 'senior boom.' So first, and above all, we must save Social Security for the 21st century. We will save Social Security now."

They say the Starr Report cost about 40 million dollars. Extract from the report: "Ms. Lewinsky gave him, among other things, six neckties, an antique paperweight showing the White House, a silver tabletop holder for cigars or cigarettes, a pair of sunglasses, a casual shirt, a mug emblazoned 'Santa Monica,' a frog figurine, a letter opener depicting a frog, several novels, a humorous book of quotations, and several antique books. He gave her, among other things, a hat pin, two brooches, a blanket, a marble bear figurine, and a special edition of Walt Whitman's *Leaves of Grass.*"

Forty million dollars. That's less than the sixty-three million *Matrix* cost, and less than the sixty-five million *Eyes Wide Shut* cost, but more than the thirty-one million *eXistenZ* cost.

Leaves of Grass was first published by Whitman himself in 1855. "Song of Myself," the first poem in the book, begins like this: "I CELEBRATE myself,/And what I assume you should assume,/For every atom belonging to me as good belongs to you."

Previous spread: Prose, I Am in the Capital of the Capitalism, New York City, text by Patterson Beckwith, Purple #3

PURPLE 3, 4, PURPLE SEXE 4, 5

In his *Histoire(s) du cinéma*, Jean-Luc Godard makes a huge mistake. I suspect he did so on purpose, setting a trap. At the beginning of section 3A, entitled "La Monnaie de l'Absolu," a section that draws on fragments of a 1876 Victor Hugo text called *À la Serbie* [To Serbia], Godard says, "The scriptures tell us that before setting out on their travels, Lot's daughters wanted to turn and look back one last time, and they were transformed into salt statues." Lot's daughters transformed into salt statues! That's a good one! Look what the scriptures really say. Go to Genesis 19:26, "The Destruction of Sodom and Gomorrah" and you'll see, "But his wife looked back from behind him, and she became a pillar of salt." As if by way of reminder, Luke 17:32 tells us to "Remember Lot's wife!" So, Godard misquotes the Bible in the work some consider to be his masterpiece. One of his favorite quotes is, "Cinema places a world before us that corresponds to our desire," isn't it?

In the end, it's so typically Protestant to substitute Lot's daughters for their mother in the telling of the story. Bravo! Well done. Very practical. Neither seen nor understood: one of the worst episodes of incest in the entire history of humanity, rendered null and void.

Julien Donkey Boy says. "Midnight Chaos Eternity Chaos Morning Chaos Eternity Chaos Noon Chaos Eternity Chaos Evening Chaos Eternity Chaos Midnight Chaos Eternity Chaos Morning Chaos Eternity Chaos Noon Chaos Evening Chaos Eternity Chaos Midnight Chaos Eternity Chaos Morning Chaos Eternity Chaos…"

Isabel gently leads Pierre. They sit side-by-side on the edge of Isabel's bed. She invites Pierre to rest his head on her thighs. She lays her right hand gently on Pierre's desperate looking face. He says he's a Christian. He repeats that he wanted to do no harm, and he apologizes for something he calls swindling.

Isabel tells him she doesn't understand what he means. Pierre answers that he wanted to give her everything, but that he has nothing. Isabel tells him that they're together, and that's all that counts. "But where are we?" wonders Pierre aloud. "Outside of everything." answers Isabel.

It is indeed strange that we needed the film adaptation of a mid-nineteenth century New York gothic novel to grasp what's been happening in Eastern Europe for the last ten years. On January 8, 1852, Herman Melville brought the manuscript of *Pierre: or, The Ambiguities* to Harper & Brothers, his publisher in New York. On January 9, 1852, Victor Hugo is officially expulsed from France by decree, "for reasons of general safety."

That year, Marines were posted in Buenos Aires to protect American interests in the face of revolutionary movements. This all took place before the birth of Joseph Stalin.

On May 7, as part of Operation "Allied Force," NATO bombs hit the Chinese Embassy in Belgrade, Serbia, killing three Chinese journalists. The White House says it's a terrible mistake.

On June 14, the eleventh president of the Republic of South Africa, Nelson Mandela, the hero, retires.

I think back to a painting by Mark Rothko I discovered the spring of that year at The Museum of Modern Art in Paris. Red. Rothko red. I remember the tremendous impression I had of passing through the very substance of the color for a fraction of a second. Rothko said, "Maybe you have noticed two characteristics exist in my paintings: either their surfaces are expansive and push outward in all directions, or their surfaces contract and rush inward in all directions. Between these two poles you can find everything I want to say. "

Cover, photograph by Anders Edström, Purple #3
Run 7 264 Canal Street, Susan Cianciolo Summer collection 1999, Purple #3

Fashion, Blues Explosion, with Jon Spencer Blues Explosion, Jon Spencer,
Russell Simins and Judah Bauer, photographs by Terry Richardson, Purple #3

Fashion, Martin Margiela Summer 1999, style by Karl Plewka,
photographs by Alex Antitch, Purple #3
Fashion, A Night Without Armor, style by Benjamin Sturgill, concept by Alex Bag,
photographs by Patterson Beckwith, Purple #3
Beauty, Beauty for Schizophrenics, beauty for kids, photographs by Chris Moor,
Purple #3

Fashion, New Look, Junya Watanabe Summer 1999, style by Marion Meyer,
photographs by Marcelo Krasilcic, Purple #3
Fashion, A Night Without Armor, style by Benjamin Sturgill,
concept by Alex Bag, photographs by Patterson Beckwith, Purple #3

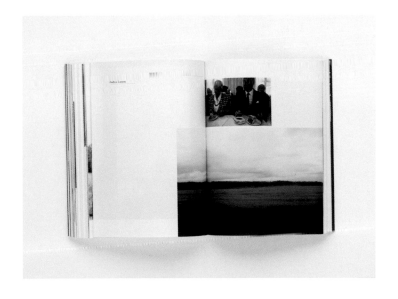

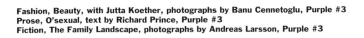

Fashion, Beauty, with Jutta Koether, photographs by Banu Cennetoglu, Purple #3
Prose, O'sexual, text by Richard Prince, Purple #3
Fiction, The Family Landscape, photographs by Andreas Larsson, Purple #3

Fashion, Beauty, with Jutta Koether, photographs by Banu Cennetoglu, Purple #3
Fiction, The Family Landscape, photographs by Andreas Larsson, Purple #3

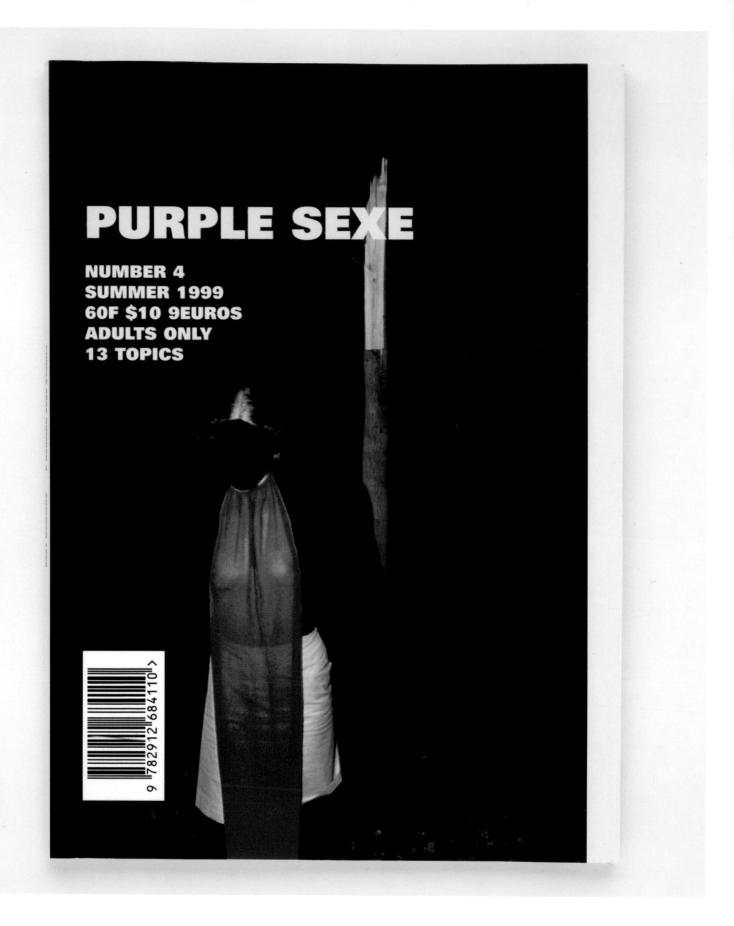

PURPLE SEXE

NUMBER 4
SUMMER 1999
60F $10 9EUROS
ADULTS ONLY
13 TOPICS

Cover, photograph by Vivianne Sassen, Purple Sexe #4

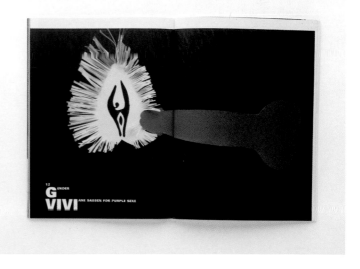

1 Girl, photographs by Mark Borthwick, Purple Sexe #4
Couple, photographs by Marcelo Krasilcic, Purple Sexe #4
Gender, photographs by Viviane Sassen, Purple Sexe #4

Couple, photographs by Marcelo Krasilcic, Purple Sexe #4
Gender, photographs by Viviane Sassen, Purple Sexe #4

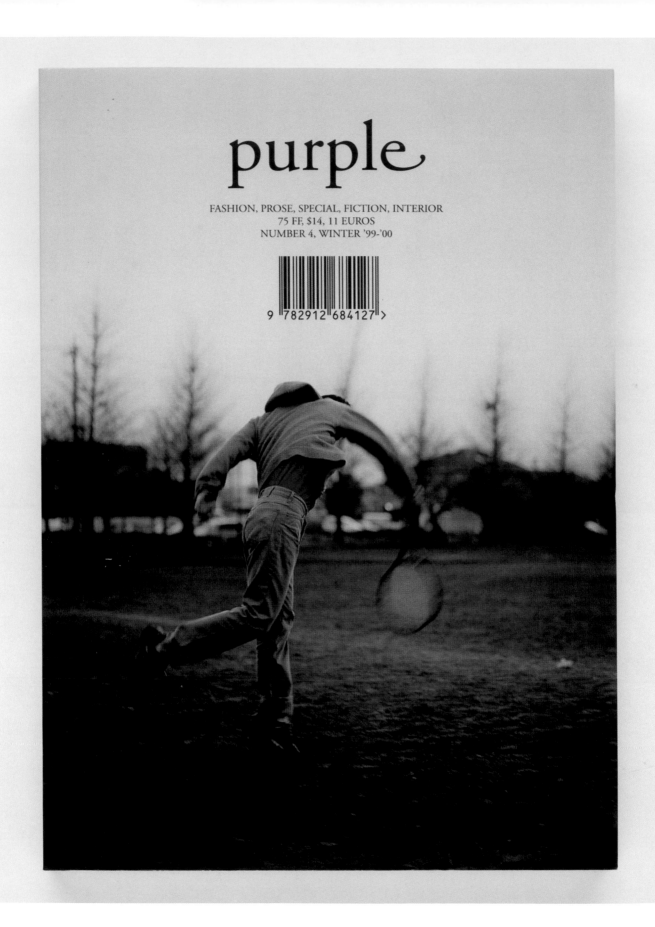

Cover, photograph by Masafumi Sanai, Purple #4

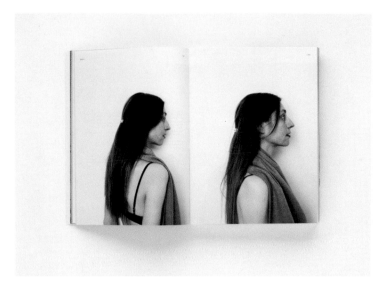

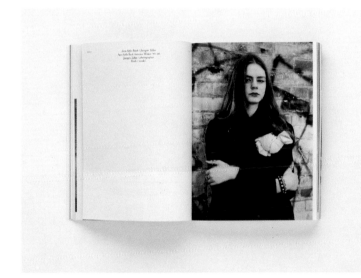

**Fashion, Hermès, Autumn/Winter 1999/2000, with Jutta Koether,
photographs by Mark Borthwick, Purple #4**
**Fashion, Ann-Sofie Back Autumn/Winter 1999/2000, photographs by Juergen Teller,
Purple #4**
**Fashion, 1999/2000, style by Yoshiko Shiojiri, photographs by Anders Edström,
Purple #4**

**Fashion, Hermès, Autumn/Winter 1999/2000, with Jutta Koether,
photographs by Mark Borthwick, Purple #4**
**Fashion, Ann-Sofie Back Autumn/Winter 1999/2000, photographs by Juergen Teller,
Purple #4**
**Fashion, 1999/2000, style by Yoshiko Shiojiri, photographs by Anders Edström,
Purple #4**

fashion

Helmut Lang / Jack Pierson
Helmut Lang Autumn Winter '99-'00
<u>Jack Pierson</u> / photographer
Annette Monheim (Streeters) / stylist
Tom Borgese / stylist for Brad
Sarra'NA (Atlantis) / hair
Rosemarie Swift (Streeters) / make-up
John Arsenault and George Perkins / assistants
Caroline, Debbie and Jen (Marilyn Agency) / models
with Nico Lou, Rosemarie, Brad, Jeff, Lyle, Matthew, Michael, Uri
Tom and Walter Schupfer / photostudio
Tracey Baran and Tim Smith / prints
Thanks to China Forbes, Romina Herrera and Joseph McKee, John Derian,
Paul Likens and Betty at Marilyn Agency

Fashion, Helmut Lang Autumn/Winter 1999/2000, with Brad Pitt,
style by Tom Borgese, photographs by Jack Pierson, Purple #4

Fiction, Far and Wide: William Eggleston, photograph by Kyoji Takahashi, Purple #4

Interior, Bedroom, with Iggy Pop, photographs by Doug Aitken, Purple #4

Fashion, Harmony Korine, photographs by Terry Richardson, Purple #4

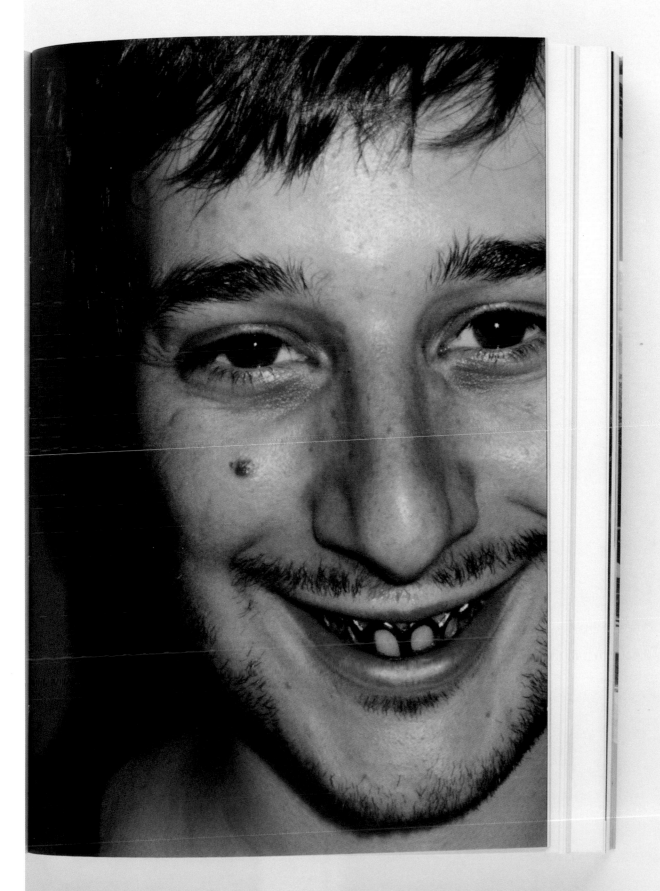

Fashion, Harmony Korine, photographs by Terry Richardson, Purple #4

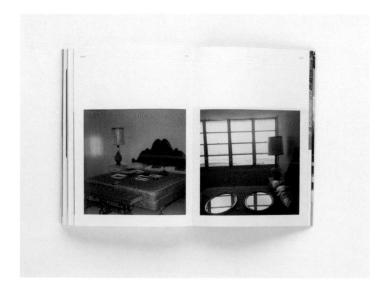

Prose, Newports, the cigarette of the street, text by Bruce Benderson, Purple #4
Fashion, French Kiss, photographs by Ange Leccia, Purple #4
Interior, The Seventies, photographs by Stéphanie Campos, Purple #4

Prose, Soft Clothes Already Broken Inn, text by Mark Gonzales, Purple #4
Fiction, Far and Wide, 5 Pictures, Black Sea, photographs by Kyoji Takahashi,
Purple #4

Cover, photograph by Marcelo Krasilcic, Purple Sexe #5
Neca With Her Dogs Maya and Ivalú in Her House, photographs by Marcelo Krasilcic,
Purple Sexe #5

On New Year's Eve, December 31, 1999–a little more than a year and eight months before that notorious event of September 11–New York was still patting itself on the back for being the well-admired center of the world. But at the same time, New Yorkers were imagining that somehow the new millennium would bring them an undefined tragedy. Vain about their popular culture, new technologies, their country's military might, and, most of all, their economic universe, they were suddenly seized with a weird panic. Was it victor guilt? I don't really know. But many resorted to survivalist measures, such as hoarding batteries, gallons of water, and even antibiotics and bandages, as a precaution against the possible devastations of Y2K.

Y2K? What does this acronym mean? Just seven years later, it's about as memorable as a former hairstyle, so let me remind you: "Y2K" stood for the ominous "Year 2000." Apparently, because the time-function systems of millions of computers, electronic calendars, and military devices had been blithely designed with only two digits, as long as fifty years ago, the very first nanosecond of the twenty-first century had a good chance of plunging us into chaos and deprivation. Every apparatus dependent upon time for its functioning was going to go bonkers, leaving us lightless, heatless, waterless, without any of the comforts we'd begun to take for granted in the last six or so decades. We'd be plunged into a new Middle Ages.

It was like a replay of the 1950s in America, when a great number of middle-class families, terrified by the risks of the Cold War, began building underground bomb shelters stocked with food, water, and pharmaceuticals–as well as guns to protect them from those who lacked such securities after the detonation of an atomic bomb. (Talk about victor guilt!)

Correlating with these fears was another, though lesser, fantasy of punishment: the threat of terrorism. Not only terrorism coming from the outside, but also from America's provincial interior, from neo-Nazi sects and born-again apocalyptic Christians, some of whom were certain that the end of the world as described in the New Testament's Revelations meant that the battle against the forces of darkness (Jews, homosexuals, centralized government, and the United Nations) would begin at exactly 12:0000000000001 AM, on January 1, 2000, and that they, as warriors of God, had the responsibility of being the first to fight on the right side. (Weren't they aware that certain mathematicians were pointing out that the millennium would actually start in 2001, and not 2000, since our counting system is based on sets of ten, not nine? And did they really think that God had such a modern, well-calibrated timepiece?)

For all these reasons, New Year's celebration in New York was a hybrid of collective joy and quasi-military mobilization. Almost a million revelers visited Times Square, and the sound and light shows lasted all day and all night, for twenty-four hours. The concept called for a new, brief presentation every hour on the hour, to represent each country in the world just as its time zone struck midnight.

However, this celebration was not, in my opinion, about world unity, but about the expansion of the tentacles of the American Market. Everyone was entertained by dances from Bali or by African drums–which took place just steps away from Times Square's mega Disney Store, turning the whole celebration into one big hallucinated cartoon. Meanwhile, approximately 7,000 sinister cops circulated through the crowd, on the lookout for evil-doers.

Previous spread: Purple special, Richard Prince, Only in America, text by Jeff Rian, photographs Richard Prince, Purple #6

PURPLE 5, 6, PURPLE SEXE 6, 7

As I sat alone in front of my television set and thought of
the millions of others in front of theirs, I was gripped, I'll
admit, by a sour fantasy. Perhaps it was just a symptom of
my alienation, or bitterness about having to spend such a
landmark occasion by myself, or the after-effect of all the
previous anxiety about our non-existent Y2K crisis.
But I found myself thinking of a sallow-skinned man
in the crowd of mindless revelers, who wasn't smiling,
and who was wearing a knapsack containing a miniature
atomic bomb, and who was about to press a button.
I saw the glass of our TV sets exploding just a second
afterward, and New York transformed into a city of
skeletons celebrating the New Year in front of screens
that had become black holes.

But as early as January 1, the day after the big bash,
it became obvious that we had entered 2000 without
problems, and everyone seemed strangely disappointed
and directionless, as if we'd been led astray, or duped.
Where was the enemy? The new paradise, with its
extraordinary technical inventions, its limitless possibilities
of communication, would go on, but at the expense,
it seemed, of leaving everyone voiceless—or at least
thoughtless.

We had fallen strangely out of touch with our new world.
Living underwater like that, we existed in an oppressive
stillness, which, as I've said, would only be shattered, once
and for all, one year, eight months and eleven days later.
Could the delay have had anything to do with Y2K?

Cover, drawing by Maria Finn, Purple #5
Fashion, Spring/Summer 2000, with Chloë Sevigny, photographs by Mark Borthwick, Purple #5

**Fashion, Spring/Summer 2000, with Chloë Sevigny, photographs by Mark Borthwick,
Purple #5**

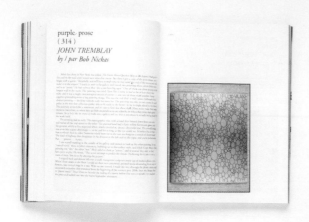

Prose, John Tremblay, text by Bob Nickas, Purple #5
Prose, Franz Ackermann, text by Joshua Decter, Purple #5
Prose, Tony Feher, text by John Lindell, Purple #5

Prose, Vija Celmins, text by Jeff Rian, Purple #5
Prose, Stanley Brouwn, text by Pierre Leguillon, Purple #5
Prose, Blake Rayne, text by Tim Griffin, Purple #5

Look, Bob Richardson, photographs by Terry Richardson, Purple #5
Look, J'adore, photographs by Wolfgang Tillmans, Purple #5

Look, Bob Richardson, photographs by Terry Richardson, Purple #5
Look, J'adore, photographs by Wolfgang Tillmans, Purple #5

Special, General Idea, AA Bronson, 1976; three men, 1976, Purple #5
Special, General Idea, Jorge Zontal, circa 1971, Purple #5
Special, General Idea, AA Bronson, circa 1973; Jorge Zontal, 1973, Purple #5

Special, General Idea, Felix Partz, 1968; Jorge Zontal, 1969, Purple #5
Special, General Idea, Jorge, Felix, and AA; Felix and AA, Purple #5

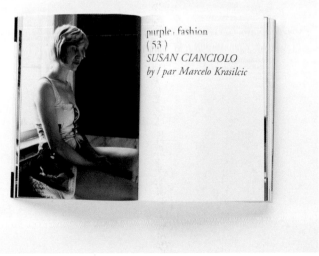

Fiction, Amendoin Japones, photograph by Elein Fleiss, Purple #5
Helmut Lang's new collection, photographs by Lodge Kerrigan, Purple #5
Fashion, Susan Cianciolo, style Haidée Findlay-Levin,
photographs by Marcelo Krasilcic, Purple #5

Helmut Lang's new collection, photographs by Lodge Kerrigan, Purple #5
Fashion, Susan Cianciolo, style Haidée Findlay-Levin,
photographs by Marcelo Krasilcic, Purple #5

left
Volume 2, Number 3 of *FILE* magazine, 1973, the special *IFEL* issue created especially for the Musée d'Art Moderne de la Ville de Paris.

right
Photoshoot for *FILE* magazine, circa 1973: Felix Partz dresses a model.

Special, General Idea, Volume 2, Number 3 of File magazine, 1973; Felix Partz, Purple #5

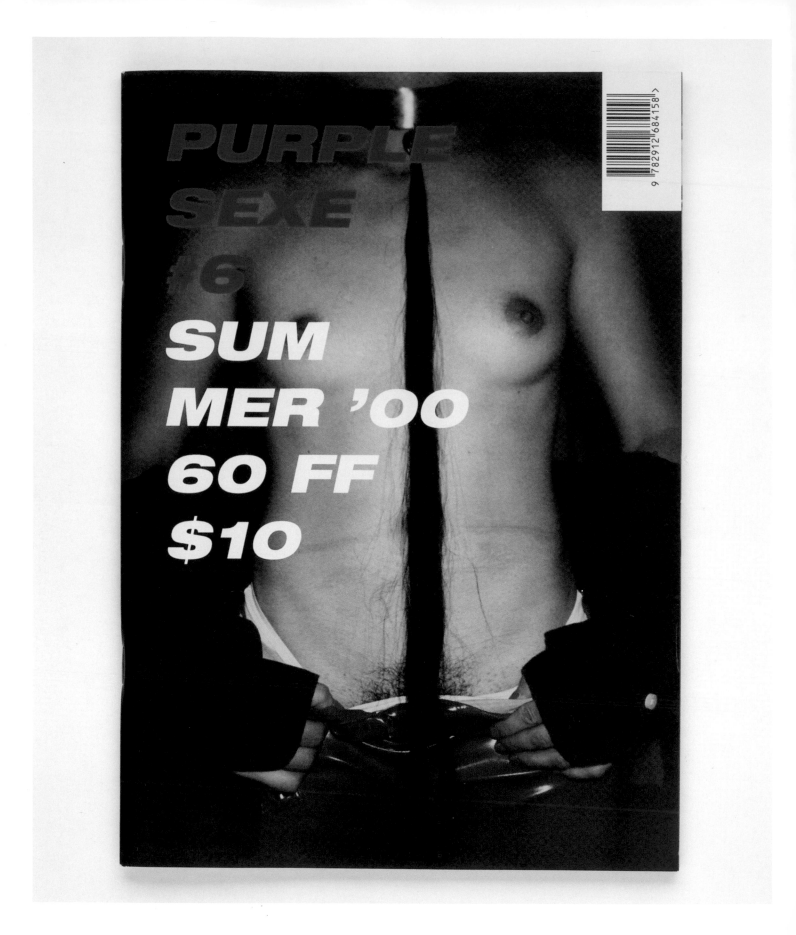

Cover, photograph by Giasco Bertolli, Purple Sexe #6

Red Two, photographs by Giasco Bertoli, Purple Sexe #6
Celeste, photographs by Giasco Bertoli, Purple Sexe #6

Red One, photographs by Giasco Bertoli, Purple Sexe #6

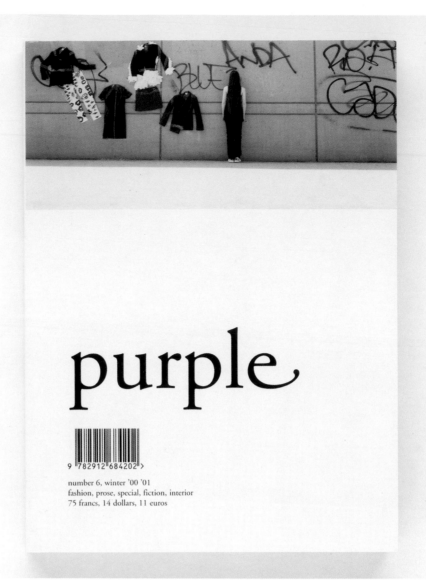

purple

9 782912 684202

number 6, winter '00 '01
fashion, prose, special, fiction, interior
75 francs, 14 dollars, 11 euros

Cover, photograph by Mark Borthwick, Purple #6
Purple Fashion, Friends Winter collections 2000/2001,
photographs by Mark Borthwick, Purple #6

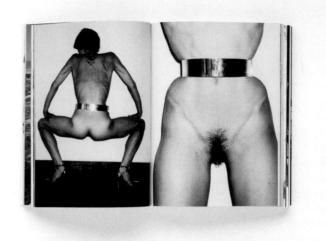

Fashion, Fendi, Gang Deluxe, photographs by Terry Richardson, Purple #6
Fashion, Balenciaga, Attitudes Revisited, photographs by Vanina Sorrenti, Purple #6

Fashion, Fendi, Gang Deluxe, photographs by Terry Richardson, Purple #6
Fashion, Lutz, Working Girl, photographs by Giasco Bertoli, Purple #6

Special Richard Prince, Only in America, text by Jeff Rian,
photographs Richard Prince, Purple #6
Fiction, Blue Meridian, photographs by Torbjørn Rødland, Purple #6

Special Richard Prince, Only in America, text by Jeff Rian,
photographs Richard Prince, Purple #6

Cover, photograph by Katja Rahlwes, Purple Sexe #7
I Kill You First, drawings by Rita Ackermann, Purple Sexe #7

Catherine, top by Patrick van Ommeslaeghe and her YSL Haute Couture jacket
Chan, all clothes by Prada

For many years to come, 2001 will be remembered as the year of September 11. But the question is, how long exactly is "for many years to come"? That is to say, will the event really set the tone for the new century, as it has for the past six years? Or can we expect that another event will one day relegate September 11 to the status of anecdote?

Since 1789, the coordinates and references were clear —the stirrings of thought and practice over almost two centuries, even in their variety, pointed to a shared meaning and truth, which could be applied infinitely. There was progress and reaction, on the left and on the right, Hegelian-Marxism and Nietzschean-Heideggarianism….

The year 1789, it seemed, was the year theology was liquidated in favor of politics. Theological-politics were born when the Roman Emperor converted to Christianity. Theological-politics were meant to hide politics entirely behind theology. In 1789, in one fell swoop, the universal apprehension of The Thing was reversed. The theological would henceforth, and forever, it was thought, be the ideological propaganda masking most political relationships in human society. Hegel exemplarily understood this, and Marx would sum it up in his famous maxim, "Religion is the opiate of the masses." The left strived for emancipation, progress and equality of all mankind; the right for the preservation of old privileges. In 1917, in the face of the expected triumph of the "left's vision of the world," the right understood that it could not simply represent conservative reaction and nostalgia for the old world. It had to prove that it could also represent the radical new, a new that had nothing to do with the new of the Republican, Democrat, Egalitarian, Bolshevik enemy, nor anything to do with old theological-politics. This involved creating new theological-politics. In thirteen short years, Nazism would sink humanity into an abyss, "the abyss of theological-politics as is," Lacoue-Labarthe said, from which it would never recover.

Nazism wanted to produce an operation. Beyond its final "failure," the abyss exposed by this operation continues to exist.

For the thirty years after 1945, the left still seemed to be alive and well. There was real socialism, revolution, liberation of blacks and women, third-world empowerment. Nazism and Fascism had failed to defeat Communism, but another enemy—with a more human face, because it promised to be the enemy of Communism itself—that is, American Capitalism, strove to eliminate "the left" throughout the world. It did so by the means of armed financial corruption, by means of torture training, by means of the systematic support of all local fascism in poor countries, even those in Europe (Iberia and Greece for example). At the end of the 1970s, from behind the scenes, the dye was case. A key event? The war in Afghanistan. For the first time, the word jihad, up until then used strictly as a theological term, now also inferred a political meaning. "Real" Communism would never recover from this war; backup forces from the United States, and the Taliban forces, drove the Communists to loose ends. "What is to be done?" asked Lenin.

During the exact same period, in France, a fundamentalist country, in the literal sense of the word, there emerged what I call "democratic nihilism." To my mind, democracy is not necessarily nihilist; this determination was nevertheless established as absolute by historical fascists, including the most brilliant among them, Nietzsche and Heidegger. Democracy is nihilism (that is, for these historical fascists, and for the Nazis, it's monotheism, the French Revolution, Rousseau, Socialism, Bolshevism, etc). The secondary ideology of democratic nihilism was disseminated throughout France by a group called the "New Philosophers." They imported 1930s American ideology, adding only an argument about mass crimes, those starting with Auschwitz and the Gulag. Everything that wasn't "democracy"—meaning the upholding of formal rights and the freedom of the market—was

Previous spread: **Fashion, Spring/Summer, with Catherine Deneuve and Chan Marshall, photographs by Terry Richardson, Purple #8**

inevitably bound to transform into "totalitarianism."
A few decades later, these "democratic" and "humanist" ideologues, known for being "on the left," were leaning very much to the right, even to the far right. In the name of human rights (the right to food, shelter, and health care are not considered human rights in the United States), the war in Iraq, the Patriot Act and Guantanamo. That the "philosophy" of these "thinkers" did not amount to much was well known—at the very moment they appeared to "triumph" politically, their ideology was crumbling. Let us assume that, when evaluating the politics of a given country, the central issue is crime committed by its State. How then can the unconditional support of the country whose State is by far the most criminal since the death of Stalin be justified?
To take the issue further, this is what seems to me to be the challenge. Hegel had a philosophy about the absolute. He was the first to make the death of God a theme, and wrote explicitly about the revolutionary Reign of Terror (which for Hegel meant the advent of the absolute freedom of man in the face of man). When leading thinkers—Kant, Nietzsche, Heidegger, for example—reflected on their times, they didn't support or collaborate on political impostures in ways that we know. They theorized that man without God was a finite man. Which, in other words, means that man under democratic nihilism is the first in the entire history of mankind to not have the right to an absolute.
It is therefore not Osama bin Laden alone who brought History back to Earth. As Lacoue-Labarthe noted, the United States is no less a theocratic state (evangelism) than the Islamic countries or Israel. As long as our "spiritual" definition of democracy is the lack of an absolute, old forms of the absolute will continue to arbitrate the world, with fire and blood. If we refuse the challenge, it's pointless to continue moaning. Let the GIs, the kamikazes, and Tzahal take care of serious stuff. Democratic nihilism will continue to lose ground, as the last presidential elections in France so poignantly proved, to something that, in any case, is stronger: mankind in possession of an absolute. Because mankind is defined by being the only known species to have never lived only in the absolute, or in its banal element.

Cover, photographs by Richard Prnce, Purple #7

**Fashion Spring/Summer 2001, style by Yasmine Eslami,
photographs by Richard Prince, Purple #7**

Special, New Jersey, text by Dan Graham, photographs by Dan Graham, Purple #7
Special, New Jersey, photographs by Roe Ethridge, Purple #7

Gucci & Seth Shapiro, The Way We Were, photographs by Terry Richardson, Purple #7
Lutz & Comme des Garçons #1, English Friends, photographs by Juergen Teller, Purple #7

Beauty, Bambou, photographs by Mauricio Guillen, Purple #7
Lutz & Comme des Garçons #1, English Friends, photographs by Juergen Teller, Purple #7

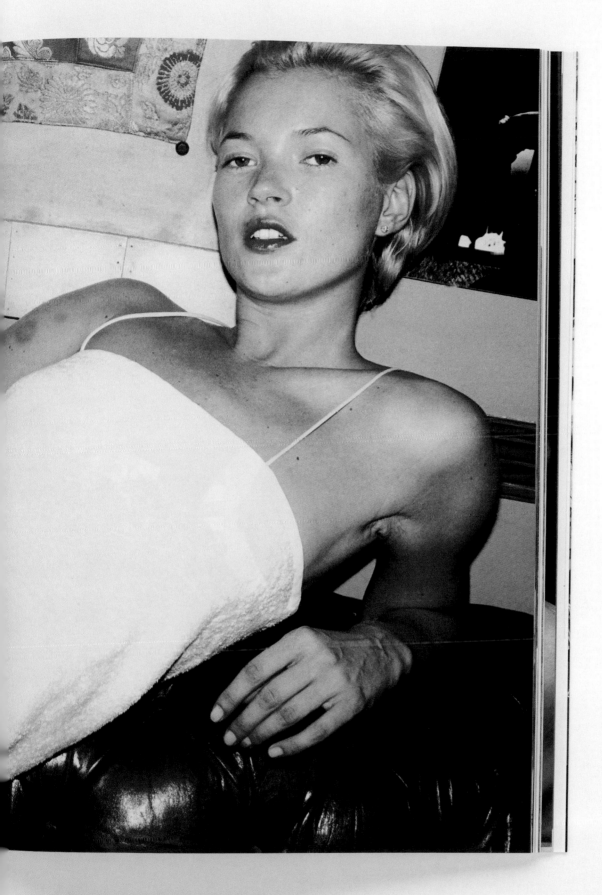

Lutz & Comme des Garçons #1, English Friends, photographs by Juergen Teller,
Purple #7

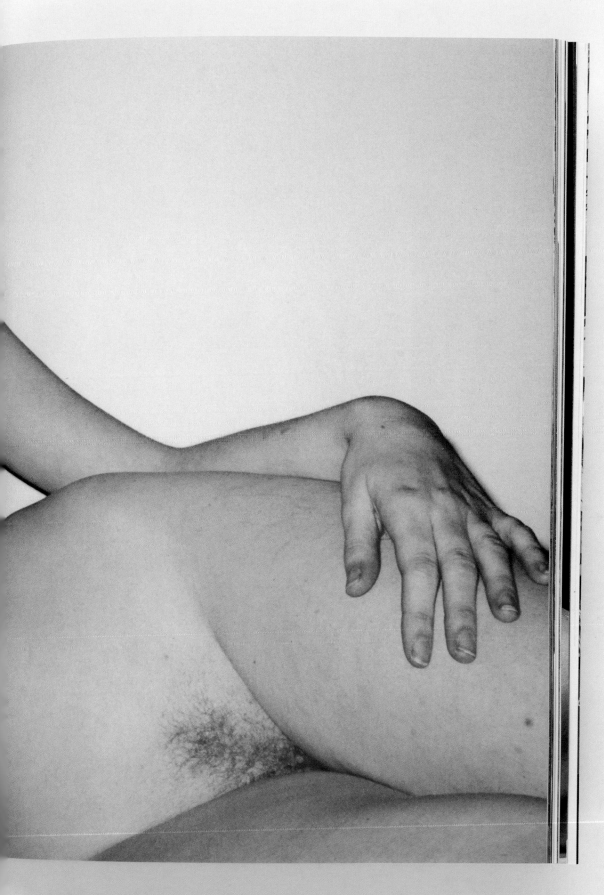

Gucci & Seth Shapiro, The Way We Were, photographs by Terry Richardson,
Purple #7

Cover, photograph by Terry Richardson, Purple #8

Purple Fashion Spring/Summer

by Terry Richardson

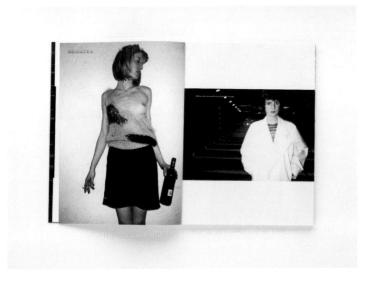

Fashion Spring/Summer, photographs Terry Richardson, Purple #8

167

Marc Jacobs and Kate Moss

Chloe in Balenciaga and Terry

Fashion Spring/Summer, with Marc Jacobs and Kate Moss; with Chloë Sevigny and Terry, photographs by Terry Richardson, Purple #7

Fashion, Martin Margiela Femme, Kim's Place, photographs by Chris Moor, Purple #8
Fashion, Burberry, Brighton Drizzle, photographs by Anders Edström, Purple #8
Fashion, Martin Margiela Homme, Six New York Guys, photographs by Alex Antitch, Purple #8

Fashion, Martin Margiela Femme, Kim's Place, photographs by Chris Moor, Purple #8
Fashion, Burberry, Brighton Drizzle, photographs by Anders Edström, Purple #8
Fashion, Martin Margiela Homme, Six New York Guys, photographs by Alex Antitch, Purple #8

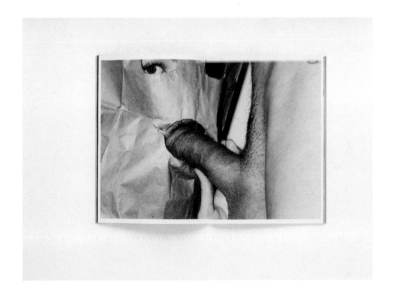

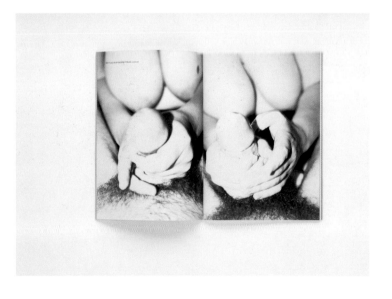

Cover, photograph by Terry Richardson, Purple Sexe #8
Phantom of the Paradise, photographs by Terry Richardson, Purple Sexe #8

Untitled (for Sigmar Polke), photographs by Richard Prince, Purple Sexe #8

Cover, photograph by Anders Edstöm, Purple #9
Fashion, Top Floor, photographs by Juergen Teller, Purple #9

Fashion, Top Floor, photographs by Juergen Teller, Purple #9

Column, Ceryth Win Evans, photographs by Wolfgang Tillmans, Purple #9
Fashion, Diamonds and Shadows, photographs by Laetitia Benat, Purple #9
Fashion, Afternoon Noir, photographs by Masafumi Sanai, Purple #9

Fashion, Portrait of the Creator as a Young Man, photographs by Takashi Homma, Purple #9

Two thousand two was just five years ago, but it might as well have been a million. Do you know where you were five years ago? What you were thinking? What you were doing? How you felt about the world around you? I've kept every appointment book I've used since 1978. Do they come anywhere close to helping me answer these questions, from one year to the next? At best, you can only account for your general whereabouts–whom you had dinner with, whom you slept with, what movies or bands you saw. Which, in the end, is not a real accounting of a life. It's just the mundane movement from one appointment to the next, from this opening to that dinner, from one body to another. How can it help but make us feel insignificant? It's just life, and it happens…to all of us. History–history with a capital H–wants us to believe that there are significant moments that resonate for us all, collectively, and, yes, some moments actually do. But the simple fact is that the world goes on, and, for better or worse, we're in it–implicated, pulled into its ebb and flow. In these times, events don't so much resonate as scare the hell out of us. Make our blood boil. But how self-involved and self-important we must be to even conceive of the world revolving around us–as if humans are somehow at the center of its gravitational pull, and not merely extras in some grand, or not so grand, scheme. Let's face it, we don't matter all that much, and every one of us is going to end up as just so much dust. I've said it before: so you're going to end up finer and more powdery. So what? Do people learn from the mistakes of the past? History tells us NO. There's no use fighting it, because fate will not be denied, and fate is, I suppose, what we're talking about here. We'd be fools to think otherwise. Life happens to us. It's not controlled by us. We're the puppets, not the puppet masters.

When Chris and Kurt Kirkwood formed a band in Phoenix, Arizona, in 1980, they decided to call themselves The Meat Puppets, acknowledging not only that we as humans are at the mercy of larger forces, but that there is a psycho-sexual element at play, both on and off the concert stage. The performer is a phallic symbol, a meat puppet, and he–being almost always a male figure–bobs up and down in a public display that can be both celebratory and demeaning. (A meat puppet is also what hangs, or stands, between a man's legs.)

Music has always provided a way out for me, a brief release from the horrors and banality of the day-to-day. Moreover, the ritual/communal aspect of a concert, to my mind, is found almost nowhere else in modern life. Flipping through my 2002 appointment book, it's clear that I went to see a lot of bands that year. Some of the most memorable shows were by bands from the '60s, '70s and '80s that had reformed. Bands like Suicide, Television, Wire, and Love, originally led by the late, great Arthur Lee (RIP). One of the more transporting of these live experiences was a concert by Ghost, the Japanese group who somehow brought together a heady psychedelia with the gentle, unhurried music of a medieval troubadour– Masaki Batoh as the hurdy-gurdy man. (When I recently asked someone why Ghost hasn't been around in years, I was told that they refuse to play in America until George Bush leaves office.) On a number of occasions I saw Electrophilia, the group Steven Parrino (RIP) formed with Jutta Koether. There were a few great free summer shows: The Sun Ra Arkestra and Sonic Youth in Central Park. Sun Ra (RIP); N.E.R.D. (No one Ever Really Dies), also in the park; Lightning Bolt, Forcefield, !!! (chick chick chick), and a band with a name I'll never forget, Split Me Wide Open, in a Williamsburg alley. There were shows with the Scene Creamers (formed by Ian Svenonius after The Make-Up split up), Fischerspooner, The Polyphonic Spree, and the one that I traveled all the way to Chicago to see, featuring Total Sound Group Direct Action Committee, with Tim Kerr as the ring-leader of an always anarchic, joyous (political) party. I saw a number of bands, like The Melvins, Black Dice, Brother Danielson, and The White Stripes, twice. But the hands-down winner was

Previous spread: Beauty, Ludivine Sagnier, photographs by Henry Roy, Purple #10

PURPLE 10, 11, 12, 13

Dead Meadow, who I saw no less than six times. I was instantly attracted to their long, hazy songs, like "Drifting Downstreams" and the one I adopted as my own personal anthem, "Dusty Nothing." I like turning people onto new bands. Dead Meadow was my 2002 band of the year, so I always took friends to see them play. I brought Kelley Walker along to a show, and after we left he said that they were good, but that they should change their name. "Why," I asked. "They already have a great name. What should they change their name to?" With a sly, mischievous smile, he said, "Sex Meadow."

What my appointment book doesn't reflect is what official history has recorded:

Euro notes and coins were issued in Finland, Ireland, the Netherlands, Belgium, Luxembourg, France, Germany, Austria, Italy, Spain, Portugal, and Greece, replacing those countries' own currencies. Switzerland still has its own money, and England keeps the pound, each country smug in its own respective "neutrality" and isolation.

The United States Department of Justice began a criminal investigation of Enron. America: a country with almost no sense of justice, where the bad guys usually get a slap on the wrist and laugh all the way to the bank.

Among a group of Taliban fighters captured in the 2001 invasion of Afghanistan was a man who turned out to be an American, John Walker Lindh. Referred to as "Jihad Johnny" and the "American Taliban," he was sentenced to twenty years in prison. Lindh won't see the light of day until 2022.

Wall Street Journal reporter Daniel Pearl was kidnapped in Pakistan, accused by his captors of being a CIA agent. His murder, by decapitation, was filmed and widely broadcast to a totally shocked world. Had anyone ever seen a man, alive and conscious, have his head cut off? This was the first and most truly searing image of the new age of brutality in which we live, and Hollywood took notice. Pearl's terrible story was turned into a movie starring Angelina Jolie. A tragic end to a tragedy.

Former Yugoslavian President Slobodan Milosevic went on trial at the United Nations war crimes tribunal in The Hague.

RIP: Singer Peggy Lee ("Is That All There Is?"), Freddie Heineken, Traudl Junge, the secretary to Adolf Hitler, dead at the age of 82, Waylon Jennings ("Mammas Don't Let Your Babies Grow Up To Be Cowboys"), animator Chuck Jones, director Billy Wilder, Linda Bareman (better known as the actress Linda Lovelace from the movie *Deep Throat*), Lisa "Left Eye" Lopes of TLC, Niki de Saint Phalle, Dee Dee Ramone, musicologist Alan Lomax, Jam Master Jay of Run DMC, child murderer Myra Hindley, and Joe Strummer of The Clash.

Almost forty years after his crime, a jury convicted former Ku Klux Klan member Bobby Frank Cherry of the 1963 murders of four young girls who died in the bombing of the 16th Street Baptist Church in Birmingham, Alabama.

The Beltway sniper attacks began with five shootings in Maryland. After terrorizing the public for over three weeks, and randomly killing ten people, John Allen Muhammad and his 17-year-old accomplice, Lee Boyd Malvi, were arrested.

The United Nations Security Council unanimously approved UN Security Council Resolution 1441, forcing Saddam Hussein to disarm, or face "serious consequences."

President Bush established the Department of Homeland Security.

Last, but not least, at a Sotheby's auction in London, Lord Thomson paid a record $76.2 million for a Peter Paul Rubens' painting, *The Massacre of the Innocents*.

Is that all there is?

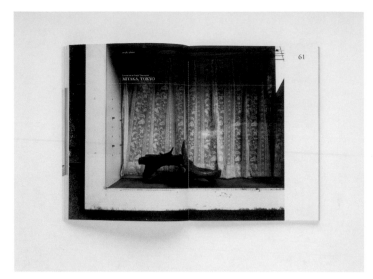

Cover, photograph by Mark Borthwick, Purple #10
Fashion, Latest Pictures of Tara St Hill, style Tara, photographs by Corinne Day,
Purple #10

Column, Landscape, photographs by Kyoji Takahashi Mitaki, Purple #10
Fashion, Latest Pictures of Tara St Hill, style Tara, photographs by Corinne Day,
Purple #10

Interview, L'eXistenZ selon MBK, Mehdi Belhaj Kacem interviewed
by Olivier Zahm and Bernard Joisten, drawings by Laetitia Benat, Purple #10
Portraits, Laetitia Benat, by Pierre Leguillon, photograph by Pierre Leguillon,
Purple #10
Portraits, Maurizio Cattelan, text by Olivier Zahm, photograph by Armin Linke,
Purple #10

Portraits, Anders Edström, text by Jeff Rian, photograph by Maurizio Cattelan,
Purple #10
Portraits, David Berman, text by Bennett Simpson, photograph by Gregh Humphries,
Purple #10
Portraits, Rita Ackermann, text by Kim Gordon, photograph by Laetitia Benat,
Purple #10

Interview, Miguel's Angels, Miguel Calderon interviewed by Pablo León de la Barra,
photographs of Miguel Calderon's grandfather, Purple #10

Cover, photograph by Alex Antitch, Purple #11
Beauty, Uslu Airlines, photographs by Banu Cennetoglu, Purple #11
Fashion, Julia & Mehdi, Après, photographs by Laetitia Benat, Purple #11

Column, Portrait: Miss Kitten, photograph by Wolfgang Tillmans, Purple #11
Beauty, Green, Blue, Pink, Charlotte, photographs by Henry Roy, Purple #11
Fashion, Julia & Mehdi, Après, photographs by Laetitia Benat, Purple #11

Fiction, Seven Pink Drawings, drawings by Tomoo Gokita, Purple #11

La mer, Nakako in Kamakura, photograph by Mark Borthwick, Purple #11

LES ROCHES NOIRES, TROUVILLE by Elein Fleiss

La mer, Les Roches Noires, Trouville, photograph by Elein Fleiss, Purple #11

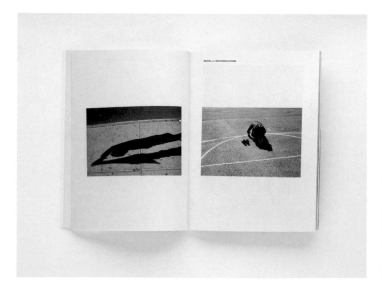

Cover, photograph by Mark Borthwick, Purple #12
Fashion Spring/Summer 2002, photographs by Mark Borthwick
and Maurizio Cattelan, Purple #12

**Fashion Spring/Summer 2002, photographs by Mark Borthwick
and Maurizio Cattelan, Purple #12**

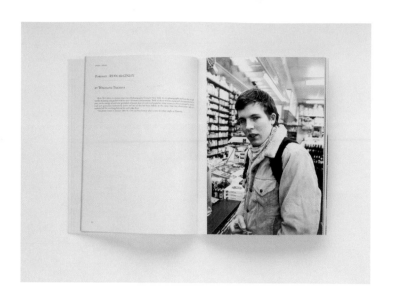

Column, Portrait: Ryan McGinley, photograph by Wolfgang Tillmans, Purple #12
Fashion, Art Scene Tokyo, photographs by Takashi Homma, Purple #12
Fashion, Martin Margiela Homme/Van Cleef & Arpels, photographs by Laetitia Benat, Purple #12

Fashion, Art Scene Tokyo, photographs by Takashi Homma, Purple #12
Fashion, Martin Margiela Homme/Van Cleef & Arpels, photographs by Laetitia Benat, Purple # 12

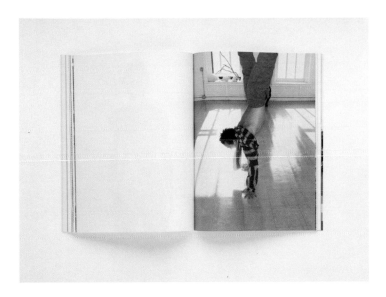

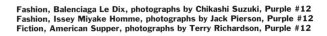

Fashion, Balenciaga Le Dix, photographs by Chikashi Suzuki, Purple #12
Fashion, Issey Miyake Homme, photographs by Jack Pierson, Purple #12
Fiction, American Supper, photographs by Terry Richardson, Purple #12

Fashion, Balenciaga Le Dix, photographs by Chikashi Suzuki, Purple #12
Visual Essay, photographs by Maurizio Cattelan, Purple #12

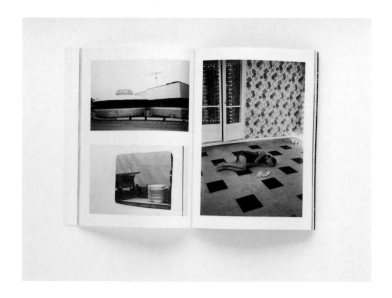

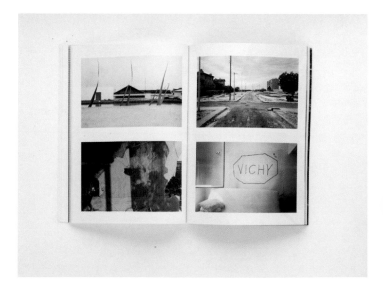

Cover, photograph by Giasco Bertoli, Purple #13
Visual Essay, photographs by Claude Lévêque, Purple #13

Column, Portrait: Isa Genzken, photograph by Wolfgang Tillmans, Purple #13
Visual Essay, photographs by Claude Lévêque, Purple #13

Beauty, Anna Thompson, Hotel Saint Germain, photograph by Serge Leblon, Purple #13

Fiction, Lifestyle, photographs by Henry Roy, Purple #12

"I'm also not very analytical. You know I don't spend a lot of time thinking about myself, about why I do things." George W. Bush, June 4, 2003

Two thousand three was the year George W. Bush–let's call him "Oedipus Wreck"–concocted a war on terrorism, and lashed out against his self-created "axis of evil," making the world a more dangerous place.

He kicked the year off by telling then Secretary of State Colin Powell that he–King Wreck–had decided to declare war against Iraq. In February, Powell told the UN all about the "irrefutable and undeniable" evidence that Iraq was concealing weapons of mass destruction (WMD). Abetting Oedipus Wreck, British Prime Minister Tony Blair on March 1st compared, through innuendo, Saddam Hussein to Hitler. On March 16, after a meeting with Blair and Prime Minster Jose Maria Aznar of Spain, Oedipus Wreck announced: "Tomorrow is a moment of truth for the world."

Air strikes against Iraq began on March 19. American, British, Australian and Polish troops invaded on March 20. Two days later the U.S. and Britain instigated "shock and awe" attacks, a mix of godlike power and mediated sublimity, on Baghdad. By April 23, Paul Bremer had been put in charge of Iraq. He would only go on to make a grand mess an epic mess. Untold, until 2007, was the story of the twelve billion dollars of Iraq's impounded money–363 tons of hundred-dollar bills wrapped in plastic–flown from New York to Baghdad during 2003, disbursed as handouts, and ultimately disappearing into Iraq's catastrophic void.

Few journalists would question Bush or Powell, though millions of people worldwide would condemn the decision to go to war. Christopher Hitchens, for example, said it was the right thing to do, shocking the many of us who thought he had leftist tendencies. Thus began several years of journalistic kowtowing to the war.

By April 15, 2003 (tax day in the U.S.), the war was considered a fait accompli. On May 1, off the coast of San Diego, on the deck of the aircraft carrier USS Abraham Lincoln, Bush proclaimed: "In the battle of Iraq, the United States and our allies have prevailed. And now our coalition is engaged in securing and reconstructing that country." To most of the world it seemed that Wreck's sole interest was conquest, for reasons no one then fully fathomed, or indeed, can comprehend today. Some claimed that an obsession with his father's failure to oust Saddam in 1991 drove him on, and he wanted to prove himself capable of doing the job. By June, one U.S. soldier a day was being killed in Iraq. That number would increase as Iraqi insurgents reacted more vehemently. Wreck's response: "Bring 'em on." On July 22, Saddam's sons Uday and Qusay were killed. On December 13, Hussein was captured, and out of every 1,000 people in Iraq 5.84 were dead. And the killing was just beginning.

Other events of the year included the presentation of a "Road Map" for peace between Israel and Palestine, outlined and endorsed by the U.S., the European Union, and Russia. It called for an end to terror and a normalization of Palestinian life and institutions.

In February the space shuttle Columbia disintegrated as it re-entered the Earth's atmosphere, killing all seven astronauts aboard. On the Horn of Africa, on April 25, the Darfur Liberation Front (now split into the Sudan Liberation Movement and Sudanese Liberation Army) began fighting against the Sudanese government in Khartoum. About 2.5 million people would eventually be displaced. In June, the dictatorial president of Zimbabwe, Robert Mugabe, cracked down on the Movement for Democratic Change, arresting its leader, Morgan Tsvangirai, tipping the country into violent chaos. That same month in Chechnya, a female suicide bomber blew herself up near a bus carrying Russian soldiers and civilians.

Previous spread: Fashion Spring/Summer 2003, We are not going back, photographs by Wolfgang Tillmans, Purple #15

PURPLE 14, 15, 16

A deadly virus in southern China called Severe Acute Respiratory Syndrome (SARS) attracted world attention. In August, a heat wave in Paris killed 3,000 people, and an electrical power blackout affected major cities in the northern U.S. and parts of Canada, some of them for days. In September, Bush asked for an additional $87 billion for Iraq, which he called the "central front" in his global war against terror. In September, singer Johnny Cash died. In October, North Korea claimed it was extracting plutonium from spent nuclear fuel rods to make atomic weapons, China became the third country to send a man into outer space, and Arnold Schwarzenegger became the governor of California–only a month before Michael Jackson was arrested on sexual abuse charges. In my world that winter, the last, unified issue of *Purple* magazine was published, before it branched into two magazines, *The Purple Journal* and *Purple Fashion*.

During the lead-up to the war, and in the ensuing months, I was stunned by emails from my liberal American friends written in support of a war I considered insane as well as illegal. These people were sixties-style social reformers now claiming that America's influence could redirect Iraq toward democracy. American naïveté has often been a factor in its folly. Most politicians, including Hillary Clinton, also backed the war. The name "Bush" became for many a litmus test. Those against him were silenced by his supporters. France was contra, and therefore treated as Evil's assumed accomplice.

I spent October working in Tucson. French wine was rare and expensive. Arizonans didn't talk much about Iraq, Speech was guarded. When I passed through New York City, friends talked about a lingering post-9/11 anxiety. No attack of such scale had occurred since Pearl Harbor. Amateurs had attacked the U.S., and succeeded. No one attacks the U.S. and gets away with it, especially not terrorists. Terror was criminal, not political. Reactionary Islamist radicals were the culprits. Wreck instigated controls and tactics associated with the repressive Cold War machinations of his father's generation. Comparisons between the respective casualty rates, careless ineptitude, and inevitable corruption of the Vietnam and Iraq wars were still years away. Meanwhile, political positions began drifting ever rightward. The Left disintegrated, here, there, and everywhere, to quote an old song. This occurred as political consciousness gave way to paranoid insecurity. Terror became a political football linked to problems of immigration and globalization. Problems like global warming and excessive U.S. carbon emissions were put on the back burner by Oedipus Wreck, Prince of the oil industry and the war on terror. His rhetoric of terror would enflame conservatism of every stripe–Christian, Islamic, and Jewish. The Left remained directionless in its approach towards religious conflict.

And the future loomed darkly. Predictions were apocalyptic. Summers will get hotter. Europe will become as cold as Canada. Bangladesh will be swamped. Hungry hordes will invade. China will take over and saturate Ol' Blue's atmosphere with pollutants.

Forty years ago astronauts photographed our planet from outer space, and on that day (or night) Earth became an artwork and we its custodians. We, being this one murderous family, genetically related, fighting for property and power like the gods of Greek theater. American power became linked to its command of the sky. The world would be America's by proxy–and the country's consumption of 25 percent of its natural resources made this proportionally true. Wreck's rhetoric of terror, with its so-called "axis of evil," overshadowed the wastefulness that was generated, not only of human life, but also of the life of our universe's greatest artwork.

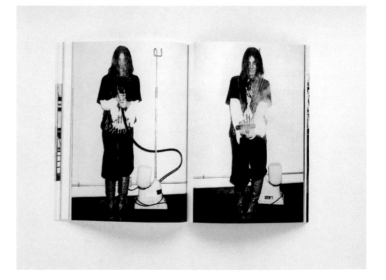

Cover, photograph by Laetitia Benat, Purple #14
Column, Portrait: Peter Saville, photograph by Wolfgang Tillmans, Purple #14
Fashion, Grand National Styling, photographs by Terry Richardson, Purple #14

Fashion Fall/Winter 2002/2003, photographs by Laetitia Benat,
Alexandra Koubichkine and Mehdi Belhaj Kacem, Purple #14
Fashion, Grand National Styling, photographs by Terry Richardson, Purple #14

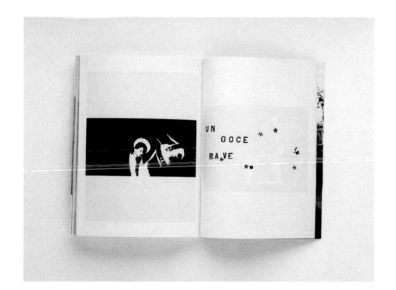

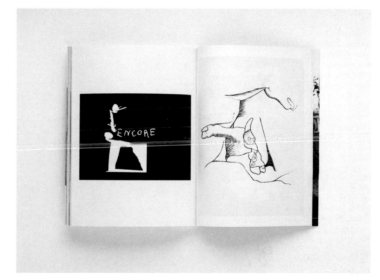

Fiction, Rock Feller, paintings by Christophe Brunnquell, Purple #14

Interview, Peckinpah's daughter, Lupita Peckinpah interviewed
by Pablo León de la Barra, Purple #14

Cover, photograph by Wolfgang Tillmans, Purple #15

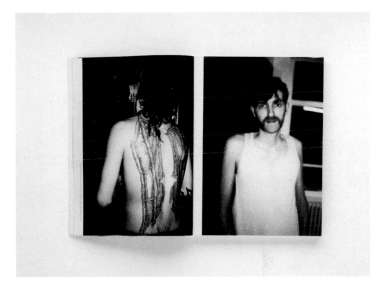

**Fashion Spring/Summer 2003, We Are Not Going Back, photographs
by Wolfgang Tillmans, Purple #15
Fashion Spring/Summer 2003, We Are Not Going Back, photographs
by Wolfgang Tillmans; Peasant Boy, painting by Wilhelm Leibl, Purple #15
Fashion Spring/Summer 2003, We Are Not Going Back,
photographs by Wolfgang Tillmans, Purple #15**

**Fashion Spring/Summer 2003, We Are Not Going Back,
photographs by Wolfgang Tillmans, Purple #15**

Fashion Colour, photographs by Cris Moor, Purple #15
Fashion Black & White, with John Waters, photographs by Terry Richardson, Purple #15

Fashion Black & White, photographs by Richard Kern; photograph by Lizzi Bougatsos, Purple #15

Cover, photograph by Takashi Homma, Purple #16

Fashion Black & White, Rita Ackermann, photographs by Mark Borthwick, Purple #16
Fashion Colour, photographs by Chikashi Suzuki, Purple #16
Fashion Black & White, photographs by Terry Richardson, Purple #16

Fashion Colour, photographs by Chikashi Suzuki, Purple #16
Fashion Fall/Winter 2003/2004, Tender Tokyo by Takashi Homma,
with Mikako Ichikawa, photographs by Takuma Nakahira, Purple #16
Fiction, Democracy by Maurizio Cattelan, Purple #16

Money, texts by Ken Lechter, Lewis Baltz, Jeff Rian, Marina Faust, Mark Fishman,
Peter Nadin and Mehdi Belhaj Kacem, Purple #16

DANA, SHORTS AND NECKLACE BY A.P.C.,
TIE BY HEDI SLIMANE FOR DIOR HOMME

I remember remembering 2004. It wasn't so long ago, but it's as blank in its way as riverbed clay. I think it's the year I've hated the most so far, as far as I can remember. But memory is so arbitrary. Tomorrow it might be 1993 that I can't bear. Sometimes I can hardly remember 2004, except that my kid, Oscar, turned three that year and all of that was good. He had a good year; he started dancing and telling jokes. But aside from that, the year seems pretty vague in retrospect. Its history is unclear, too. It's a year that needs a microscope trained on it, to watch history escape from it like worms on the run.

The good thing about being three years old is that you don't know what year it is, and therefore understand the meaninglessness of years. Three year olds know that history is a game, and that the ball is in the air. Are they all so different from one another, these years? I could write about 1844. It's almost as fresh in my mind, but I couldn't ask my friends about it.

Well, 2004 saw the first recorded South Atlantic hurricane to hit land. It was the Year of the Monkey, and being a leap year, had 366 days. The 4,701st year in the Chinese reckoning and 5,764th in the Hebrew reckoning. And I remember that on my Pisces birthday NASA announced that the Mars rover Opportunity had transmitted information suggesting that the area it was exploring had once been covered in water.

Maybe 2004 is best remembered for the tsunami in the Indian Ocean, and the nearly 200,000 deaths it caused. But I mostly recall it as being the year George Bush was re-elected President of the United States. Maybe that's why it seems so vague in my memory: some things you just want to try and forget. He was elected over John Kerry, a candidate so uninspired even his membership in Yale's Skull and Bones Society, alongside Bush, began to seem almost interesting.

In August 2004, the Republican Party held their convention at Madison Square Garden in New York City. Ex-mayor Rudy Giuliani compared George Bush to Winston Churchill, and quoted Bush's "Either you're with us or you're with the terrorists" line to the assembled faithful. Outside hundreds of thousands of peaceful protesters, herded meekly into pens, were mostly ignored by the media, although the unlucky among them were arrested for no reason by the New York City Police Department, which is always brave when it comes to dealing with unarmed, middle class people. If you're not with the Republicans, not only are you with the terrorists, you are a terrorist.

The election of 2004 was a strange, anti-climactic affair, especially after the impending constitutional crisis of 2000, when more than half a million more votes were cast for Al Gore than George Bush. The Democrats found a popular, forceful leader in Howard Dean, a fresh face from outside the Washington establishment who transformed campaign organizing and fundraising through enlightened use of the Internet. He suggested that change might be possible. But Dean was blackballed by the media after he was filmed emitting a sort of Jim Morrison scream at a campaign rally. The clip of this was replayed endlessly on national television using only the feed from Dean's microphone, making it appear as if the candidate had gone berserk, when in fact he was screaming along with the crowd.

The good news was that although the Democrats nominated the diffident patrician John Kerry, Howard Dean became Chairman of the Party. And despite Kerry's wooden personality, he almost won the 2004 election. The crucial votes came from the state of Ohio, where there was evidence of irregularities, including fraud. In 2003, Warren O'Dell, the chairman of Diebold, the voting machine manufacturer, wrote to fellow Republicans that he was "committed to helping Ohio deliver its electoral votes to the president next year." Meanwhile, Ohio's Secretary of State attempted to bar voters whose registrations were not written on eighty pound stock paper. The extraordinary disparity between

Previous spread: Purple Spring/Summer 2004, Seth & Dana, photographs by Terry Richardson, Purple Fashion #1

THE PURPLE JOURNAL 0, 1, 2, PURPLE FASHION MAGAZINE 1, 2

exit polls and the final results led to widespread suspicions of monkey business.

And so George W. Bush, today generally considered the worst President in American history, stayed in office, even though the continuing war in Iraq began to dissipate the dream of "Mission Accomplished." Two thousand four was the year when people began to wake up from the dream of September, 2001, and wonder what had really happened, how history had been hijacked. But we still had a long way to go.

The way forward was in some ways illuminated by Michael Moore's documentary *Fahrenheit 9/11* which showed, amongst other things, President Bush continuing to read *My Pet Goat* to a class of schoolchildren while the World Trade Center towers burned. The film was given an R-rating by the "industry watchdog" MPAA, meaning that no person under seventeen years of age could be admitted without parental consent, the same restriction enforced for admission to the United States Armed Forces.

The same day Bush was "re-elected," the Dutch writer and filmmaker Theo van Gogh, who made *Submission*, the film about violence against women in Islamic societies, was assassinated in Amsterdam by Mohammed Bouyeri, an Islamic militant.

The Iraq war was escalating, and although it wasn't obvious, there were signs of increasing militarism. The Russian military, Cossacks, and the tribes of Ghengis Khan were cited as influences on the fall fashion collections. Fur was back, on collars and Ugg boots, and lots of ladies with no horse in the stable were still dressed for equestrian pursuits, even though in 2004 Britain outlawed fox hunting.

In the same months, thieves stole *The Scream* and other paintings from The Edvard Munch Museum in Oslo. Until I visited Oslo, I thought that the best *Scream* was the version in The National Museum. But no, it's the one in The Munch Museum. I've got to admit that I never really appreciated the greatness of Munch until I visited The National Museum in Oslo.

Oh, and Ireland banned smoking in pubs. Janet Jackson flashed a nipple during Super Bowl XXXVIII and it was called "a wardrobe malfunction." San Francisco issued marriage licenses to same sex partners, and Massachusetts soon followed suit. South Korean scientists announced they were cloning human embryos. The ceiling of the terminal where I always changed planes at Charles De Gaulle Airport in Paris collapsed, shaking my faith in modernism. The pickled heart of Louis XVII was buried. The spacecraft Cassini (named after the astronomer Giovanni, not the designer Oleg) flew by Titan, a moon of Saturn. On *The Sopranos*, Silvio killed Adriana after she admitted to Christopher that she'd been wearing a wire. Richard Avedon died of natural causes.

And I wrote this:

Change Artist

Did you ever notice how much
Robert Lowell looked like Clark Kent?
God is design, even our ugliness
Is the goodness of his random will.
It gives me chills the microscope shows
The abstract expressions of the spirochete
Swimming upstream in blood toward madness.
Even the smallest find words when the worm turns
To speak in the ear of the cat in the catbird Seat.

Cover, Susan Eldrige, photograph by Terry Richardson, Purple Fashion #1

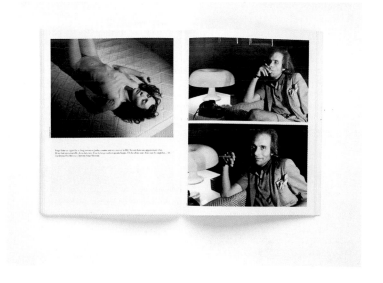

Cover, Purple Journal #0
Serge Manzon, Purple Journal #0
Photographs by Anders Edström, Purple Journal #0

Le tournage de Lola, dernier film de Rainer Werner Fassbinder,
photograph by Marina Faust, Purple Journal #0
Eve Bitoune, photograph by Camille Vivier; Serge Manzon, Purple Journal #0
Théâtre National Populaire, photograph by Laetitia Benat;
photograph by Jonathan Hallam, Purple Journal #0

Best of the Season, photographs by Katja Rahlwes, Purple Fashion #1
Interview, Michael Lonsdale interviewed by Matthieu Orléan,
photographs by Hélène Jeanbrau, 1969, Purple Fashion #1
Fashion, The Maritime Hotel, New York, photographs by Terry Richardson,
Purple Fashion #1

Best of the Season, photographs by Katja Rahlwes, Purple Fashion #1
Interview, Michael Lonsdale interviewed by Matthieu Orléan,
photographs by Erica Lennard, 1974, Purple Fashion #1
Fashion, The Maritime Hotel, New York, photographs by Terry Richardson,
Purple Fashion #1

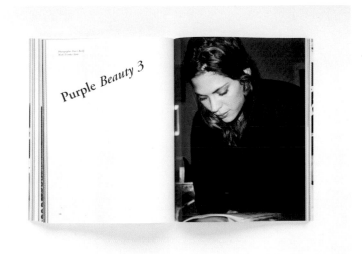

Purple Beauty 3

Seth & Dana

Beauty, photographs by Pierre Bailly, Purple Fashion #1
Fashion, Seth & Dana, photographs by Terry Richardson, Purple Fashion #1
People, photograph by Paolo Roversi, Purple Fashion #1

Purple Beauty, photographs by Pierre Bailly, Purple Fashion #1
Fashion, Seth & Dana, photographs by Terry Richardson, Purple Fashion #1
People, Zora Star, photograph by Paolo Roversi, Purple Fashion #1

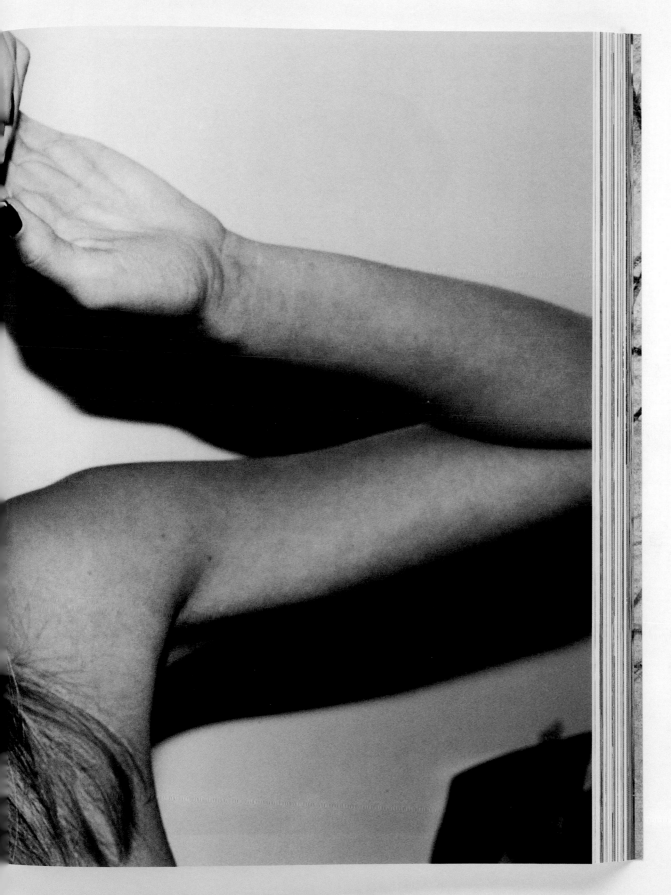

Fashion, Julia Stegner, photograph by Katja Rahlwes, Purple Fashion #2

Cover, The Purple Journal #1
Photograph by Laetitia Benat; photograph by Camille Vivier, Purple Journal #1
Photograph by Jonathan Hallam, Purple Journal #1

Photograph by Mark Borthwick; drawing by Tomoo Gokita, Purple Journal #1
Elliott Roy, photograph by Henry Roy; photograph by Chikashi Suzuki,
Purple Journal #1
Takuma Nakahira, photographs Takashi Homma, Purple Journal #1

Cover, The Purple Journal #2
Anxious Days in Kinshasa, text by Henry Roy, photograph by Laetitia Benat,
Purple Journal #2
Portrait of Reine, photographs by Amit Berlowitz, Purple Journal #2

Anna Dubosc, photographs by Laetitia Benat, Purple Journal #2
In the Shadows of the Signposts on the Road, text by David Berman,
photographs by Jonathan Hallam, Purple Journal #2.
Four-by-foured to Oblivion, text by Jeff Rian,
The Power-Bar Guy's Widow (You Can Have Her, I Don't Want Her, She's Too Old
For Me), text by Nick Tosches, Purple Journal #2

Cover, Angela Lindvall, photograph by Terry Richardson, Purple Fashion #2
Terry, The Terry Richardson Book, Purple Book #1

ELIZABETH
PEYTON

PORTRAITS BY ANNETTE AURELL

Fashion, Fall/Winter 2004/2005, Elizabeth Peyton, photographs by Annette Aurell, Purple Fashion #2
Fashion, Balenciaga by Nicolas Ghesquière, A First Retrospective, Summer 1998, Winter 2004, Spring/Summer 2000, Purple Fashion #2

Fashion, Fall/Winter 2004/2005, Elizabeth Peyton, photographs by Annette Aurell, Purple Fashion #2
Fashion, Balenciaga by Nicolas Ghesquière, A First Retrospective, Summer 1998, Winter 2004, Spring/Summer 2000, Purple Fashion #2

SPRING/SUMMER 2002

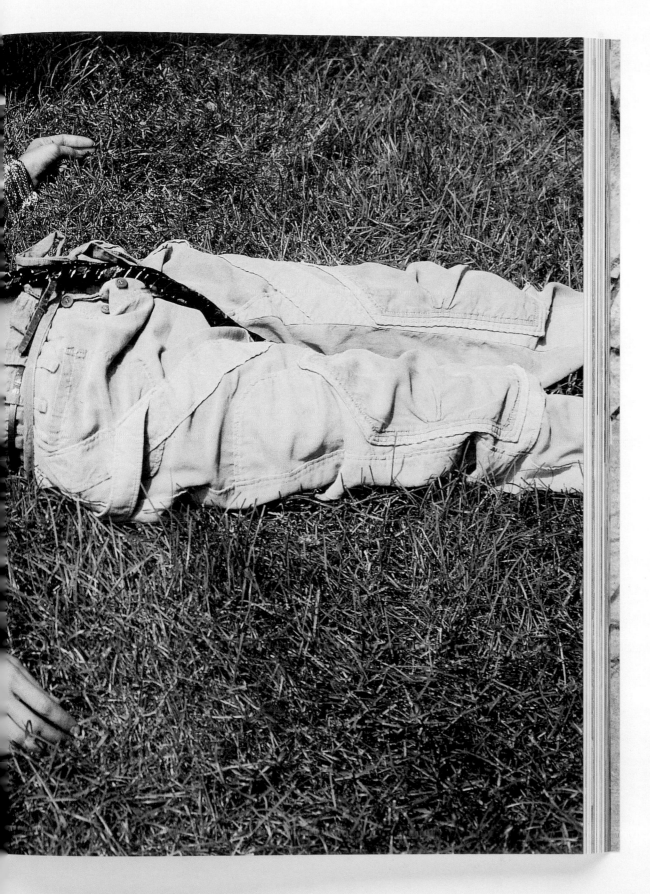

Fashion, Balenciaga by Nicolas Ghesquière, A First Retrospective, Summer 1998,
Winter 2004, Spring/Summer 2002, Purple Fashion #2

Interviews, Objectif lune, John Armleder interviewed by Stéphanie Moisdon, photographs Claudia Lisa Riedel, Purple Fashion #2
Fashion, Fall/Winter 2004/2005, All Around Kim, photographs by Mark Borthwick, Purple Fashion #2
Fashion, Fall/Winter 2004/2005, 5 O'Clock Dracula, photographs by Terry Richardson, Purple Fashion #2

Interviews, Objectif lune, John Armleder interviewed by Stéphanie Moisdon, photographs Claudia Lisa Riedel, Purple Fashion #2
Fashion, Fall/Winter 2004/2005, All Around Kim, photographs by Mark Borthwick, Purple Fashion #2

RITA ACKERMANN
COLLAGES FOR PURPLE

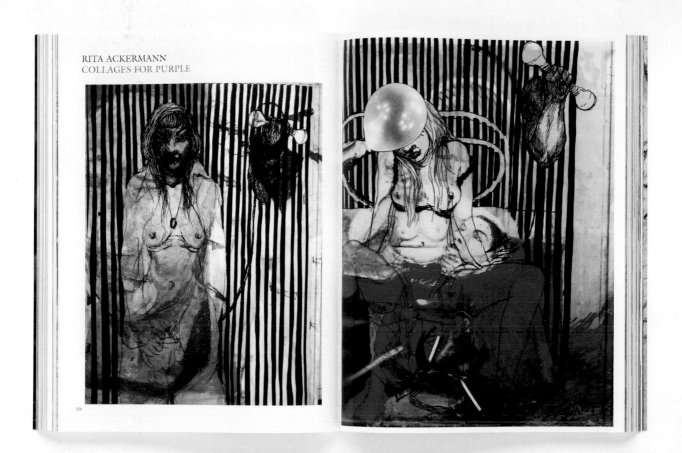

CHORUS 1
Arc arc
Rumble and rise
Tie a leash to oblivion.

Meet four men at the city gates
And tie a leash to oblivion.

Darkened days are in their eyes
Though lowly talk will bore you.

Know less than you the price you pay
And tie a leash to oblivion

What happened in the few of years of struggle and hope that separate the France of the 1960s from the France of the wonder boys and propagandists? We act as if the short detour of 1968 never happened, or as if it were a dream, something we'd like to be rid of when we wake up, a stain.

We went from hating power to adoring it. From wanting "to be" to wanting "to be part of." From systematic questioning to the ecstasy of consent. From the candor and intransigence of imminent uprising to the postures and impostures of servile groveling. From egalitarian combat to a pure and simple offensive against equality, against the Other, in every form. We went from cultural avant-garde to ever-present kitsch. From the body's liberation to its guilty and immediate consumption. From radical critique to praise of the fait accompli, of merit and work. We swung from discord to consensus, from teenage dreams to nightmares about our security. The spirit of the 2000s is, above all, about the insidious naturalization of change–and there's as much debate about it as there is about a natural disaster.

Change suddenly lost the logical power it had in the last century to invite critique.

Two thousand and five is the year I've been asked to recall. I can only think of the people who died that year. It was a good year for obituary columnists. Pope John Paul II died on April 2, at age 84, after more than 26 years as pontiff. Shortly after, Prince Rainier III died at age 82, after 56 years of rule. The wedding of Prince Charles and Camilla Parker Bowles was pushed back a day because of the Pope's funeral ceremonies. The great bell of Notre Dame in Paris, which only rings on special occasions, rang the death knell. In this hysterical atmosphere of slackening awareness, it's more a toll for the secular republic that sounded. Flags on public buildings were flown at half-mast. The mayor of Paris decided to rename the square in front of Notre Dame after John Paul II. The few card-carrying agnostics, myself included, "fall from the closet" (to use Jacques Chirac's favorite expression). In his inaugural address the mayor, Bertrand Delanoë, saluted the memory of John Paul II, calling him a "major sentinel of modern times." To which Act Up-Paris answered, "The fact that the Catholic hierarchy insists on condemning the use of condoms … and thrusts its followers into shame, suffering and death is one thing. It's another when an elected republican, who claims to be progressive, and who, furthermore, is himself the target of discriminatory remarks, sullies his city with plaques glorifying murderers."

CHORUS 2
We met a man,
Nice shoes had he,
He filled the world with stuff stuff stuff
We beat his head then held his death.
Oh love of good intentions!

On August 29, a stupefied world is enlightened about the poverty of the black population, and the realities of class relations, in America. It's never too late. Hurricane Katrina strikes Louisiana and Mississippi, claiming almost two thousand victims. In Biloxi, a gambling center and Mecca for Mississippi's underprivileged, a large percentage of whom come seeking work in the hotels and casinos, "Many people did not have the means to escape," declared Alan LeBreton, a 41-year-old porter who lived on the sea front. "It's a crime and people can't accept it." The wealthiest residents, anticipating official instruction, for the most part headed north of Mississippi, and to neighboring Alabama and Georgia, cramming into motels, and emptying service stations and small markets of their last reserves. As the American photographer Stanley Greene explained, "In the white neighborhoods, supermarkets were opened to people, out of solidarity. In the black neighborhoods, guards were posted to prevent people from going in! The goal isn't to bring people back, but rather to turn New Orleans into a lucrative white city. Investors are looking everywhere for destroyed houses, which they can buy for $10,000. Katrina is the biggest despoilment operation of all time."

CHORUS 3
Hands chalked by earth
And clouded expect
A rock to end your anger!

On October 27, in France, two minors being chased by the police are fatally electrocuted at a power substation. The tragedy triggers 18 days of rioting. On November 8, a state of emergency is declared in France. The French National Assembly votes in favor of adopting a proposal to extend it for three months. At Doug Aitken's opening at l'Arc, Doug tells me he wants to film the action over in the ghetto we call the *banlieue*. He seems very excited about the exoticism of the images broadcast the night before on the television channel TF1. Social outlaws! Not understanding a word of French, he missed the best part, which is always in the apocalyptic comments, the bombastic statements, the clichés, and the soundtrack that accompanies this fascinating spectacle—the beautiful

images of cars on fire, the bands of teenagers united by rage. I turn down the invitation for a nighttime drive-through. Born in France, I know better than to mess with Sarkozy's brigades. My love of art has its limits.

CHORUS 4
Yes the light that takes
The light that takes!
(It's true it's true. see you not?! its true!)
By the water of the ever changing river
We swear death comes as essay.

June 13: Michael Jackson is acquitted of pedophilia. I was fascinated by the trial, by the intoxication of a people calling for Bambi's execution. They're the same ones who cried so hard when the real Bambi's mother was killed by a hunter. I'm like Pierre Huyghe and Arnaud Viviant in that I like trials, both fictional and real ones. I've a bit of a fetish for them. Jackson's plight especially interests me because since 2000 I myself have been prosecuted for "diffusion of images of a pornographic or violent nature accessible to minors." This stems from my involvement in an exhibition in Bordeaux, an exhibition like many others in being critical and contemplative in its examination of a subject that is, in the end, rather banal, yet has become an unacceptable fixation, an off-limits subject. The child advocacy organization La Mouette is calling for prison sentences for the curators and director of the institution where the show was mounted, and for the destruction of the works by 24 artists, including Cindy Sherman, Dan Graham, Ugo Rondinone, Elke Krystufek, Annette Messager, Mike Kelley, Larry Clark, Carsten Höller. Is another Kristallnacht is upon us? As I write this essay, the outcome of the trial remains entirely uncertain.

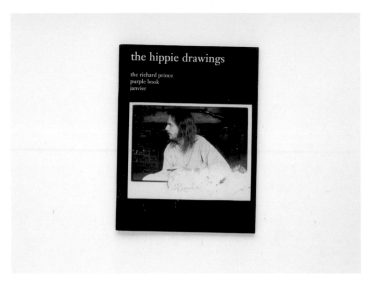

Cover, Chloë Sevigny, photograph by Terry Richardson, Purple Fashion #3
Best of the Season with Chloë, art direction by Olivier Zahm, style by Katja Rahlwes,
photographs by Terry Richardson, Purple Fashion #3

Cover, The Hippie Drawings, The Richard Prince Book, Purple Book #2

Best of the Season with Chloë, art direction by Olivier Zahm, style by Katja Rahlwes, photographs by Terry Richardson, Purple Fashion #3

**Visual Essay, Kate Moss, 1999; Final Fantasy-Wendy, 1993, photographs
by Inez van Lamsweerde & Vinoodh Matadin, Purple Fashion #3
Interview Literature, photographs by Hélène Bamberger, 1982, 1991,
Purple Fashion #3
Purple Beauty, Fifteen, photographs by Martynka Wawrzyniak, Purple Fashion #3**

**Purple Beauty, Bijou, photographs by Vava Ribeiro, Purple Fashion #3
Purple Interview Literature, photograph by Hélène Bamberger, 1991,
Purple Fashion #3
Purple Beauty, Fifteen, photographs by Martynka Wawrzyniak, Purple Fashion #3**

Woman Spring/Summer 2005, Just Married Béatrice Dalle, text by Sheila Single, photographs by Pierre Even, paintings by Christophe Brunnquell, Purple Fashion #3
Interview, Jonathan Meese interviewed by Christine Macel, photographs by Jonathan Meese, 2004, Purple Fashion #3
Men Spring/Summer 2005, 853 Kamikaze, photographs by Hedi Slimane, Purple Fashion #3

Woman Spring/Summer 2005, Just Married Béatrice Dalle, text by Sheila Single, photographs by Pierre Even, paintings by Christophe Brunnquell, Purple Fashion #3
Woman Spring/Summer 2005, Gracepunk, style by Benjamin Sturgill, photographs by Anette Aurell, Purple Fashion #3
Interviews, Divergent Tropical Zone, Ashley Bickerton interviewed by Alison M. Gingeras, Purple Fashion #3

It's shit i
wi

ople have to go
ut things.

Visual Essay, Leave a Dog Alone, a Tribute to Ol'Dirty Bastard,
collage by Rita Ackermann, Purple Fashion #3

THE PURPLE JOURNAL

PUBLISHED EACH SAISON, NUMBER 3, WINTER 05
ESSAYS, STORIES, PORTRAITS, CHRONICLES, PHOTOGRAPHS
7,5 EUROS (FRARNCE), ENGLISH VERSION

In this time of extreme historical mediocrity, betrayal and shame: Let's live! Let's welcome chaos! Let's affirm with joy our non-participation in the world as it destroys itself! Let's adopt the speed of melody! Let's not please anyone! Let's love! Let's sigh in the traitor's ears! Let's not belong to anything! Let's cherish our American friends! Let's laugh at the parade! Let's be the wind! Let's be the rain! Let's not be afraid of anything! Let's live, because it's official: we're dying!

3 760090 840104 >

Cover, The Purple Journal #3

Komazawa Olympic stadium, Tokyo; Silhouette for Winter 2004/2005,
photograph by Dorothée Perret, Purple Journal #3
Constance Crémer and Hen Yanni, photographs by Noriko Tezuka, Purple Journal #3
Cover, The Purple Journal #4

Berlin, winter 2004, Spring/Summer 1999, Purple Journal #3
Meiji Jingu, Tokyo, photographs by Chikashi Suzuki, Purple Journal #3
Photograph Sarah Adler, 2004, Purple Journal #4

Purple *fashion*

MICKEY ROURKE *P.106*

STEPHANIE SEYMOUR *P.10*
JOHN BALDESSARI *P.92*
RICK OWENS *P.228*
JUN TAKAHASHI *P.96*
NICOLLE MEYER *P.122*
KRISTEN McMENAMY *P.106*
RITA ACKERMANN *P.872*
STEFANO PILATI *P.500*
MILTOS MANETAS *P.376*
BROOKE SHIELDS *P.868*

L.A.'S BEAUTY *P.601*
PIERRE HARDY *P.126*
PARADISE FOUND *P.10*

NUMBER 4
BI-ANNUAL
FALL/WINTER
2005/06

Purple *fashion*

interzone

the hedi slimane book
purple / janvier

Cover, Mickey Rourke, photograph by Terry Richardson, Purple Fashion #4
Cover, Stephanie Seymour, photograph by Terry Richardson, Purple Fashion #4

Cover, Interzone, The Hedi Slimane Book, Purple Book #4

Interview, Back in the Ring, Mickey Rourke interviewed by Olivier Zahm, photographs by Terry Richardson, Purple Fashion #4
Best of the Season, Stephanie Seymour, photographs by Terry Richardson, Purple Fashion #4

Interview, Back in the Ring, Mickey Rourke interviewed by Olivier Zahm, photographs by Terry Richardson, Purple Fashion #4
Best of the Season, Stephanie Seymour, photographs by Terry Richardson, Purple Fashion #4

Quilted coat John Galliano
Gold and amethyst necklace VanCleef & Arpels
CREATIVE TEAM
Art direction Olivier Zahm & Leslie Lessin
Stylist Masha Orlov
Assistant Nicolas Klam

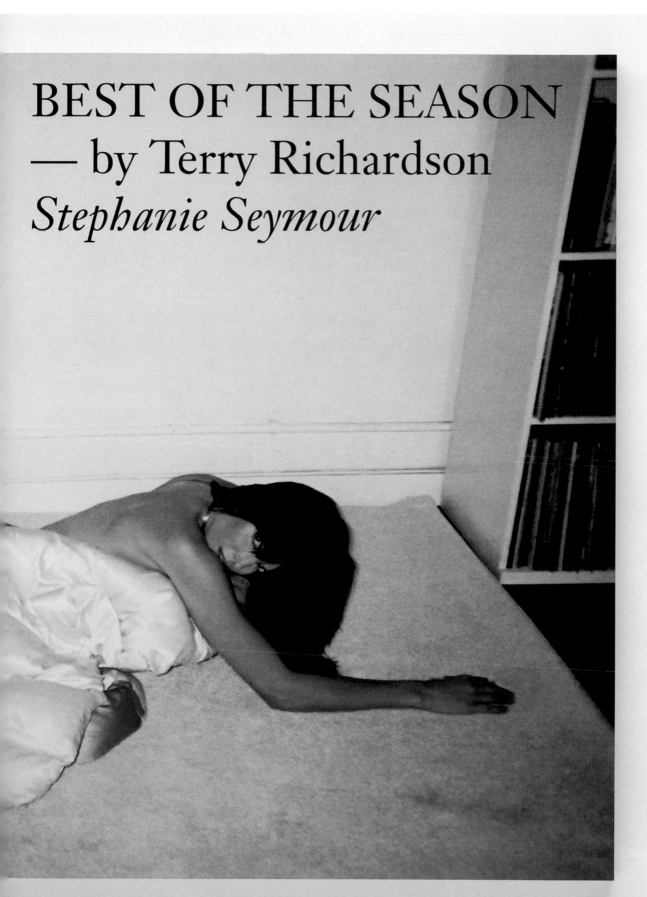

BEST OF THE SEASON
— by Terry Richardson
Stephanie Seymour

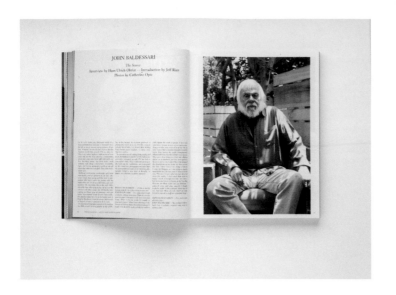

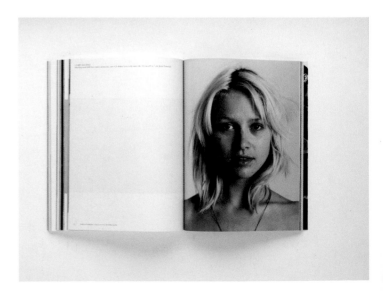

Interview, The Source, John Baldessari interviewed by Hans Ulrich Obrist,
photographs by Catherine Opie, Purple Fashion #4
Interview, From Freeway to Runway, Rick Owens interviewed by Olivier Zahm,
photographs by Rick Owens, Purple Fashion #4
Beauty, New Generation Hollywood, photographs by Vava Ribeiro, Purple Fashion #4

Interview, The Source, John Baldessari interviewed by Hans Ulrich Obrist,
photographs by Catherine Opie, Purple Fashion #4
Interview, From Freeway to Runway, Rick Owens interviewed by Olivier Zahm,
photographs by Rick Owens, Purple Fashion #4
Beauty, New Generation Hollywood, photographs by Vava Ribeiro, Purple Fashion #4

**Visual Essay, Marc Jacobs, Fall/Winter 2005/2006, photographs by Juergen Teller,
Purple Fashion #4**

Visual Essay, The Feast of the Beast, photographs by Rita Ackermann,
Purple Fashion #4
Visual Essay, Spiritual America, Rephotography Revisited/ Brooke Shields
text by Jeff Rian, photographs by Sante D'Orazio and Richard Prince,
Purple Fashion #4

Purple Beauty, Versailles in June, photographs by Laetitia Benat, Purple Fashion #4

Cover, The Purple Journal #5
Arsinée Khanjian, photograhs by Amit Berlowitz, Purple Journal #5
Dossier autour d'un bâtiment; D'ailleurs, ici...faits divers d'actualité
et photographies, Purple Journal #5

D'ailleurs, ici...faits divers d' actualité et photographies, photograph by Elein Fleiss,
photograph by Laetitia Benat, photograph by Camille Vivier, Purple Journal #5
Collection de vêtements d'été, photographs by Takashi Homma, Purple Journal #5

Cover, The Purple Journal #6
David Kroll, photographs by Amit Berlowitz, Purple Journal #6

David Kroll, photographs by Amit Berlowitz, Purple Journal #6
Lettre de Belgrade, text by Jonathan Boulting, photographs by Katarina Radovic,
Purple Journal #5

Black T-shirt dress LANVIN, *leather belt* GIVENCHY, *necklace by the artist* CÉSAR.

It's blind stamped. That means you can feel it, but you can't see it.

Emerging from the cipher of the first five years of the third millennium, identity is precious. That there's even a rush in popular culture to identify the decade in which we haven't yet lived is a testament to a self-awareness that is felt more acutely than ever before. We call this era the aughts. And this is a great word for how we live now because aught as an archaic pronoun means "anything at all"; however, when used as an archaic verb, it signifies ownership, possession. Possession/possibility: a dialectical entitlement that's assumed as we emerge from the twentieth century molded and anxiety-ridden by such expansiveness.

This attitude isn't anything new. In a post-war context, Jean-Paul Sartre articulated a similar reflexive dilemma, couched in the individual's obligation both to oneself and society. Sartre also published periodicals, a gesture by one for many, and his 1945 *Les Temps Modernes* and 1973 *Libération* are still to this day accountable to their bodies of readers.

In speaking, the periodical is the tie between individual and community—the encyclopedia of and for a larger culture. But when the cultural moment is laden with catastrophic worldwide events and a relentless media awareness of (and fascination with) them, how do you respond as the editor of a fashion and art magazine? You put on your best outfit, go out all night, and be yourself, damn it.

Fashion is a way to combat banality, sadness, and ennui.
It pushes you to be happier.

In 2006, *Purple Fashion* traipsed out from this five-year post-millennial adolescence and put on its face without much shame. Dressing up in fashion and art editorial wasn't an act of resignation—it was a reaction. Some take for granted the notion of fashion as a provocative assertion of identity when, especially in 2006, search engines and social networking databases gave us increased ability to calibrate our interests and desires with others. Magazines are just as responsible for courting niche interests, but in a more patient way that allows time for their development and reaction. The most expressive subcultures forged intimate connections over time based on the recognition and trading of symbolic affects.

But is there a magazine today that chronicles this process now assumed by MySpace? If we look closely at *Purple Fashion* in 2006, we see that this action/reaction fashion dialectic is exercised in the bi-annual self-portrait of one man—Olivier Zahm.

Both Vincent Gallo and Terry Richardson goaded Zahm to break down the fourth wall, so to speak, and involve himself not just as the editor of the magazine, but also as a photogenic photographed subject. French *Vogue*'s editor, Carine Roitfeld, had already made an appearance on *Purple Fashion*'s spring 2006 cover in an act of fashion industry reflexivity. This idea evolved to the point where Zahm and Gallo dressed in women's clothes before Richardson's lens. In a stark white composition typical of Richardson's style, Gallo is consumed by his surreal parallel identity with an almost meditative gaze, stroking the chest he wished he had; but Zahm still reserves himself. His apprehension would all but wash away in the following issues as he made regular appearances, but this was an important transformation in the concept of a periodical that underscored this era of heightened self-awareness and possibility.

Whether knowingly or not, the entire story was an almost direct reference to Man Ray's photographs of Marcel Duchamp dolled up as his self-indulgent female alter ego Rrose Sélavy—a moniker meant to evoke the phrase, "Eros, c'est la vie." And from this new optic of love, or even self-love, *Purple Fashion* settled into capturing a community of the fearless.

Celebrity culture became vulgar while the Old Garde became jealous.

The magazine was working its way to this point anyway.
A large chunk of editorial content in *Purple*'s 1990s
editions dealt with manipulated identity and the transfer
of self-presentation from the street to venues such as
the Internet. In some of their solicited contributions,
photographers Inez Van Lamsweerde & Vinoodh
Matadin rendered subjects obnoxiously pixilated in altered
states, while Zahm explored exhibitionism not only as
the editor of *Purple Sexe*, but also in interviews with idols
of cyberspace porn, a phenomenon that was, at the time
philosophically still up for grabs.
And in 2006, we have Zahm in places other than *Purple
Fashion*, a facsimile of identity rendered both in society
pages and web pages. There's no doubt that a generation
younger than his would relate to such an absurd
performance in a year where a heightened celebrity
culture spawned not only more curious voyeurs, but also
the first chapters of the mass media-chronicled narrative
of Britney Spears's fall from pop grace.
Zahm's seasonal accounts of the world's fashion weeks
and art fairs are writ glossy in a recklessly stylish grand
tour of night appearances in clubs, photo shoots, and
frank interviews. His pageantry runs parallel to the
effusive self-promotion of personalities on websites like
YouTube and MySpace. So, it was only a matter of time
before the social networking of *Purple Fashion* merged
with MySpace. The magazine and the man became more
muddled and this amalgam garnered the fascination of a
much larger and younger community beyond the already
established coterie of the fashion world, who may or may
not have been eclipsed by these new sensibilities.
For those left behind, Olivier Zahm might not be
recognizable. But, just as the Romantic poet Lord Byron,
who notoriously circulated in London's most fashionable
salons "awoke one morning and found (himself) famous,"
Zahm and *Purple Fashion* operate on this exhilarating
threshold between personality and possibility.
For aught we know, this is the only way to live in 2006.

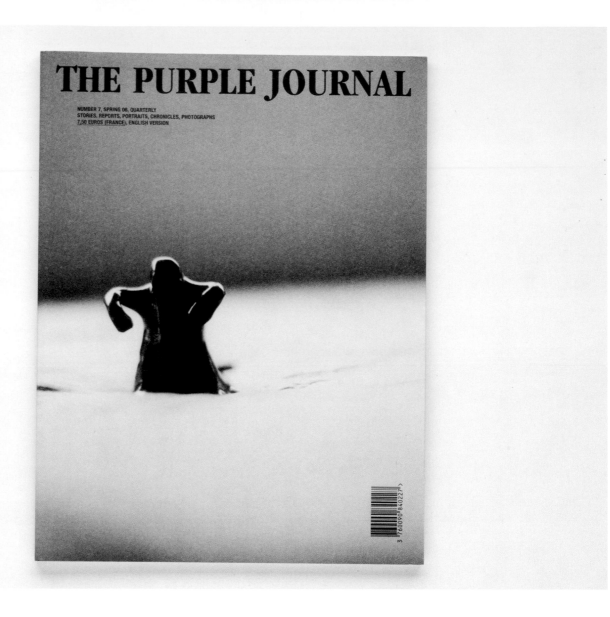

Cover, The Purple Journal #7
Fashion Collections of Garments for Spring/Summer 2006, Maison Martin Margiela,
Paris, photographs by Daniel Riera and Maison Martin Margiela; Von Sono, by
Stephane Oberg, photographs by Von Sonno, Purple Journal #7

Galerie, Cap Blanca, photograph by Henry Roy, 2004, Ibiza,
photograph by Henry Roy, 2005, Purple Journal #7

Cities Around Paris, Alfortville; Letter from Belgrade, Poisson à la merde,
text by Jonathan Boulting, Purple Journal #7
Fashion Collections of Garments for Spring/Summer 2006, Cosmic Wonder
by Yukinori Maeda, photographs by Laetitia Benat, Purple Journal #7

Topography of a City, The Turin Chronicles; Cities around Paris, Alfortville,
Purple Journal #7

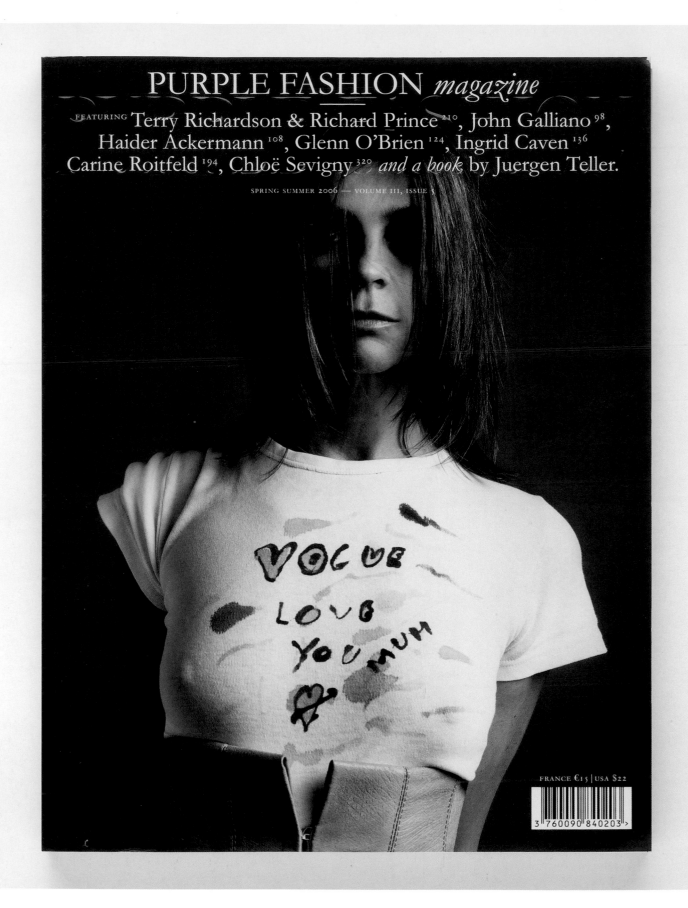

Cover, Carine Roitfeld, photograph by Inez van Lamsweerde and Vinoodh Matadin,
Purple Fashion Magazine #5

Cover, Ed in Japan, The Juergen Teller Book, Purple Book #5
Interview, Never Eat Fan Mail, Glenn O'Brien interviewed by Olivier Zahm,
photographs by Terry Richardson, Purple Fashion Magazine #5
Interview, L'Ange noir; aurait dit Marlène, Ingrid Caven interviewed by Olivier Zahm,
photograph, 1974, Purple Fashion Magazine #5

Interview, Never Eat Fan Mail, Glenn O'Brien interviewed by Olivier Zahm,
photograph by Bobby Grossman, Purple Fashion Magazine #5
Interview, L'Ange noir; aurait dit Marlène, Ingrid Caven interviewed by Olivier Zahm,
photograph, 2005, Purple Fashion Magazine #5

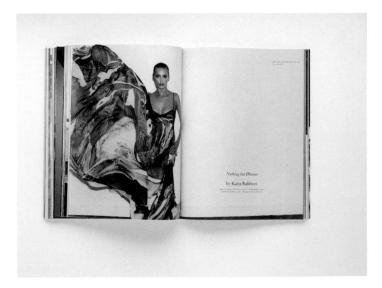

Fashion Woman, The Private Case, photographs by Terry Richardson and Richard Prince, Purple Fashion Magazine #5

Fashion Woman, Nothing but Dresses, photographs by Katja Rahlwes, Purple Fashion Magazine #5

Fashion Men, Peter Saville's Estate, photographs by Donald Christie,
Purple Fashion Magazine #5
Best of the Season, Spring Summer 2006, photographs by Terry Richardson,
Purple Fashion Magazine #5

Fashion Men, Gotham City, photographs by Terry Richardson,
Purple Fashion Magazine #5

Fashion Woman, Chloë nue, photographs by Inez van Lamsweerde
& Vinoodh Matadin, Purple Fashion Magazine #5

Villa La Cañada, Acapulco

Photos by Todd Cole, text by Pablo León de la Barra

R.J. Shaughnessy, *photo assistant* — Maripili Sanderos, *hair & make-up* — Shelly Jiménez, *model*

Interview, Ombres et Lumières, Haider Ackermann interviewed by Olivier Zahm and Samuel Drira, photographs by Johan Sandberg, Purple Fashion Magazine #5
Travel, Villa La Cañada, text by Pablo León de la Barra, photographs by Todd Cole, Purple Fashion Magazine #5

Travel, Villa La Cañada, text by Pablo León de la Barra, photographs by Todd Cole, Purple Fashion Magazine #5

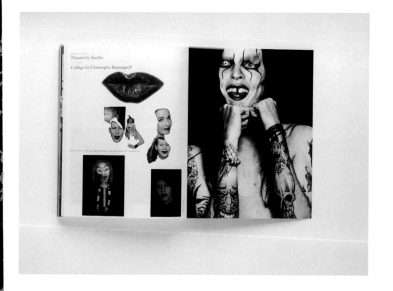

Visual Essay, Memorial Tribute to Bob Richardson, 1928-2005,
photograph by Annie Richardson and Bob Richardson, Purple Fashion Magazine #5
Visual Essay, Memorial Tribute to Bob Richardson, 1928-2005,
photographs by Bob Richardson and Terry Richardson, Purple Fashion Magazine #5
Last Page, Haunted by Marilyn, collage by Christophe Brunnquell,
Purple Fashion Magazine #5

Visual Essay, Memorial Tribute to Bob Richardson, 1928-2005,
photograph by Bob Richardson, Purple Fashion Magazine #5
Visual Essay, Memorial Tribute to Bob Richardson, 1928-2005,
photographs by Bob Richardson and Terry Richardson, Purple Fashion Magazine #5

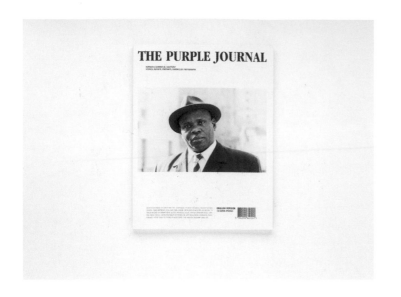

Cover, The Purple Journal #8
Pelican Avenue, Erban Collection, Purple Journal #8
Photographes, photographs Jorge Matsuhiro, Purple Journal #8

Photographes, Purple Journal #8
Letter from Vienna, text by Gaelle Obiégly; View from Rio de Janeiro,
photographs by Elein Fleiss, Purple Journal #8
New York Demonstrations, text and photographs by Alex Antitch, Purple Journal #8

Cover, The Purple Journal #9
Cities Around Paris, Boulogne-Billancourt, Purple Journal #9
Fashion Collections of Garments for Fall/Winter 2006/2007, Cosmic Wonder
by Yukinori Maeda; photographs Cosmic Wonder, Purple Journal #9

Portrait Lizzi Bougatsos, photograph by Laetitia Benat, Purple Journal #9
Purple Gallery, photograph by Laetitia Benat, Purple Journal #9
Fashion Collections of Garments for Fall/Winter 2006/2007, Susan Cianciolo,
New York, photographs Mark Borthwick, Purple Journal #9

PURPLE FASHION *magazine*

FEATURING Vincent Gallo [81], Charlotte Gainsbourg [114], M. Blash [180], Christopher Wool [409], Helena Christensen [222], Riccardo Tisci [126], Leelee Sobieski [174], Proenza Schouler [152], Pete Doherty [328]...

FALL WINTER 2006 / 2007 — VOLUME III, ISSUE 6

FRANCE €15 | USA $22

Cover, Vincent Gallo, photograph by Terry Richardson, Purple Fashion Magazine #6

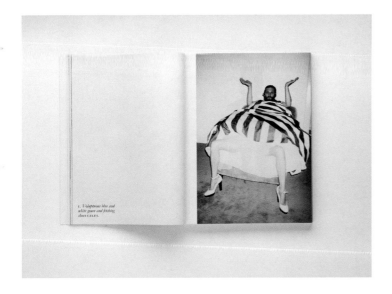

Cover, The Rita Ackermann Purple Book, Good morning New York, Purple Book #6
Best of the season, Fall/Winter 2006/2007, Vincent Gallo,
photographs by Terry Richardson, Purple Fashion Magazine #6

XII. *Winter in the army dress* LOUIS VUITTON, *boots* RICK OWENS.

XIII. *Shaggy scarf* ANN DEMEULEMEESTER, *trenchcoat* VIKTOR&ROLF, *shoes* HUSSEIN CHALAYAN.

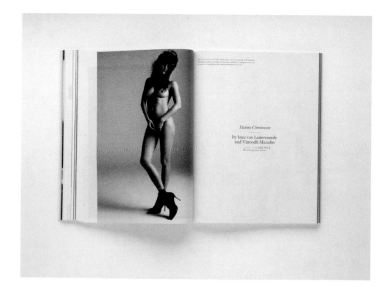

Interview, Dolce Vita, Leelee Sobieski interviewed by Olivier Zahm,
photographs by Terry Richardson, Purple Fashion Magazine #6
Fashion Woman, Fall/Winter 2006/2007, Camille Bidault-Waddington,
photographs by Horst Diekgerdes, Purple Fashion Magazine #6
Fashion Woman, Helena Christensen, photographs by Inez van Lamsweerde
& Vinoodh Matadin, Purple Fashion Magazine #6

Interview, Sometimes I close my eyes, Christopher Wool interviewed
by Glenn O'Brien, photograph by Terry Richardson, Purple Fashion Magazine #6
Fashion Woman, Fall/Winter 2006/2007, Camille Bidault-Waddington,
photographs by Horst Diekgerdes, Purple Fashion Magazine #6
Fashion Woman, Helena Christensen, photographs by Inez van Lamsweerde
& Vinoodh Matadin, Purple Fashion Magazine #6

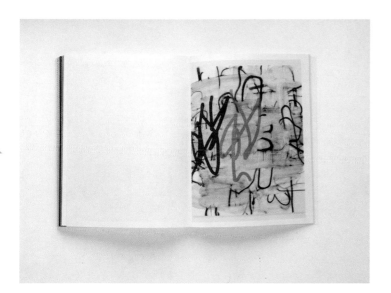

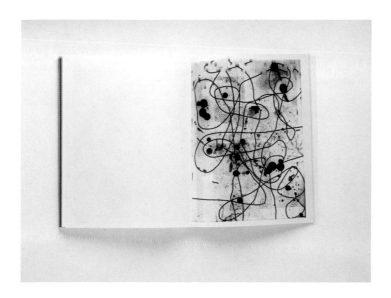

Fashion Men, Marc Jacobs Winter 2006/2007, Dick & James,
A True Story, photographs by Juergen Teller, Purple Fashion Magazine #6
Visual Essay, She Smiles For The Camera, paintings by Christopher Wool,
Purple Fashion Magazine #6

Fashion Men, Marc Jacobs Winter 2006/2007, Dick & James,
A True Story, photographs by Juergen Teller, Purple Fashion Magazine #6
Visual Essay, She Smiles For The Camera, paintings by Christopher Wool,
Purple Fashion Magazine #6

Travel, Air, painting by Heinz Peter Knes, Purple Fashion Magazine #6

1992   **1993**

PURPLE PROSE 1
INDIAN SUMMER
Fall

64 pages
black & white
24.5 x 19 cm
9.6 x 7.5 in

COVER
Jeanne Dunning

COLUMNS
Tilt by Bernard Joisten;
Memo from the Institute
for Advanced Comedic
Behavior by David
Robbins; Un point sur
la critique Blurg by
Vitaly Glabel; Materiaux
intermediaires; Cultural
Tourist by Peter
Fleissig; La tentation
biographique by
Dominique Gonzalez-
Foerster; Squirts
by Dike Blair; Notes
on... by Henry Bond;
Handicraft by Daniel
Jasiak

INTERVIEWS
Patrick van
Caeckenbergh with
Lieven Van Den Abeele;
Kitten with Jutta
Koether; Andrea Zittel
with Benjamin Weil;
Patrick Bouchitey with
Elein Fleiss; Jean-Luc
Vilmouth with Siam;
François Roche and
Xavier Veilhan with
Olivier Zahm

INDIAN SUMMER
Urban Notations
by Joshua Decter;
Quelques principes
sioux personnels by
Jean-Christophe Menu;
Et l'on s'aimera encore
by Olivier Zahm; The
Sunset Effects by Jeff
Rian; Hachivi Edgar
Heep of Birds by Olivier
Zahm; The Maine
Thing by Daniel Lerner;
Crossing the Desert by
Jan Avgikos; The Return
of Something Precious
by Denise Olelslczuk;
The Indians by John
S. Hall; The World's a
Mess, It's in My Kiss by
Roddy Bogawa; Courrier
by Martin Kippenberger

PURPLE PROSE 2
TO DREAM
Winter

82 pages
black & white
24.5 x 19 cm
9.6 x 7.5 in

COVER
Henry Bond

COLUMNS
Tilt by Bernard Joisten;
Notes on... by Henry
Bond; Memo from the
Institute for Advanced
Comedic Behavior by
David Robbins; Cultural
Tourist by Peter
Fleissig; Laboratoire by
Jacques-Arthur Weil;
Flux by Olivier Badot,
Bernard Cova and
Anne-Charlotte Rouelle;
Squirts by Dike Blair;
Architecture(s); Archive
by Anne Frémy; Purple
Bustes; Materiaux
intermediaires

INTERVIEWS
Martine Aballéa with
Elein Fleiss; Julia Scher
with Barbara Osborn;
Valerie Pigato with
Olivier Zahm; R.U.
Serius with Dike Blair;
Eva Marisaldi with
Tomasso Corvi-Mora;
Un Acarien with Jean-
Luc Vilmouth; John S.
Hall with Elein Fleiss
& Olivier Zahm; Isaac
Julien with Simon Lee

TO DREAM
The Wound, the Woman
and the Monster by
Liz Dalton; Rêve
de terre, d'eau,
d'enfouissement et
peut-être d'architecture
by François Roche;
Real Life by Isabelle
Graw; Un rêve collectif
by Michel Maffesoli;
L'existence onirique by
Dominique Gonzalez-
Foerster; Dream and
Purpose by Jeff Rian;
On the Bus the Same
Thing by Tom Verlaine;
Well by Jutta Koether;
Rêve d'apesanteur by
Olivíer Zahm; Du rêve
comme acteur de la
vie by Ariel Kyrou; Le
rêve de la voie lactée
by Thomas Johnson;
Ich Kampfe um Dich by
Lothar Hempel; Rêver
by Johanna Schipper;
Exister c'est écrire sa
vie by Vitaly Glabel

**PURPLE PROSE 3
IT'S MORE LIKE
POST-ART**
Summer

98 pages
black & white
24.5 x 19 cm
9.6 x 7.5 in

COVER
Catherine Bret-
Brownstone

COLUMNS
Tilt by Bernard Joisten;
Noir et blanc by Martin
Margiela; Good Luck
to Humans by Stephen
Joannon; Squirts by
Dike Blair; Materiaux
intermédiaires;
Tendance by Olivier
Zahm; Purple Bustes;
Architecture(s) by Anne
Frémy

INTERVIEWS
Maurizio Cattelan with
Tommaso Corvi-Mora;
Serge Brussolo with
Dominique Gonzalez-
Foerster & Bernard
Joisten; Encore by
Olivier Zahm; Sarah
Lucas & Tracey Emin
with Pauline Daly
& Brendan Quick;
Carole Scotta with
Elein Fleiss; Adrian
Piper with Benjamin
Weil; Marylene Negro
with Claude Closky
and Olivier Zahm; Un
poisson with Jean-Luc
Vilmouth; Jean Touitou
with Elein Fleiss

**IT'S MORE LIKE
POST-ART**
By Dominique Gonzalez-
Foerster and Olivier
Zahm; Re-Post-Art by
Roddy Bogawa; Vous
avez dit post-art? by
Stephen Germer; Body
Count by Jan Avgikos;
Souvenirs des
immateriaux by
Benjamin Weil; Pre-
Post-Art by Helen
Molesworth; Origami de
néon fluide by Bernard
Joisten; Theory of a
Final Dream by Laura
Emrick; Comic by Ugo
Rondinone; Un été, trois
Expositions by Yves
Aupetitallot, Jennifer
Flay, Christian Bernard

**PURPLE PROSE 4
MULTIPLE
PERSONALITY
DISORDER**
Fall

114 pages
black & white
24.5 x 19 cm
9.6 x 7.5 in

COVER
Viktor & Rolf

COLUMNS
Tilt by Bernard Joisten
Collection n°1:
Detachement by Viktor
& Rolf; Correspondance
from the Institute for
Advanced Comedic
Behavior by David
Robbins; Squirts
by Dike Blair;
Architecture(s);
Archives by Anne
Frémy; Purples
Bustes; La tentation
biographique by
Dominique Gonzalez-
Foerster; Villes sans
cités by François Roche;
Peace Movement by
Wolfgang Tillmans

INTERVIEWS
Hans Moravec with
Dike Blair; Lorenzo
Strik Lievers with
Tommaso Corvi Mora;
Philippe Parreno with
Olivier Zahm; Sister
Windy Brikett with Mat
Collishaw; Siri Hustvedt
with Benjamin Weil;
Jack Persekian with
Jean-Luc Vilmouth;
William Forsythe and
Thom Willems with
Dominique Gonzalez-
Foerster and Olivier
Zahm; Ilan Flammer
with Elein Fleiss and
Olivier Zahm

**MULTIPLE
PERSONALITY
DISORDER**
Ces personnalités
multiples qui désormais
errent dans la société
qui fit l'art et ceux qui
le font by Maria Wurtz;
Des territoires sans
terre by Gil Gonzalez-
Foerster; Walker by
Tom Verlaine; Faces of
Eve and Ego of Adam
by Laura Cottingham;
Le troisième scénario by
Dominique Gonzalez-
Foerster; Jeu by Encore;
Of Two Minds by David
Deitcher; Morphing, Inc.
by Bernard Joisten; Out
of Character by Jutta
Koether; Ritournelles
(extraits) by Félix
Guattari; Centers,
Margins, and the
Morphology of Science
by Jeff Rian; Illustration
by Emma Mafille

**PURPLE PROSE 5
POST SEXE**
Winter

96 pages
black & white
monochrome
24.5 x 19 cm
9.6 x 7.5 in

COVER
Wolfgang Tillmans

COLUMNS
Tilt by Bernard Joisten;
Squirts by Dike Blair;
Correspondance
from the Institute for
Advanced Comedic
Behavior by David
Robbins; Flux by Olivier
Badot; L'architecture,
c'est pas banal by
François Roche; House
by Peter Fleissig;
Tendances by Elein
Fleiss; Purple Bustes;
Matériaux;
intermediaires

INTERVIEWS
Claude Lévêque
with Guillaume Nez;
Therapy? with Stephen
Joannon; Markus
Hansen with Andrew
Cross; Carsten Höller
with Tommaso Corvi
Mora; Atom Egoyan with
Dominique Gonzalez-
Foerster; Francisco
Varela with Bernard
Joisten and Olivier
Zahm; Ami Garmon with
Jean-Luc Vilmouth

POST SEXE
(présentation) by Olivier
Zahm with photographs
by Jack Pierson; Post-
Penis by Joshua Decter;
Andre Durandeau,
Danielle Flaumenbaum
and Ginette Lemaitre
with Elein Fleiss and
Olivier Zahm; Post Post
Sex, Or Why Don't We
do it in the Road? by
Bob Nickas; Detachable
Penis by John S. Hall;
The G-spot, the Big
Dildo and That Muscle
Between Her Thighs
by Liz Dalton; Olivier
Blanckart with Elein
Fleiss; Greg Bordowitz
by Benjamin Weil;
Trespassing by Loïs
E. Nesbitt; Vydia with
Elein Fleiss & Jean-Luc
Vilmouth; Alberto
Sorbelli with Valentine
de Ganay; Post Sexe by
Wolfgang Tillmans; Post
Sexe by Shugi Ariyoshi

**PURPLE PROSE 6
LES ANNÉES 10**
Summer

96 pages
black & white
monochrome
24.5 x 19 cm
9.6 x 7.5 in

COVER
Vanessa Beecroft

COLUMNS
Tilt by Bernard Joisten
Correspondance;
from the Institute for
Advanced Comedic
Behavior by David
Robbins; Squirts by
Dike Blair; Images by
Anne Frémy; Cowboys
and Girls de la Danse
by Ami Garmon;
Une architecture
d'infiltration entre
bricolage, Jardinage
et mecanique auto by
François Roche; Purple
Bustes with Vanessa
Beecroft; Materiaux
intermediaires; Old
Habits Die Hard by
Travis

LES ANNÉES 10
(présentation)
In the Future, Everyone
Will be Thinking About
the Future (or, the
Remembrance of
Things to Come) by
Joshua Decter; Little
Pricks by Lee Ranaldo
and Leah Singer; Les
Années 10 by Amy
Davis; Fear of Music by
Bernard Joisten; Une
rencontre with Francis
Yellow; Artiste Sioux by
Dominique Godrèche;
Symptoms of the 90's
by Michaël Krome; Les
Années 10 by Anders
Edström; Marvellous
Margiela by Olivier
Zahm; Les Années 10
by Wolfgang Tillmans;
Rocket Scientists by
Laura Emrick; Music
Machine by Stephen
Joannon; Les Années 10
by Ange Leccia; Leonard
Cohen Afterworld
by Olivier Zahm; Les
Années 10 by Inez van
Lamsweerde; Picture of
a New God by Jeff Rian;
Softworld with Benjamin
Weil

OTHERS
Marie-Ange Guilleminot
with Guillaume Nez; Jon
Moritsugu with Elein
Fleiss; Tania Mouraud
with Elein Fleiss &
Ginette Le Maître; The
Vegas Manifesto by
Dave Hickey; Christine
Hill with Pauline Daly
Leslie Thornton: The
Art Process and The
(Process) Art of Film
Making by Roddy
Bogawa; Eyal Sivan
with Elein Fleiss
& Corine Lesage;
Diabologum with
Rebecca Bournigault
and Elein Fleiss; Le
pays des merveilles ou
quelques remarques
sur le paradis by Nika
Dubrovsky & Alexandre
Daymand

**PURPLE PROSE 7
VIOLET VIOLENCE**
Fall

96 pages
black & white
monochrome
24.5 x 19 cm
9.6 x 7.5 in

COVER
Vidya & Jean-Michel

COLUMNS
Tilt by Bernard Joisten;
Instincts d'architecture
by Jean-Michel Fradkin;
Squirts by Dike Blair;
Du rapport de bon
voisinage by François
Roche; 1 Franc, t'as 4
Chansons by Stephen
Joannon; Architectures
by Anne Frémy; Purple
Bustes with Miltos
Manetas; Materiaux
intermediares

VIOLET VIOLENCE
Violet Violence by
Vidya & Jean-Michel;
This Wonderful Life by
Jeff Rian; Rape Me,
My Friend by Olivier
Zahm; Omniviolence by
Bernard Joisten; Richard
Kern with Olivier Zahm;
The Drive-By, the
Car Jack, the Club by
Roddy Bogawa; Violet
Violence by Wolfgang
Tillmans; Un scénario,
des filles des heures by
Dominique Gonzalez-
Foerster; James O'Baar
with Dike Blair; Shirin
Neshat with Octavio
Zaya; False-False, Real-
Real and False-Real
by William Scheferine;
Viktor & Rolf with Elein
Fleiss; Mild Thing by
Dike Blair; Gregory
Green with Benjamin
Weil; Every Cloud Has a
Scooby-Doo Ending by
Travis

OTHERS
Claude Closky with
Olivier Zahm; Bruce
McDonald with Bernard
Joisten & Guillaume
Nez; Chuck Nanney
with Robert Nickas;
Sarah Schwartz with
Elein Fleiss & Jeff
Rian; L'incertain with
Dominique Gonzalez-
Foerster and Bernard
Joisten

PURPLE PROSE 8
Winter

80 pages
black & white
24.5 x 19 cm
9.6 x 7.5 in

COVER
Inez van Lamsweerde &
Vinoodh Matadin

Codeine with Matthew
Connors and Olivier
Zahm; Movra Davey by
Jennifer Montgomery;
François Gadel by
Guillaume Nez; Scott
McGehee and David
Siegel with Elein Fleiss
and Olivier Zahm; Liquid
Madonnas, Vegetable
Gods by Jeff Rian; Alix
Lambert with Lionel
Bovier; Correspondance
from the Institute for
Advanced Comedic
Behavior by David
Robbins; Squirts by
Dike Blair; Elément
d'une garde-robe de
poupée by Olivier Zahm;
Georgia Starr with
Tommaso Corvi Mora;
Mimesis by François
Roche; The Japanese
Sense of Place by
Dominique Gonzalez-
Foerster; Dogbowl,
Kramer and Peter
Parker Experience
with Olivier Zahm;
Territoires occupés
vues de l'extérieur
by Jean-Michel
Fradkin; Matériaux
intermédiaires; Some
Happy Accident at
the Lancôme Factory
by Bernard Joisten;
Yasumara Morimura by
Benjamin Weil; Inez van
Lamsweerde by Olivier
Zahm; Tilt by Bernard
Joisten; Gloria Toyum
Park by Olivier Zahm;
Vanessa Beecroft by
Barbara Polla; Laurent
Faulon by Guillaume
Nez; 1F t'as quatre
chansons by Stephen
Joannon; Alan Belcher
with Elein Fleiss; Toland
Grinnell by Benjamin
Weil; Surgery with
Stephen Joannon and
Guillaume Nez

PURPLE PROSE 9
SPORTS, JAPAN,
INDEPENDENTS
Summer

159 pages
black & white
monochrome
18.5 x 13 cm
7.5 x 5.3 in

COVER
Mariko Mori

Vidya & Jean-Michel,
Serge & Christophe
with Olivier Zahm;
William Gibson with
Bernard Joisten and
Ken Lum; Robert Longo
with Dike Blair; How
Much by Wolfgang
Tillmans; Ernest T.
with Elein Fleiss; Kiki
with Bernard Joisten;
Dominique A. with
Olivier Zahm; Not Now,
Honey, the Game's On!
by Jeff Rian; Swimming
in the 21st Century by
Anne Frémy; Sporting
Dreams by Jutta
Koether; Reportage
Sport with Anders
Edström and Yoshiko
Shiojiri; La Fuite vers
le sport by Olivier
Zahm; Pascal Rivet by
Nathalie Goudinoux;
Yurie Nagashima with
Elein Fleiss; Sim Flight
by Gilles Gonzalez-
Foerster; Keiji Haino
by Izumi Kusano &
Sanemasa Mushakoji;
Tokyo Marine by Anne
Frémy; Mariko Mori
with Dike Blair; Takashi
Homma by Nakako
Hayashi; L'archipel
des catastrophes by
Dominique Pasqualini;
Boredoms by Guillaume
Nez; Espace-Digestif,
Corps-Digestif by Jean-
Michel Fradkin; Purple
Bustes with Stévenart,
Glaser, Périgot; Pierre
Huyghe with Dominique
Gonzalez-Foerster;
Fisherman, Shellac and
Tortoise by Stephen
Joannon; Matériaux
intermédiaires; Fred
Sathal with Cédric de
Saint André Perrin; The
Thing with Dike Blair;
Une enquête sur les
labels indépendants en
France by Elein Fleiss;
Kristof Mòl by Renée
Takeoff; Shoes by
Freddie Stevens; Taroop
& Glabel by Leonora
Himmelblau; Serge
Comte with Bernard
Joisten; Andreas
Angelidakis with Miltos
Manetas & Vanessa
Beecroft

PURPLE FICTION 1
June

104 pages
black & white
19 x 13.5 cm
7.5 x 5.3 in

COVER
Christophe Brunnquell

Beware of Deadly
Memories by Martine
Aballéa; Scénarios de
romans (à développer)
by Dominique Gonzalez-
Foerster; Swimming
Lesson by Jeff Rian;
Exras by Miltos
Manetas; De l'alcool
sur le feu by Stéphane
Camille; The Power of
One by Leah Singer;
Les victimes n'ont
apparemment aucune
relation entre elles by
Françoise Valéry; Songs
by Dog; Papilla's Bridge
by Dog; Late Afternoon
in the Offices of Field
and Screen David
Robbins; From the
Movie by Lee Ranaldo;
J'accepte la Critique by
Bernard Joisten

PURPLE FASHION 1

32 pages
color
black & white
18.5 x 13 cm
7.3 x 5.1 in

COVER
Anders Edström

Pascale Gatzen
by Jerome Esch;
Bernadette Corporation
by Wolfgang Tillmans;
Owen Gaster by Martine
Houghton; Viktor &
Rolf by Christophe
Brunnquell; Marcel
Verheijen by Mark
Borthwick; Fredie
Stevens by Bernard
Joisten; Lutz Huelle by
Anders Edström

PURPLE PROSE 10
NORMAL EXPLOSION
Winter

160 pages
black & white
monochrome
16 x 13 cm
6.3 x 5.1 in

COVER
Alex Bag

Swedish Erotic
Sequences by Anders
Edström; Sonic Stoll
by GA. Boyer; Gastr
del Sol/Brise Glace
by Stephen Joannon;
Ulan Bator by Stephen
Joannon; Jungle
Power by Jean-Luc
Vilmouth; About äda
web by Benjamin Weil;
Letter by Vidya &
Jean-Michel; Picture
This by Marco Boggio
Sella; Border Line by
Jean-Michel Fradkin;
Job Interview by Jeff
Rian; Identification d'un
moment by Dominique
Gonzalez-Foerster;
Remix by Olivier
Zahm; alt. PRE-FAB by
Andreas Angelidakis;
Catastrophes of the
Interior by Joshua
Decter; Pronostic Vérité
by Claude Closky;
It's Always the Same
by Dike Blair; The
Moderator Goes on
Holiday by Liam Gillick;
Chateau by Wolfgang
Tillmans; Alex Bag's Girl
World by Elein Fleiss
& Jeff Rian; Matériaux
intermédiaires; Gothique
Victorien by Bernard
Joisten; Immaculate
Camera by Helena
Papadopoulos; Giuseppe
Gabelonne by M.
Manetas & V. Beecroft;
Cleo 3000 by Bernard
Joisten; Blast by Dike
Blair & Elein Fleiss;
Sans Titre by Ange
Leccia; Autodidact by
David Robbins; Faces
and Names by Guillaume
Nez; Untitled by Marjon
Driessen; Eau Minérale
by Stephen Joannon &
Olivier Zahm; Untitled
by Bagatti-Boggio Sella
Toreno; Cellulaire et
Sexy by Bernard Joisten

PURPLE PROSE 11
Summer

208 pages
black & white
monochrome
18.5 x 13 cm
7.3 x 5.1 in

COVER
Laetitia Benat

Letter by Vidya & Jean-
Michel; Impressions of
Poise by Dog; Chiaki
Tamura by Olivier Zahm;
Sites Utopiques by
Anne Frémy & Dean
Inkster; In Town with
Boss Hogg by Jutta
Koether; Maurizio
Cattelan, World Tour
by Olivier Zahm; Carole
Chabat by Guillaume
Nez; Don't Look Back
by Elein Fleiss & Marie-
Thérèse Leccia; Go to
the Bear's by Keizo
Suhara; Humbert by
Marie-Thérèse Leccia;
Meanderings on the
Age of BLUR and blah,
blah, blah by Dike
Blair; La Maison de
thé by Elein Fleiss &
Dominique Gonzalez-
Foerster; Nathalie
Baye by Bernard
Joisten; Conscious
Clothes by Elein Fleiss;
Maura Biavi by Anaïd
Demir; Where Are You
Now? by Dominique
Gonzalez-Foerster;
Racing Cup by Anders
Edström; Intimate
Journey by Jan Aman
& Catti Lindhal; La Vie
en 3D Arnaud Viviant
by Bernard Joisten &
Olivier Zahm; Réserve
Ilnu de Mashteuiatsh
Pointe; Bleu by Anne
Cury; 69 Proposals
for an Anti-Erotic Year
by Jeff Rian; NaCl by
Jean-Michel Fradkin;
Test by Claude Closky;
Union Pour le Vêtement
by Else Skalvoll;
Florence Manlik by
Guillaume Nez; Au
Delà des Apparences;
Absence de mode by
Marie-Thérèse Leccia;
3 Photos by Yurie
Nagashima; Makeshift
Power Suit by Andreas
Angelidakis; The Logic
of the Puppeteer by
Dike Blair; La Voie
Lactée by Elein Fleiss;
Subrosa by Stephen
Joannon; Je crois
qu'il est temps de
s'interrompre by Olivier
Zahm; Beyond the
Score by Judy Elkan
Maria Finn by Simon
Sheikh; Temporary
Coalitions by Olivier
Zahm; Girls Talk by
Dike Blair; Overall Oval
by Bernard Joisten &
Camille Vivier

PURPLE FICTION 2
1996/1997

96 pages
black & white
19 x 13.5 cm
7.5 x 5.3 in

COVER
Camille Vivier

I'm the King of Everything by Jutta Koether; My Time Divided by Two by Mauricio Guillen; Momentanément by Marie-Thérèse Leccia; Kinosaki by Anders Edström; The Boy Made Out of Bone China by John S. Hall; Diarreah Nose by John S. Hall; C40-C60 by Mark Borthwick; Dress by Mark Borthwick; 1978 by Mark Borthwick; Transformation by Stéphanie Hope; Flooded Fire by Stephanie Hope; Rough Sketch for Michael (Stalagg 3) by Steven Hale; T.V. Times by Steven Hale; Visiting by Giasco Bertoli; The Drainer by Nicholas Chaikin; The Trucker Series by Nicholas Chaikin; "… Yeah, riding high on love's true blueish light" by Camille Vivier; Lisp by Amy Fusselman; Missing by Laetitia Benat; Pinhead by Dog; Substance Abuse by Dog; Naked by James Tegeder; Shift Up to Fall by Marie-Thérèse Leccia; L'homme nu devant le Pacifique by Francine Stoecklin; Marc(b)lage by Christophe Brunnquell & Anne-Iris Guyonnet; Necro by Richard Penny

PURPLE PROSE 12
INC.
Summer

176 pages
black & white
monochrome
18.5 x 13 cm
7.3 x 5.1 in

COVER
Marcelo Krasilcic

Silk Saw by Stephen Joannon; Gianni Motti with Barbara Polla; Stéphanie Arrignon with Anaïd Demir; Tommy Stoeckel with Karsten R. S. Ifversen; Cindy Dall with Bennett Simpson; Laetitia Benat with Anaïd Demir; Klaus Scherubel with Jeff Rian; Christophe Berdaguer & Marie Péjus with Guillaume Nez; Ganz Angst by Vidya & Jean-Michel; Iris-In Iris-Out by Jeff Rian; Timetrack Camera by Dike Blair; Kava Naet Long Roni Nakamal by Stéphane Camille; Bak Truppen by Else Skalvoll; Highway to Hell by Laetitia Benat & Camille Vivier; Japan Final Flash by Bernard Joisten; Intervista by Elein Fleiss & Guillaume Nez; Silver Jew by Bennett Simpson; G.T.S. by Olivier Zahm; A Japanese Store by Chapel Hiromi Eto Inc. by Jeff Rian; Style by Anders Edström; At the Office of Prop & Gander by Dog; Corporate Style by Andreas Angelidakis; Fast on His Feet by Dike Blair & Elein Fleiss; Fx, Inc. by Bernard Joisten; D&G Corporate Song by Olivier Zahm; 2000 Wasted Years by Antek Walczak; Sneakers by Mark Borthwick; Pollution en pente douce by Jean-Michel Fradkin; The Great Logo Wars by Jeff Rian; Simcity by Andreas Angelidakis; Tommy Boys (and Tommy Girls) by Joshua Decter; Better Than Life by Dike Blair

PURPLE FICTION 3

160 pages
black & white
monochrome
18.5 x 13 cm

COVER
Chikashi Suzuki

Rat Patrol by Amy Fusselman; Wagner in Tits by Harmony Korine; Swan Son of the Spick by Harmony Korine; Story and Visage… by Harmony Korine; The Killing of Randy Webster by Harmony Korine; Sei Jin Shiki by Chikashi Suzuki; Indigo Angel by O. Micaeli; Cintas de Plata by Mauricio Guillen; In by Walter Alter; Script/Photogrammes by Pierre Bismuth; Big Star by Leah Singer; Freud/Madame Tien by Gérard Duguet-Grasser One Way Ticket by Gérard Duguet-Grasser; Pauv' Solo de Trompette by Gérard Duguet-Grasser; Buffer VI and Buffer V by Bennett Simpson; The Angel Tour by Jeff Rian & Elein Fleiss; From the Short-Psychopathic-Autobiographies Series by Nicholas Chaikin; Eté by Ange Leccia; The Church-Goers' Tale by Vito Hannibal Acconci; Dialogue 04 by Maurizio Cattelan & Judy Elkan; As by Jackie Simmons; Jesus The Cockroach by Jackie Simmons; Thank You, Goodbye by Jackie Simmons; No Sleep by Jackie Simmons; La Maison Martini: des rêves d'une seconde by Dominique Gonzalez-Foerster; Andrée by Stéphane Camille; Bobby's Fluff – An Artworld Fable by Kathe Burkhart; Demanza by Miltos Manetas; Circles of Confusion by Kevin O'Sullivan; La plage by Frédéric El Bekkay; L'hiver d'après by Marie-Thérèse Leccia; Return of the Gods – The Million Year Fantasy by D'Antek; My Father by John S. Hall; Nickles for Ned by John S. Hall; Happiness by John S. Hall; Räfs by Anders Edström; Kyocera by Bernard Joisten

PURPLE FASHION 2
1997

180 pages
black & white
monochrome
full color
18.5 x 13 cm
7.3 x 5.1 in

COVER
Nathaniel Goldberg

Snow White by Armin Linke & Miltos Manetas; Chinese Ladies by Anders Edström; Else Skalvoll by François Rotger; Collection 1994, Chiaki Tamura by Anne-Iris Guyonnet Le Chic Gauschiste by Vidya & Jean-Michel Beige, Copenhagen by Elein Fleiss; Add-Ons by Laetitia Benat; Les ciseaux à la main by Marie-Thérèse Leccia; Columbus Indiana, 1996 by Dominique Gonzalez-Foerster; Junya Watanabe by Takashi Homma; Pause by Armin Linke; Hanuk Kim by Mauricio Guillen; Collegamenti by Miltos Manetas & Armin Linke; Horses, Horses, Comin' in in All Directions, White, Silver… by Mark Borthwick; Viktor & Rolf Fitting; L'institut liquéfiant by Martine Aballéa; Martin Margiela, Inevitably Here and Now by Marina Faust; Erik Halley by Camille Vivier & Sanghon Kim with text by Cécile Kizlik & Camille Sanghon; Vanessa Beecroft, 1996, Performance, Galleria Massimo de Carlo, Milan by Armin Linke, Oorla's Choice by Mauricio Guillen; Run by Marcelo Krasilcic; Details 31/08/96 by Duc Liao; Andrea Zittel by Peter Muscato; Alex's Shopping by Giasco Bertoli; Still Life by Anders Edström; 40/30 by Christophe Brunnquell; Faridi by Wolfgang Tillmans; Lingerie by Sarah; New York/Honduras by Mario Sorrenti; Quiet Sweden by Anders Edström; Standard Keyboard by Inez van Lamsveerde & Vinoodh Matadin, Koji Tatcuno by Nathaniel Goldberg; Pascale Gatzen by Saira van Essen; Bernadette Corporation by John Wayne Nguyen; Vanessa Beecroft, 1996, Miu Miu Shot, New York by Armin Linke

PURPLE FASHION 3
Summer

122 pages
full color
18.5 x 13 cm
7.3 x 5.1 in

COVER
Mark Borthwick

Martin Margiela by Anders Edström; Run #3 by Cris Moor; Approaching Cadillac of Time by Vidya & Jean-Michel; Vinter Månar Sommar Månar by Maria Finn; Eight of Maurizio Cattelan's Photos; First We Feel by Camille Vivier; Owen Gaster by Anders Edström; Whooshh by Terry Richardson; Tokyo Eye by Camille Vivier; Beauté by Sarah; Early Dark by Laetitia Benat; Don't Look Now by Giasco Bertoli; Pascale Gatzen by Joke Robaard; Sportswear by Anders Edström; Portraits by Rebecca Bournigault; Run #2 by Banu Cennetoglu; Run #1 by Mauricio Guillen; The Periodic Table by Marcelo Krasilcic; Hand Made by Laetitia Benat; After Beige by Elein Fleiss; Seijin-Shiki by Yoshiko Shiojiri by Chikashi Suzuki; Nevers 79 by Claude Lévêque; La Chava 1/2 Gabacha by Mauricio Guillen; Yoichi Nagasawa by Laetitia Benat; Frédérique Hood by Mauricio Guillen; Two Pictures by Collier Schorr; Kim by Mark Borthwick; Real World by Armin Linke; Shadows by Danielle Wessel; On The Way by Jean-François Brun & Else Skalvoll; Aa by Bernard Joisten; Marie-Ange Guilleminot by Horst Diekgerdes; Shiri Slavin by Camille Vivier; Yab Yum by Chikashi Suzuki; Comme des Garçons by Mark Borthwick

PURPLE PROSE 13
THE ABSTRACT ISSUE
Winter

158 pages
black & white
monochrome
18.5 x 13 cm
7.3 x 5.1 in

COVER
Doug Aitken

Anouchka by Olivier Zahm; Tu voulais voir Vesoul by Elein Fleiss & Jeff Rian; Darwin Alley: Interview with Serge Lehmann by Bernard Joisten & Anne Frémy; Filmaking in India by John Bhaktul; Marco, Zappa, Baadder et Moi: Interview with Rainer Oldendorf by Stéphanie Moisdon-Trembley; What Were Girls Wearing in the 90's in Tokyo by Nakako Hayashi; Face to Face: Interview with Ange Leccia by Olivier Zahm; Abstract (J'ai essayé de te décrire à quelqu'un) by Olivier Zahm & Dominique Gonzalez-Foerster; E.O.D. by Laetitia Benat; 98.6 Wetware by Bennett Simpson; Otherworldly: Interview with John McCracken by Dike Blair; Where Are You From Paleblue? by Andreas Angelidakis; Abstraction by Dominique Gonzalez-Foerster; Abstraction by John Lindell; Abstraction by Philippe Parreno; Abstraction by Seton Smith; Run Abstraction by Various On Aliens; Abstraction and 2kism by Dike Blair; Atami Mood by Dominique Gonzalez Foerster; Domenten in the Future Present: Interview with Miltos Manetas by Jeff Rian; Photos by Anders Edström; Ou bien, ou bien by Bernard Joisten; Abstractive Houses by Anne Frémy; Midi sous terre: scénario by Vidya & Jean-Michel; Forest and Trees by Jeff Rian Sound and Image, Self and Place: Interview with Doug Aitken by Dike Blair

**PURPLE 1
POLYTIX**
Summer

384 pages
black & white
monochrome
full color
21.5 x 15.5 cm
8.5 x 6.1 in

COVER
Takashi Noguchi

POLYTICS BY:
Jeff Rian; Olivier Zahm;
Stephen Joannon;
Maurizio Cattelan;
Lee Ranaldo; Bennet
Simpson; Xavier Veilhan
Jutta Koether; Rudolf
Stingel; David Robbins;
David C. Berman;
Jean-Michel Fradkin;
Amy Fusselman; Serge
Comte; Jordan Crandall
Laetitia Benat; John S.
Hall; Martine Abálléa;
Dominique Gonzalez-
Foerster; Dike Blair
Pete; Antek Walczak;
Zoe Leonard; Bernard
Joisten; Thurston
Moore; John Lindell;
Jop Van Bennekom;
Karl Holmqvist; Claude
Closky; Rebecca
Bournigault

**PURPLE FASHION
SUMMER**
Calvin Klein Collection
by Cris Moor; Linda
Björg Amadottir by
Anders Edström;
Transcontinents by
Takashi Noguchi; Martin
Margiela by Wolfgang
Tillmans; Klaartje
Martens by Rosell
Heymen; Viktor & Rolf
by Anuschka Blommers;
Siri Harr Steinvik by
Torbjørn Rødland; Susan
Cianciolo by Takashi
Homma; Y's by Chikashi
Suzuki; Junya Watanabe
by Donald Christie;
Jérome Dreyfuss by
Matt Jones; Véronique
Branquinho by Ronald
Stoops; Miho Sekine
by Hirokazu Sugita;
Hussein Chalayan
by Camille Vivier;
Owen Gaster by Katja
Rahlwes; Koji Tatsuno
by Nathaniel Goldberg;
Helmut Lang by Giasco
Bertoli; Comme des
Garçons by Anette
Aurell

PURPLE BEAUTY
Make Up by Leonhard
Stark; Morning Beauty
by Mark Borthwick;
Make Up Retrospective
by Various
Photographers

STORIES
Remember the Waves
by Doug Aitken;
Dimanche by Anders
Edström; Wien 98
by Bettina Komenda;
Galaxy 2000 by Elein
Fleiss; Blue in Green by
Torbjørn Rødland; Moon
System by Dominique
Gonzalez-Foerster;
Images by Claude
Lévêque; Weedville, PA
by Terry Richardson

PURPLE FICTION
Dishwasher by Henry
Baum; Squares are
Human Inventions by
Marcelo Krasilcic; Line
After Line by Hunter
Kennedy; The Cold
Cut Crackpot Life of
Al Goldstein by Bart
Plantega; Poems by
Bennett Simpson; 3
P.M. by Masafumi
Sanaï; The American
Anti-Revenant League
by Neil Hagerty;
The Call by Delphine
Zempetti; Watching by
Beth Yahp; Amarillo
by Didier Courbot;
Environmentalist in the
Bottle by Richard Roger

PURPLE SEXE 2
Photography by:
Katja Rahlwes; Terry
Richardson; Chikashi
Kasai; Viviane Sassen;
Takashi Homma; Mark
Borthwick; Anne-Iris
Guyonnet; Mauricio
Guillen

PURPLE 2
Winter 1998/1999

448 pages
black & white
monochrome
full color
21.5 x 15.5 cm
8.5 x 6.1 in

COVER
Anuschka Blommers

**PURPLE FASHION
CITIES**
Paris: Comme des
Garçons by Anuschka
Blommers; Martin
Margiela by Banu
Cennetoglu; Koji
Tatsuno by Masafumi
Sanaï; Sun Young Song
by Marc Demonaz;
Carrefour by Bettina
Komenda; Sharon
Wauchob by Ange
Leccia; Gaspard
Yurkievich by Martin
Laporte; Hermès by
Johnny Gembitsky;
Antwerpen: Véronique
Branquinho by Cédrick
Eymenier; New York:
Susan Cianciolo by
Laetitia Bénat; Helmut
Lang by Richard Prince;
Bruce by Alex Antitch;
Tokyo: Chiaki Tamura
by Takashi Nogushi;
Munich: Kostas
Murkudis by Ellen
Nolan; London: Hussein
Chalayan by Torbjørn
Rødland; Ann-Sophie
Back by Mauricio
Guillen; Amsterdam:
Viktor & Rolf by Terry
Richardson

PURPLE BEAUTY
Inge Grognard by
Nathaniel Goldberg;
Bernadette Van-Huy by
Katja Rahlwes; Elein
Fleiss by Anne-Iris
Guyonnet; Kenshu
Shintsubo by Chiaki
Tamura; Patterson
Beckwith by Alex Bag

PURPLE LOOKS
Colin De Land, Dan
Graham, David Karlin
and Debra Kinery by
Marcelo Krasilcic; Form
and Function by Mark
Borthwick; Global Echo
by Antek Walczak

INSERT: LEXICON
An Excerpt From a
Work In Progress by
Jeff Rian, photographs
by Anders Edström

INSERT
Takashi Homma
Photographs

**PURPLE PROSE
COLORS**
Rose fluorescent
& irisé by Bernard
Joisten; Black & White
by Pascale Gatzen;
An Abstract Minimal
Pattern in Flourescent
Orange on a Slightly
Textured, Pale Olive-
Green Background by
Andreas Heuch; Klein
Blue by Arto Lindsay;
Bleu by Philippe
Parreno; Bondi Blue by
Dike Blair; Ombre by
Dominique Gonzalez-
Foerster; Green/Blue
by Jutta Koether; Silver
by Hunter Kennedy;
Orange by Antek
Walczak; Gris by Michel
Sitbon: Interview; Blanc
et rouge by Serge
Comte; Grey by Denis
Dalquist; Transparent by
Joshua Decter; Brown
by Helena Sundström;
Rouge/Vert by Jean-
Michel Fradkin; Fire by
Pete; Gris by Olivier
Zahm; White by Bennett
Simpson; RGB by S.
Lockhart: Interview
Gris/Transparent by
Manon de Boer; White
by V. Gastaldon & J.M
Wicker; Glauque by
Roche, DSV & SIE.
P & Ammar Eloueini;
Black/Silver by Dora
Garcia; BlueBlack by
Yukihisa Nakase; Purple
by Yasuhiko Hamachi

PURPLE FICTION
Above & Beyond by
Sabine Schründer;
Looking the Other Way
by Elein Fleiss; Tracks
by Claude Lévêque;
Summer Games by
Maria Finn; Seeing Out
Loud by Camille Vivier;
Neon Dark by Doug
Aitken; Electricidad by
Mauricio Guillen; It's
About Love by Maurizio
Cattelan; Brown Walls,
Chandeliers by Linda
Healey; The 3rd Avenue
el by Gerard Malanga;
Triggers/4 Dead Birds
by Risa Mickenberg;
Janie/Lilacs by Larry
Griffin; Saint-Projet by
Michel Zumpf; Rubber/I
Can Hear Dogs Speak
by Adam J. Maynard;
Dancing With an Emu
by Christine Gillespie;
When I Say That I Love
Her by Gérard Duguet-
Grasser; Container
Island by Stéphane
Camille

PURPLE INTERIORS
Vues d'exposition by
Dominique Gonzalez-
Foerster; Raugh'n'Ready
by Andrea Zittel; FX by
Ariko; Transcendental
Decoration by Dike
Blair; Jajouka by Leah
Singer; Home and Office
by Jean Prouvé

PURPLE FICTION 4
Winter

128 pages
monochrome
18.5 x 13 cm
7.3 x 5.1 in

COVER
Mauricio Guillen

Random by Vidya
& Jean-Michel; Self
Portrait at 28 by
David Berman; Silver
by Giasco Bertoli;
Domestic Life by John
S. Hall; Does That
Make Me Gay?... by
John S. Hall; In-Sights
by Aurélie Monier
& Anne Cottreel; I'll
Be Good (I Promise)
by Karl Holmqvist;
Babies in Space by Karl
Holmqvist; Hot in AZ
by Vanessa Beecroft
and Miltos Manetas;
Softcore by Mai-Thu
Perret; Tourism-Three
Extracts by Bernard
Cohen; Tempered
by Laetitia Benat;
Cinéma by Frédéric
El-Bekkay; Tropicide by
Katja Rahlwes; Août
by Gérard Duguet-
Grasser; Three Poems
by Franklin Sirmans and
photographs by Giasco
Bertoli; Excerpt from
Cocaine Diary by Kayla
Allen; Travelvet by Dike
Blair; Something I Didn't
Ask by Jen Budney;
Flower Bubbles by Marc
Demonaz; Requited
Love by Mark Fishman

PURPLE FASHION 4
Winter

122 pages
color
black & white
18.5 x 13 cm
7.3 x 5.1 in

COVER
Chikashi Suzuki

CONTENTS
Martin Margiela by
Chikashi Suzuki;
Selfridges! by Anders
Edström; Street Style
by Andreas Angelidakis;
Spice Girl by Ellen
Treasure; Collier
Schorr; Raf Simons by
Anne-Iris Guyonnet;
Pascale Gatzen by Mark
Borthwick; Carolien
Huizinga by Olaf
Klaasseni; Viktor & Rolf
Exhibition; Riverside
by Laura Scicovelli;
Zuckerzeit by Banu
Cennetoglu; File #1 by
Mauricio Guillen; File
#2 by Mauricio Guillen;
File #3 by Mauricio
Guillen; Koji Tatsuno
by François Rotger;
Bless by Laetita Benat;
Comme des Garçons by
Mark Borthwick; Sleep,
Éat But Don't Walk by
Takashi Homma; Junya
Watanabe by Miguel
Gori; London by Jack
Pierson; Calendar by
Marcelo Krasilcic;
Helmut Lang by Terry
Richardson; Auto
Show by Dike Blair;
Bernadette Corporation
by John Minh Nguyen;
Sabina Schreder by
Marcelo Krasilcic;
235 Berry Street by
Vanessa Beecroft &
Miltos Manetas; Vidya
& Jean-Michel by Mark
Borthwick; Leaving
Helsinki by Elein Fleiss;
A Minor Mode by
Camille Vivier; Eriko
by Kenshu Shintsubo;
Torbjørn Rødland
Home Away Home by
Claude Levêque; Blue
Grass by Laetitia Benat;
Hussein Chalayan by
Mark Borthwick; Noriko
Shiojiri by Dominique
Gonzalez-Foerster;
Susan Cianciolo by
Annette Aurell; Yab
Yum by Chikashi Suzuki;
Red by Maria Finn; APC
by Bernard Joisten;
Tender Sports by Banu
Cennetoglu

PURPLE SEXE 1
Winter

66 pages
full color
18.5 x 13.5 cm
7.3 x 5.1 in

COVER
Terry Richardson

Monochromes by
Camille Vivier; Link
by Mauricio Guillen;
Stretch by Marcelo
Krasilcic; Big Red Lips
by Katja Rahlwes;
French Kids by Hiromix;
Super maginie by
Anders Edström;
Moon Hearts by Terry
Richardson; Blond-
age by Armin Linke;
Georges Tony Stoll;
Nataly by Giasco
Bertoli; Cuba by Banu
Cennetoglu; Boot Camp
by Katja Rahlwes; The
Dynamic Duo by Terry
Richardson

PURPLE SEXE 3
16 TOPICS
October

88 pages
full color
21.5 x 15.5 cm
8.3 x 6.1 in

COVER
Terry Richardson

ART
Vanessa Beecroft,
Leipzig 1998; Virtue
in Vice by Noritoshi
Hirakawa; Lady by
Richard Kern; Singles
by Claude Olosky, 1998
Portraits; Singles &
Doubles by Annette
Aurell; Fashion
Special Missoni by
Terry Richardson; TBH
by Vanessa Beecroft;
Tender Sticks by Katja
Rahlwes; Fleurs by Cris
Moor and Bernadette
Van-Huy; T&A; Joy
Dish Liquid by Terry
Richardson; The Purple
Girl by Katja Rahlwes;
Leisure Summer
Pictures by Jack
Pierson; Kisses Wet by
François Rotger; Car;
Hummer by Jamil; GS;
Diary; Bethany Ritz by
Gilles Toledano; Fiction;
Hunters and Hustlers by
Justine Parsons

PURPLE 3
Summer

448 pages
black & white
monochrome
full color
21.5 x 15.5 cm
8.5 x 6.1 in

COVER
Anders Edström

PURPLE FASHION
Run #7 264 Canal
Street by Anders
Edström; Rio Ouaba
by Bettina Komenda;
Nuit Blanche by
Donald Christie; Blues
Explosion by Terry
Richardson; Printemps
tardif by Kenshu
Shintsubo; Reprise
by Alex Antitch;
After Rock by Giasco
Bertoli; Art moderne by
Marcelo Krasilcic; Look
by Marcelo Krasilcic;
Women's Wear by
Mark Borthwick; A
Night Without Armor
by Patterson Beckwith;
Check-In by Chikashi
Suzuki; Balenciaga
Maintenant by Katja
Rahlwes; Two Halves
Make a Whole by
Martien Mulders; Jocks
& Jills by Blommers &
Schumm; Job Interview
by Martien Mulders;
Affective Phrenology by
Camille Vivier; Bareback
by Patrick Katzman;
Original Geometry by
Tokyo Spiral 3; Fluid
by Giasco Bertoli; In a
Silent Way by Takashi
Noguchi; Helmut Lang
U.S.A. by Collier
Schorr; Beauty by
Ronald Stoops; Beauty
for Schizophrenics by
Cris Moor; Lipstick
T-Shirts (Juicy Details)
by Maria Finn; Jutta
Koether by Banu
Cennetoglu

PURPLE PROSE
Interview Questions by:
Dike Blair, Claude
Closky, Elein Fleiss,
Dominique Gonzalez-
Foerster, Bernard
Joisten, Jutta Koether,
Jeff Rian, David
Robbins, François
Roche, Antek Walczak,
Olivier Zahm
Answers by: Martine
Aballéa, Rita
Ackermann, Alex Bag,
Laetitia Benat, Susan
Cianciolo, Kim Gordon,
Jutta Koether, Alix
Lambert, Sonia
Marques, Julia Scher,
Collier Schorr, Lisa
Yuskavage, Patterson
Beckwith, Dike Blair,
Claude Closky, Nicolas
Franck, John S. Hall,
Bernard Joisten, Claude
Lévêque, John Lindell,
Miltos Manetas, Maison
Martin Margiela, John
McCracken, Eric
Minkkinen, Richard
Prince, Lee Ranaldo,
David Robbins, Alain
Séchas, Kyle Statham,
Georges Tony Stoll,
Jean-Luc Vilmouth

PURPLE SPECIAL
By Laetitia Benat

PURPLE FICTION
Two Minutes by James
Gooding; Alabama,
Roma by Alex Antitch;
Fla 85 by Dike Blair;
Earth Pix by Lila Heller;
Basic Linguistics by
Rainer Ganahl; Devotion
by Torbjørn Rødland;
Family Landscape
by Andreas Larsson;
Fire Flies by André
Passos; Investigation
of Delusion & Delirium
by Daniel Pinchbeck;
Dear Ashley/Mommy is
So Disgusting by Risa
Mickenberg; 2 Poems
by Gerard Malanga;
Typing Test by Michael
Drake & Dike Blair;
Two Guys in a Car by
Jeff Rian; Copeaux by
Saül Yurkievich; Pissing
in the Wind by Mark
Mordue; Italian Movie
by Tim Griffin; Novel
in Progress by Richard
Hell

PURPLE INTERIOR
Modules by Mark
Borthwick; Architecture
by Katja Rahlwes; Walls
by Banu Cennetoglu;
Vehicules by Laetitia
Benat; Second Homes
by Helen Nollan;
Atmosphere by
Christopher Sturman

PURPLE 4
Winter 1999/2000

496 pages
full color
21.5 x 15.5 cm
8.5 x 6.1 in

COVER
Masafumi Sanaï

PURPLE FASHION
Hermès by Mark
Borthwick; Trace
by Koji Tatsuno by
Camille Vivier; Prada
by Torbjørn Rødland;
Junya Watanabe by
Laetitia Benat; Van
Ommeslaeghe by
Jork Weismann; Jurgi
Persoons by Johnny
Gembitsky; Ann-Sofie
Back by Juergen Teller;
Black Birds by Banu
Cennetoglu; Helmut
Lang by Jack Pierson;
André Walker by Bettina
Komenda; '99–'00 by
Anders Edström; Ruffo
Research by Giasco
Bertoli; Xavier Delcour
by Laetitia Benat

PURPLE LOOK
Harmony Korine by
Terry Richardson;
Berenice Mendez by
Mauricio Guillen; Cover:
Versions by Maria Finn;
Japan Today by Takashi
Homma; Status: Quo by
Patterson Beckwith

PURPLE BEAUTY
Kim Gordon by Alex
Antitch; Nouvelle Vague
by Sabine Schründer;
French Kiss by Ange
Leccia

**PURPLE PROSE:
THE FOOD, DRUG AND
CLOTHES ISSUE**
Strange Haze: Drugs,
Artists and Art,
Interviews by Dike
Blair with Richard
Prince, Fred Tomaselli,
Motohiko Tokuta and
Stephen Pesce, M.S.W.
Kookaïne by Bernard
Joisten; The Invention
of Lifestyle by Jeff Rian;
Flex Appeal by Mary
Clarke; In the Air For
Ever by Olivier Zahm;
Clothes are Desire by
Lewis Baltz; Newports,
the cigarettes of
the street by Bruce
Benderson; Power
Ballads in the Form of
a Gel Cap by Jeremy
Blake; Nudity by Mark
Borthwick; Easy E.
Frayed Jeans, Mohawk
by Lizzi Bougatsos;
Prince of Whales by
Judy Elkan; Sure I take
seconds. I even take
thirds and fourths. But
I don't take fifths by
Experimental Jet Set;

I wish more people, in
general, would
do magazines as a
pastime, like gardening
by Amy Fusselman;
Coffee, Fish, Green
Vegetables and Coca-
Cola by Maurice Ganis;
Soft Clothes Already
Broken Inn by Mark
Gonzales; Today I Ate
Nikudofu by Nakako
Hayashi; I'm Always
Affected by Clothes by
Mary Heilmann; I used
to think smoking pot
would deliver me from
the things in the world
I don't like by Yvonne
Hildebrandt; Those who
fall, fall. I shalln't by
Harmony Korine; Alka
Seltzer by Liz Larner
1) Lost Opportunity,
2) Calories, 3) Fit
and Breathability, 4)
Laundering by Hand,
5) Telemarketing by
Tan Lin; Food Absorbs
Drugs, Drugs Alter
Taste, Food Stains
Clothes by Leah Singer;
Food and Drugs are the
Everyday Philosophy
of the People by Aya
Tanizaki; In the next
decade, a top fashion
designer will be hired to
create T-shirts for the
pharmaceutical giant,
Hoffmann La Roche by
Antek Walczak

PURPLE SPECIAL
Dominique Gonzalez-
Foerster

PURPLE FICTION
Headache by Henry
Roy; Gelée blanche by
Charlotte Beaurepaire;
Points of Orientation
by Sabine Schründer;
Evaporate Girl by Lila
Heller; Far and Wide
by Kyoji Takahashi;
Solfège by Masafumi
Sanaï; Sunday Night
by Olivier Kartak; The
Bear-Boy of Lithuania
by Amy Gerstler;
Rondo by Bennett
Simpson; Abduction by
Benjamin Weissman;
The Fecality of It All
by Karl Holmqvist;
Elevator Music/Among
the Faeries by Lodge
Kerrigan; From Ambient
Stylistics by Tan Lin;
Intempérie (Baltimore
Pictures) by Saul
Yurkievich; Frankfurt
Like No Other (86
Minutes) by Antek
Walczak

PURPLE INTERIOR
Bless by Mark
Borthwick; Bedroom
by Doug Aitken;
The Seventies by
Stephanie Campos;
Stationwagon by Olivier
Zahm; Jungle Gym
by Cédrick Eymenier;
Urban Species by Fujita
Kazuhiro; Swimming
Pools by Giasco Bertoli

PURPLE SEXE 4
13 TOPICS
Summer

96 pages
full color
21.5 x 15.5 cm
8.5 x 6.1 in

COVER
Viviane Sassen

CONTENTS
Videotape by Donald
Christie; For Purple
Sexe by Mark
Borthwick; Privacy
by Johnny Gembitsky;
Professional by Terry
Richardson; Laetitia
by Katja Rahlwes;
Auto-Eroticism by
Marcelo Krasilcic;
Women Underwear by
Martin Laporte; Couple
by Marcelo Krasilcic;
Drawings by Jack
Pierson; Hair by Thomas
Schenk; The Brides of
Drunken Frankenstein
by Dike Blair; T&A by
Richard Kern; Gender
by Viviane Sassen

PURPLE SEXE 5
ESPECIAL BRASIL BY
MARCELO KRASILCIC
Winter 1999/2000

92 pages
full color
25.5 x 18 cm
10 x 7.1 in

COVER
Marcelo Krasilcic

PURPLE 5
Summer

512 pages
full color
21.5 x 15.5 cm
8.5 x 6.1 in

COVER
Maria Finn

PURPLE FASHION
Gaspard Yurkievich
by Chikashi Suzuki;
Dorothée Perret by
Frederike Helwig; Susan
Cianciolo by Marcelo
Krasilcic; Fredie
Stevens by Bianca Pilet;
Van Ommeslaeghe by
Camille Vivier; Bernhard
Willhelm by Kenshu
Shintsubo; Comme des
Garçons by Torbjørn
Rødland; Summer '00
by Mark Borthwick;
Jurgi Persoons by Cris
Moor; Helmut Lang by
Logde Kerrigan; Miu
Miu by Masafumi Sanaï;
Yab Yum by Chikashi
Suzuki; Yohji Yamamoto
by Jork Weismann;
Bless by Katja Rahlwes;
Raf Simons by Armin
Linke

PURPLE LOOK
Bob Richardson by
Terry Richardson; Suits
& Coats by Anders
Edström; J'adore by
Wolfgang Tillmans;
Maru Alfonso by Sergio
Guillen

PURPLE BEAUTY
Lightning by Maria Finn;
Patterns by Blommers
& Schumm; Nuit Noire
by Alex Antitch

PURPLE PROSE
Pierre Vadi with Sylvia
Alberton; Barry La
Va with Lewis Baltz;
Sture Johannesson with
Lars Bang Larsen; Le
chevallier with Olivier
Bardin; Isamu Noguchi
with Dike Blair; Fabrice
Gygi with Lionel Bovier;
Diego Gutierrez with
Jen Budney; Lisa
Beck with Jimi Dams;
Franz Ackermann
with Joshua Decter;
Gérard Fromanger with
Gilles Deleuze; Alain
Declercq with Anaïd
Demir; Jenny Gage with
Edith Doove; Uri Tzaig
with Theresa Duncan;
Arturo Herrera with
Nicolas Franck; Miwa
Yanagi with Dominique
Gonzalez-Foerster;
Yvette Brackman with
Michelle Grabner; Blake
Rayne with Tim Griffin;
Stephen Prina with
David Grubbs; Anne
Daems with Nakako
Hayashi; Andrea Zittel
with Karl Holmqvist;
Jacques Monory with
Bernard Joisten; Antonio

Allegri Da Correggio
with Herwig Kempinger;
Stanley Brouwn with
Pierre Leguillon; Allen
Ruppersberg with Tan
Lin; Tony Feher with
John Lindell; Rosemarie
Trockel with Stéphanie
Moisdon; Lawrence
Alma-Tadema with
Pierre Nadin; Jeremy
Deller with Guillaume
Nez; John Tremblay
with Bob Nickas; Olaf
Breuning with Michelle
Nicol; Richard Prince
with Glenn O'Brian;
Ceryth Wyn Evans with
Hans Ulrich Obrist;
Vija Celmins with Jeff
Rian; Bas Jan Ader
with Bennett Simpson;
Amy Sillman with
Michael Smith; Daniel
Pflumm with Wolfgang
Staehle; Jack Goldstein
with Thomas Zummer;
Photographs with Pierre
Leguillon

PURPLE FICTION
Particles and Waves by
Laetitia Benat; The Fish
and The Fire by Andreas
Larsson; Thinking
of the Days by Jin
Osashi; Superstition by
Henry Roy; Horizontal
Terminus by Banu
Cennetoglu; Amendoin
Japones by Elein Fleiss
The Most Ridiculous
Moment by Amy
Fusselman; Perfect
Ten by Peter Josephs;
Yours Truly by Lauren
Davis; The Air Traffic
Controller by Adam J.
Maynard; I Look Myself
in the Mirror by Edy
Poppy; The Tallest Man
in The World by Natasha
Sho; Saint-Omer by
Arnaud Viviant

PURPLE SPECIAL
General Idea

PURPLE INTERIOR
Streets of New York
by Mark Borthwick;
Big Studio, Bangkok by
Dominique Gonzalez-
Foerster; Palm
Springs, Pasadena by
Dominique Gonzalez-
Foerster; Kew Gardens,
London by Frederike
Helwig; Excerpts
From Forthcoming
Book by Armin Linke;
Habitat, 1998 by Klaus
Scherubel; Burger
King, 1998 by Klaus
Scherubel; The Deep
Gallery, Tokyo by
Chikashi Suzuki; China
Arts Objects Galleries
by Amy Yao; Jungle
Science 2 by Jean-Luc
Vilmouth

PURPLE 6
Winter 2000/2001

512 pages
full color
21.5 x 15.5 cm
8.5 x 6.1 in

COVER
Mark Borthwick

PURPLE FASHION
Susan Cianciolo by Cris
Moor; Lutz by Giasco
Bertoli; Junya Watanabe
by Lars Botten;
Bernhard Willhelm by
Camille Vivier; Fendi by
Terry Richardson; Street
Fashion by Anders
Edström; Balenciaga
by Vanina Sorrenti;
Helmut Lang by Banu
Cennetoglu; Véronique
Branquinho by Chikashi
Suzuki; Marc Jacobs by
Lodge Kerrigan; Friends
by Mark Borthwick

PURPLE LOOK
Marieke Stolk by
Blommers & Schumm;
Bridemaids by Alex
Antitch; School Days by
Johnny Gembitsky

PURPLE BEAUTY
Lips and Looks by
Sassen & Grognard;
Non-Fiction by Mauricio
Guillen; Marie by
Laetitia Benat

PURPLE PROSE
Post-Cinema by Olivier
Zahm; Crumb by Jeff
Rian; Dans la peau
de John Malkovich by
Bernard Joisten; Cobra
Verde by Jutta Koether;
Female on the Beach
by Bruce Benderson;
Pasolini's Salo by Andy
Stillpass; Nashville's
Campaign Song by
Bennett Simpson;
Image-Image by
Dominique Gonzalez-
Foerster; Taxi Driver by
Pete Taylor; Entr'acte's
Last Clean Shirt by
Jason Simon; Starwars
in the Desert by Pablo
León de la Barra; Film
and Freedom in Iran by
Panu Aree; Point Blank
by Tim Griffin; Edge by
Dayton Taylor; Cube
by Dike Blair; Godard's
Birds by Gareth James;
The State of Things
by Michael Drake;
L'arche de Noé by Antek
Walczak; Le cercle
rouge by Guillaume Nez;
Heat by Tom Betterton;
3 American Actresses
by John Kelsey; A Man
Escaped by Cheryl
Donegan; Odd Man Out
by Mark Fishman; The
Matrix by Ole Scheeren;
Butterfield 8 by Sarah
Gavlak; Star Wars as a
Remake of The Wizard
of Olivier Zahm by Alix
Lambert

PURPLE SPECIAL
Richard Prince

PURPLE FICTION
Fig. 1A by Tan Lin;
Lonely Tylenol by
Sharon Mesmer; I'm
Not Sorry by Sharon
Mesmer; Continuum
by Peter Josephs;
My Two Sons by
Benjamin Weissman;
A Playground in Belize
by Jordan Davis; Hat-
Head and Bed-Clothes
by Jordan Davis; Café
crème by Fred El
Bekkay; Photo Island
by Michael Danner;
Hearts and Windows
by Giasco Bertoli;
Life Lines by Andreas
Larsson; Nowhere at the
Same Time by James
Gooding; Forty Bucks a
Night by Alex Antitch;
Screen Psychology by
Elein Fleiss; Looking
in Looking at by Henry
Roy; Night's Eyes by
Rami Maymon; Blue
Meridian by Torbjørn
Rødland; Call Me by
Marcello Simeoni;
In Another Tense by
Delphine Roque

PURPLE INTERIOR
Interior by Michael
Danner; Interior by
Elein Fleiss; Interior by
Pablo León de la Barra;
Interior by Stefan Ruiz

**PURPLE SEXE 6
SPECIAL MILAN BY
GIASCO BERTOLI**
Summer

96 pages
full color
25.5 x 18 cm
10 x 7.1 in

COVER
Giasco Bertoli

**PURPLE SEXE 7
9 SERIES BY WOMEN**
Winter 2000/2001

66 pages
full color
25.5 x 18 cm
10 x 7.1 in

COVER
Katja Rahlwes

TABLE OF CONTENTS
Heather, 21Yrs Old,
Un-Employed, L.A. by
Katja Rahlwes, Desire
Circulating Over the
Rooftops by Katja
Rahlwes; Life is Sweet
by Julie Sleaford;
Good Sex Party in a
Good House by Viviane
Sassen; Sex on Earth by
Viviane Sassen; Me, My
Bed and My Panties by
Hiromix; Irgendwas ist
Immer by Julie Sleaford;
White Skin by Vanina
Sorrenti; I Kill You First
by Rita Ackermann

PURPLE 7
Spring

242 pages
full color
27 x 20 cm
10.6 x 7.1

COVER
Richard Prince

SPRING/SUMMER
2001 By Richard Prince

PURPLE COLUMNS
The Imaginary World by
Jeff Rian; Ma couleur
préférée by Claude
Closky; Landscape
by Kyoji Takahashi;
New York Lowdown
by Bruce Benderson;
Portrait by Wolfgang
Tillmans; France: Bad
Reception by Antek
Walczak; Naked by
Masafumi Sanaï; Some
of 1971 by Bob Nickas;
Surface by Dominique
Gonzalez-Foerster;
Advanced Economics
by Experimental
Jetset; Paris Collection
Individuals by Nakako
Hayashi

PURPLE SPECIAL
New Jersey: New
Jersey Portfolio by
Roe Ethridge & Dan
Torop; New Jersey
Photographs by Dan
Graham; Atlantic City by
Bennett Simpson and
Dike Blair; Yo La Tengo
by Alan Licht; Michael
Ashkin by Jeff Rian;
New Jersey and the
Boss Belt by Dike Blair;
Deal by John Kelsey &
Marlene Marino; Asbury
Park by Jeff Rian and
Elein Fleiss

PURPLE FASHION
Gucci & Seth Shapiro
by Terry Richardson;
Helmut Lang by Richard
Kern; Lutz & Comme
des Garçons #1 by
Juergen Teller; Lutz &
Comme des Garçons
#2 by Anders Edström;
Tokyo Story by Kyoji
Takahashi; Louis Vuitton
by Banu Cennetoglu;
Cosmic Wonder &
Gaspard Yurkievich by
Masafumi Sanaï; Hotel
Palenque by Pablo
León de la Barra; Bless
Recent History by
Olivier Zahm

PURPLE INTERIOR
Interior/Exterior by
Pablo León de la Barra

PURPLE FICTION
Weekend by Ola Rindal;
Seven Figures Lying DN
NR a Butterfly by Tan
Lin; Drawings by Rita
Ackermann; Introverted
Edy Poppy

PURPLE BEAUTY
Bambou by Mauricio
Guillen; German Lenses
by Bless; Jules et Jim by
Collier Schorr

PURPLE 8
Summer

224 pages
full color
27 x 20 cm
10.6 x 7.9 in

COVER
Terry Richardson

**SPRING/
SUMMER 2001**
By Terry Richardson

PURPLE COLUMNS
The Imaginary World
by Jeff Rian; New York
Lowdown by Bruce
Benderson; Youth by
Antek Walczak; Some
of 1981 by Bob Nickas;
Ma couleur préférée
by Claude Closky;
Advanced Economics
by Experimental Jetset;
Landscape by Kyoji
Takahashi; Portrait by
Wolfgang Tillmans;
Naked by Masafumi
Sanaï; Surface by
Dominique Gonzalez-
Foerster; Paris
Collection Individuals by
Nakako Hayashi

PURPLE TRISTESSE
Tristesse Portfolio by
Roe Ethridge, Cédrick
Eymenier, Henry Roy,
Andreas Larsson;
Mourning: The Ten
Essential Elements by
Mark Kingwell; The
Empty Place by Bennett
Simpson & Gareth
James; Towards Total
Tristesse by Olivier
Zahm; Journal Japonais
by Bernard Joisten;
Michael Smith's Bland
Ambition by Dike Blair;
So Nice by Anaïd Demir
& Laetitia Benat; Pantin
Abstracts by Michel
Bumpf; Nevers Love
by Arnaud Viviant and
Claude Lévêque

PURPLE FASHION
Burberry by Anders
Edström; Martin
Margiela Homme by
Alex Antitch; Jutta's
International Style by
Vanina Sorrenti; Martin
Margiela Femme by Cris
Moor; Balenciaga Le Dix
& Susan Cianciolo Run
11 by Marc Borthwick;
Summer Shoes by
Richard Kern

PURPLE TRAVEL
Clio's Fulcrum: An
E-mail from the Palm
Beaches by Lewis Baltz

PURPLE INTERVIEW
La Force Violette de
Martine Aballéa by Elein
Fleiss

PURPLE INTERIOR
15 Love by Giasco
Bertoli; Beaugrenelle by
Olivier Amsellem

PURPLE FICTION
Hôtel Oriental by Peter
Langer; Drawings by
Jeremy Blake; Zero
Star Hotel by Anselm
Berrigan; Tokyo Sad by
Chikashi Suzuki; Shiva
Hive by Jeff Clark

PURPLE BEAUTY
Pretty Cool by Laetitia
Benat; Hair and the
City by Ola Rindal; The
Ultimate Beauty Product
by Takashi Homma

PURPLE 9
Fall

240 pages
full color
27 x 20 cm
10.6 x 7.9 in

COVER
Anders Edström

FALL/WINTER 2001
By Anders Edström

PURPLE COLUMNS
The Imaginary World
by Jeff Rian; New York
Lowdown by Bruce
Benderson; France by
Antek Walczak; Some
of 1991 by Bob Nickas;
Ma couleur préférée
by Claude Closky;
Advanced Economics
by Experimental Jetset;
Paris Collection by Elein
Fleiss; Landscape by
Kyoji Takahashi; Portrait
by Wolfgang Tillmans;
Naked by Masafumi
Sanaï; Surface by
Dominique Gonzalez-
Foerster

**PURPLE
ARCHITECTURE**
Jerusalem by George
Dupin; Uchronicity by
Lewis Baltz; Marseille
by Jean-Michel Fradkin
and Olivier Amsellem;
Bogota by François
Roche; Maîtrise des
Apparences by Bernard
Joisten; Chinatown, NY
by Bennett Simpson and
Dike Blair; Louis Kahn's
Trenton Bath Houses by
Tan Lin & Roe Ethridge;
La Grande Motte &
Beauduc by Stéphane
Camille and Elein Fleiss;
Deadville by Olivier
Zahm; The Tree by Dike
Blair; Some Buildings in
India by Pablo León de
la Barra

PURPLE FASHION
YSL Rive Gauche &
Viktor & Rolf by Robert
Wyatt; Helmut Lang
by Juergen Teller;
Comme des Garçons
by Alix Antitch; Bless
& Van Cleef & Arpels
by Laetitia Benat;
Lutz & Andre Walker
by Masafumi Sanaï;
Hermes by Alex Antitch;
Cosmic Wonder Jeans
by Takashi Homma; Rita
Ackermann by Camille
Vivier; Adidas Football
by Giasco Bertoli

PURPLE INTERVIEW
Baltimore Song: Will Oldham with Jutta Koether; Susan Cianciolo with Nakako Hayashi

PURPLE FICTION
Some Days by Vanina Sorrenti; Drawings by Shutoku Mukai; Sexe & Autobus by Jean-Luc d'Asciano

PURPLE BEAUTY
Thirteen in LA by Kenshu Shintsubo; In Your Face by Johnny Gembitsky

PURPLE SEXE 8
Winter 2001/2002

96 pages
full color
25.5 x 18 cm
10 x 7.1 in

COVER
Terry Richardson

Untitled (for Sigmar Polke) by Richard Prince; Gucci Grey Gold Necklace by Laurent Bochet; M the Doll by Olivier Zahm; Phantom of the Paradise by Terry Richardson; Mr. Hammer and Mrs. Sweet in Forever Never by Jeff Rian; 5-6 Weeks With Katya by Petter Hegre; Introduction to the Destruction of the Couple by Antek Walczak; Perversion Action Louis Vuitton by Bernard Joisten; Fulfilled Anticipation 1,2, & 3 by Noritoshi Hirakawa; Dejeuner sur l'herbe by Richard Kern; Photos souvenirs by Marnix Goossens

PURPLE 10
Winter

224 pages
black & white
full color
27 x 20 cm
10.6 x 7.1 in

COVER
Mark Borthwick

FALL/WINTER 2002
By Mark Borthwick

PURPLE COLUMNS
The Imaginary World by Jeff Rian; New York Lowdown by Bruce Benderson; France by Antek Walczak; Some of 2001 by Bob Nickas; Ma couleur préférée by Claude Closky; Advanced Economics by Experimental Jetset; Paris Collection by Elein Fleiss; Landscape by Kyoji Takahashi; Portrait by Wolfgang Tillmans; Naked by Masafumi Sanaï; Surface by Dominique Gonzalez-Foerster

PURPLE INTERVIEW
Marnie Weber with Nicolas Trembley; Miguel Calderón with Pablo León de la Barra; Mehdi Belhaj Kacem with Olivier Zahm

PURPLE FASHION
Balenciaga le Dix by Cris Moor; Comme des Garçons Homme by Banu Cennetoglu; Bundesgartenschau Potsdam 2001 by Frederike Helwig; Maison Martin Margiela by Chikashi Suzuki; Latest Pictures of Tara St. Hill by Corinne Day

PURPLE PORTRAITS
Libby Lumpkin by Dave Hickey; John McCracken by Dike Blair & Chris Felver; Ann-Sofie Back by Elein Fleiss & Anders Edström; Ange Leccia by Emmanuelle Lequeux & Giasco Bertoli; Alix Lambert by Dike Blair & Johnny Gembitsky; David Berman by Bennett Simpson & Gregh Humphries; Rita Ackermann by Kim Gordon & Laetitia Benat; Terry Richardson by Anne-Laure Keib & Pierre Bailly; Aya Tanizaki by Olivier Zahm & Takashi Homma; David Robbins by Jeff Rian & Michael Byron; Laetitia Benat by Pierre Leguillon; Maurizio Cattelan by Olivier Zahm & Armin Linke; Lizzie Bougatsos by Bennett Simspon & Anders Edström; Mark Borthwick by John Kelsey & Marcelo Krasilcic; Maria Finn by Jeff Rian & Mark Borthwick; Anders Edström by Jeff Rian & Mauricio Guillen; Nakako Hayashi by Elein Fleiss & Mark Borthwick

PURPLE INTERIOR
Rio de Janeiro by Elein Fleiss; Acapulco by Pablo León de la Barra

PURPLE FICTION
Rituals by Camille Vivier; Glow by Anders Edström; Touching Candy Taylor by Marcy Dermansky; 3 Poems by Bennett Simpson & Nick Tosches

PURPLE BEAUTY
Ludivine Sagnier by Henry Roy; Drawings by Maria Finn; Georgina Grenville by Alex Antitch

PURPLE 11
Spring

256 pages
full color
27 x 20 cm
10.6 x 7.1 in

COVER
Alex Antitch

SUMMER 2002
By Alex Antitch

PURPLE COLUMNS
The Imaginary World by Jeff Rian; New York Lowdown by Bruce Benderson; What the Coptic Guy Said by Nick Tosches; Avenidas by Jens Hoffmann; Ma couleur préférée by Claude Closky; Therefore by Elein Fleiss; Absolute Beginners by Maurizio Cattelan; Portrait by Wolfgang Tillmans; Calme plat by Pierre Leguillon; Surface by Dominique Gonzalez-Foerster

PURPLE INTERVIEW
Lutz Huelle with Nakako Hayashi; Miltos Manetas with Olivier Zahm

PURPLE FASHION
Louis Vuitton & Miu Miu by Ola Rindal; Helmut Lang by Terry Richardson; Marc Jacobs by Mark Borthwick; Ann-Sofie Back by Giasco Bertoli; Julia and Mehdi, après by Laetitia Benat; A.F. Vandevorst by Masafumi Sanaï; Jil Sander, Men & Women by Richard Prince

LA MER
Revoir la mer by Olivier Zahm; Libre, toujours tu cheriras by Mehdi Belhaj Kacem; No Waves by Beth Yahp; The Sea is Out of Control by Bruce Benderson; Shivering by Mark Mordue; Shore by Mark Kingwell; Prendre la mer by Eve Couturier; Close to the Art of Those Fearless at Sea by Geoffrey Cruickshank-Hagenbuckle; Mercure by Claude Lévêque; Where Did All the Water Come From? by Mark Fishman; Something Like Love by Chan Marshall; Floating Square Shapes by Karl Holmqvist; Tan by Amy Fusselman; Mermaid by Richard Prince; Recreio, Trouville by Elein Fleiss The Ocean Blues by Kim Gordon; Miscou Island by Lodge Kerrigan; Glow by Dike Blair; Sea Odds by Jeff Rian; Lee-Sea by Jeff Clark; Salty Dogs by Lewis Baltz; Photographs by: Laetitia Benat, Dike Blair, Mark Borthwick, Anders Edström, Elein Fleiss, C. Wayne Gordon, Takashi Homma

PURPLE INTERIOR
Tokyo Synthesis by Claude Lévêque; Ecuador by Banu Cennetoglu; El Castillo by Pablo León de la Barra

PURPLE FICTION
Seven Pink Drawings by Tomoo Gokita; In Jerusalem and Tel Aviv by Rami Maymon; Buenos Aires Amour by Guillermo Ueno; Faces by Trinie Dalton; Uncoated Eyes by Amy Jean Porter; Kook! by Geoffrey Cruickshank-Hagenbuckle

PURPLE BEAUTY
Green, Blue, Pink, Charlotte by Henry Roy; Uslu Airlines by Banu Cennetoglu; On The Hairwaves by Tom Lingnau & Frank Schumacher

PURPLE 12
Summer

200 pages,
black & white
full color
27 x 20 cm
10.6 x 7.9 in

COVER
Mark Borthwich

**SPRING/
SUMMER 2002**
By Mark Borthwick and
Maurizio Cattelan

PURPLE COLUMNS
The Imaginary World
by Jeff Rian; New
York Lowdown by
Bruce Benderson;
What The Coptic Guy
Said by Nick Tosches;
Avenidas by Jens
Hoffmann; Ma couleur
préférée by Claude
Closky; Therefore by
Elein Fleiss; Absolute
Beginners by Maurizio
Cattelan; Portrait by
Wolfgang Tillmans;
Calme plat by Pierre
Leguillon; Surface by
Dominique Gonzalez-
Foerster

**PURPLE SPECIAL:
MAURIZIO CATTELAN**
Don't Believe in War
by Olivier Zahm;
Accidentally On Purpose
by Jeff Rian; Visual
Essay by Maurizio
Cattelan

PURPLE FASHION
Comme des Garçons
by Anuschka Blommers
& Niels Schumm; Art
Scene Tokyo by Takashi
Homma; Balenciaga Le
Dix by Chikashi Suzuki;
Givenchy & Cosmic
Wonder by Angela Hill;
Issey Miyake Hommes
by Jack Pierson; Van
Cleef & Arpels &
Margiela Hommes by
Laetitia Benat

PURPLE INTERVIEW
Shimabuku with Elein
Fleiss; Andrea Fraser
with Bennett Simpson;
Martin Walde with Jeff
Rian; Carl Zimmer with
Dike Blair

PURPLE INTERIOR
Light Valley by Andreas
Angelidakis; Base
intergalactique Veracruz
by Jer-nimo Hagerman

PURPLE FICTION
Five Drawings by Zoe
Mendelson; American
Supper by Terry
Richardson; Quelqu'un
a bien du m'aimer un
peu au début by Gérard
Duguet-Grasser; 6
Poèmes by Stéphane
Bouquet

PURPLE BEAUTY
Gymnastic Melancolia by
Camille Vivier; Beautiful
in Kazakstan by Anders
Edström

PURPLE 13
Fall

224 pages
black & white
full color
27 x 20 cm
10.6 x 7.9 in

COVER
Giasco Bertoli

FALL 2002
By Giasco Bertoli

PURPLE COLUMNS
The Imaginary World
by Jeff Rian; New York
Lowdown by Bruce
Benderson; What The
Coptic Guy Said by Nick
Tosches; Avenidas by
Jens Hoffmann; Ma
couleur préférée by
Claude Closky; Absolute
Beginners by Maurizio
Cattelan; Portrait by
Wolfgang Tillmans;
Calme plat by Pierre
Leguillon; Surface by
Dominique Gonzalez-
Foerster

**PURPLE SPECIAL:
CLAUDE LÉVÊQUE**
Révolution 14 by Olivier
Zahm

PURPLE FASHION
Ann-Sofie Back
& Sonia Rykiel by
Anders Edström;
Charles Anastase &
Emilio Pucci by Cécile
Bortoletti; Cosmic
Wonder & Helmut Lang
by Chikashi Suzuki;
Civil Disobedience by
Angela Hill; Gucci &
Wendy & Jim by Takashi
Homma; Lutz and Prada
by Viviane Sassen;
Balenciaga and Comme
des Garçons by Ola
Rindal

PURPLE INTERVIEW
Colin de Land with
Gareth James; Wendy &
Jim with Nakako Hayashi

PURPLE INTERIOR
Trees & Wheels by
Cédric Eymenier;
Cape Town by Viviane
Sassen; Souvenirs From
Erevan by Elein Fleiss;
Le Casino d'Allevard
by Laetitia Benat; La
Factory du Kremlin by
Pierre Leguillon and
Matthieu Orléan

PURPLE FICTION
Five Drawings by Leane
Shapton; Lifestyle
by Henry Roy; Cinq
histoires courtes by
Alain Lacroix; Super
bien total by Adrian
Jenkins

PURPLE BEAUTY
Anna Thompson, Hôtel
Saint-Germain by Serge
Leblon; Week-Ends by
Vava Ribeiro

**PURPLE 14
WITH PURPLE
TEN YEARS**
Winter

192 pages
black & white
full color
27 x 20 cm
10.6 x 7.9 in

COVER
Laetitia Benat

**FALL/WINTER
2002/2003**
By Laetitia Benat

PURPLE COLUMNS
The Imaginary World
by Jeff Rian; New York
Lowdown by Bruce
Benderson; Avenidas
by Jens Hoffmann; Ma
couleur préférée by
Claude Closky; Absolute
Beginners by Maurizio
Cattelan; Portrait by
Wolfgang Tillmans;
Calme plat by Pierre
Leguillon; Therefore by
Elein Fleiss; Surface by
Dominique Gonzalez-
Foerster

PURPLE INTERVIEW
Lupita Peckinpah, Pablo
León de la Barra

**PURPLE SPECIAL:
1992**
Purple by Elein Fleiss
We Represent the
Georgie Bush Kids by
Bennett Simpson; Every
Last Thought by Lee
Ranaldo; Tina Chow
by Sharon Mesmer;
There is no Such Think
as Coincidence by
Marina Faust; My Year
in Paris by Dike Blair;
The Age of Grief by
Mark Kingwell; Ces
jours passés à faire
semblant... by Claude
Forminer; What V.
Was That? By Richard
Prince; Ol' Blue in '92
by Jeff Rian; Altered
States by Tim Griffin;
Getting Thru It by John
Kelsey; Juillet by Claude
Closky; No G for W by
Sébastien Jamain; 20
Ans by Michel Cloup;
Sunrise is Imminent
Yet Slowly Yet Slowly
Far Away (Crash on the
Verge of Rampant) by
Mark Borthwick; Getting
to Know the Colonel
by Mark Fishman;
Solaris by Dominique
Gonzalez-Foerster;
La communauté X by
Olivier Zahm

PURPLE FASHION
Grand National Styling
by Terry Richardson;
Berlin Stories by Heinz
Peter Knes; Man in
the Shadows by Emma
Mafille; Raf Simons
and Louis Vuitton by
Frederike Helwig; Hotel
Okura by Masafumi
Sanaï; Dominique Sanda
by Henry Roy

PURPLE INTERIOR
Baretto by Giasco
Bertoli; Look But Don't
Touch by Mauricio
Guillen; Mexico City by
Marlene Marino; AC/OC
by Danu Connetoglu

PURPLE FICTION
Rock Feller by
Christophe Brunnquell;
Emilie by Gérard
Duguet-Grasser;
World History by Rita
Ackermann; I feel
Lucky, Oh So Lucky! by
Glen Szabo; Hope by
Alex Antitch

PURPLE 15
Spring/Summer

328 pages
black & white
full color
27 x 20 cm
10.6 x 7.9 in

COVER
Wolfgang Tillmans

**WE ARE NOT GOING
BACK, SPRING/
SUMMER 2003**
By Wolfgang Tillmans

PURPLE COLUMNS
Reading Around by
Jeff Rian; New York
Lowdown by Bruce
Benderson; Avenidas
by Jens Hoffmann;
What the Coptic Guy
Said by Nick Tosches;
Science by Dike Blair;
Neenstars Neenstar by
Miltos Manetas; Portrait
by Wolfgang Tillmans;
Calme plat by Pierre
Leguillon; Surface by
Dominique Gonzales-
Foerster

PURPLE INTERVIEW
Désirée Heiss with Ines
Kaag & Nakako Hayashi;
Kelley Walker with Bob
Nickas; Robert Wright
with Dike Blair; Yukinori
Maeda with Nakako
Hayashi; Oscar van den
Boogaard with Olivier
Zahm

**PURPLE FASHION:
BLACK & WHITE**
Rita Ackermann; Laetitia
Benat; Giasco Bertoli;
Mark Borthwick;
Cécile Bortoletti; Lizzie
Bougatsos; Anders
Edström; Richard Kern
Justine Kurland;
Emmanuelle Mafille;
Terry Richardson; Henry
Roy; Masafumi Sanaï;
Takashi Homma;

MUSIC?
Questions by Marina Faust, Elein Fleiss, Jeff Rian and Olivier Zahm for Chan Marshall, Christophe Boutin, Antek Walczak, Maurizio Cattelan, Daniel Bismuth, David Grubbs, Dietrich Dietrissen, Geoffrey Cruickshank Hagenbuckle, Jeremy Blake, Kim Gordon, Matt Cook, Michel Cloup, Mike Fellows, Will Oldham, Jean-Jacques Palix, Richard Prince, Rita Ackermann, David Robbins, Aaron Rose, Tan Lin, Lizzie Bougatsos, Steve Krauss, Medhi Belhaj Kacem, Emily Sundblad; Tom Verlaine by Jutta Koether; Head Space by Jeff Rian; Don't by Marina Faust; Old Dirty Bastard by Joseph Flammand; La mort d'Elvis by Olivier Zahm; Interview with Mark Tranmer & Gnac by Miltos Manetas; Tu sens l'essence by Sébastien Jamain; Vocalises à l'occidental by Alain Lacroix

PURPLE FASHION COLOUR
Mark Borthwick; Lizzie Bougatsos; Elein Fleiss Johnny Hallam; Angela Hill; Emmanuelle Mafille Cris Moor; Henry Roy; Masafumi Sanaï; Camille Vivier

PURPLE INTERIOR
Pavillon Madame René Coty by Elein Fleiss; Arcosanti & la Fondation Cosanti by Aurélien Froment; Paving Paradise by Miss Liz Wendelbo; Lebanon Song by Matthieu Orléan; Fresh Windows by Dike Blair; Luminy by Olivier Amsellem

PURPLE FICTION
Nature by Ola Rindal; Hawaii by Collective Project; Le bruit des mouches by Carl Watson; Artless by Lucy McKenzie; Blonde on Blonde by Maurizio Cattelan; Yaounde Slow Motion by Henry Roy

PURPLE 16
Fall/Winter 2003/2004

336 pages
black & white
full color
27 x 20 cm
10.6 x 7.9 in

COVER
Takashi Homma

TENDER TOKYO, FALL/ WINTER 2003/2004
By Takashi Homma

PURPLE COLUMN
Reading Around by Jeff Rian; New York Lowdown by Bruce Benderson; What the Coptic Guy Said by Nick Tosches; Science by Dike Blair; Neenstars Neenstar by Miltos Manetas; Portrait by Wolfgang Tillmans; Calme plat by Pierre Leguillon; Surface by Dominique Gonzalez-Foerster

PURPLE INTERVIEW
Patrick Van Ommeslaeghe with Bernadette Van Huy; Tom Friedman with Jeff Rian; Nicole Garcia with Matthieu Orléan

PURPLE FASHION BLACK & WHITE
Laetitia Benat; Bless Mark Borthwick; Lizzi Bougatsos; Anders Edström; Johnny Hallam Angela Hill; Justine Kurland; Emmanuelle Mafille; Terry Richardson; Ellen Stagg Chikashi Suzuki

MONEY
Life's Blood by Ken Lechter; Everything I Know In Exactly 495 Words by Lewis Baltz; The Hook And Crook Of It by Jeff Rian; Warhol Says Yes by Marina Faust; A Lot More Than Nothing by Mark Fishman; Corporate Ass and Oligarch Balls by Peter Nadin; Le Luxe Suprême by Mehdi Belhaj Kacem

PURPLE FASHION COLOUR
Asia Argento; Annette Aurell; Rachel Bank; Mark Borthwick; Johnny Gembitsky; Johnny Hallam; Angela Hill; Richard Prince; Terry Richardson; Torbjørn Rødland; Henry Roy; Masafumi Sanaï; Chikashi Suzuki

PURPLE INTERIOR
Ville-Appartement by Pierre Leguillon; Chili; Tous ne deviendront pas architectes by Céline Duval; All That Glimmers by Gregory Krum; Fenêtres Parisiennes by Cédrick Eymenier; Kamakura by Elein Fleiss; Small Houses by Takashi Homma; Athens Report by Pablo León de la Barra

PURPLE FICTION
Democracy by Maurizio Cattelan; Lonely In New York by Budulee Lee; Baby Hairs by Benjamin Weismann; Crossfire by Alix Lambert; Polonaise by Camille Vivier; Stella Mala by Claude Lévêque; The Seasons by Michitaro Suzuki; The Choreographer by Sophie Dubosc

PURPLE FASHION 1
Spring/Summer

416 pages
full color
27.5 x 21 cm
10.8 x 8.3 in

COVER
Terry Richardson

PURPLE NEWS
New York Lowdown by Bruce Benderson; Imaginary Word by Jeff Rian; Bird Talk by Richard Prince; Chanel 5 à 7 by Rebecca Voight; Neen by Miltos Manetas; Diamants pour homme by Seamus Nicholson; Berlin, Galerie Meerrettich by Antek Walczak; Accessories by Cécile Bortoletti; Eric Camus by Anna Dubosc; A.P.C. Enfant by Jessica Ogden; United Bamboo by Andrew Richardson; Autour de Lucie by Mark Borthwick; Pierre Hardy by Giasco Bertoli; Calme Plat by Pierre Leguillon; Van Cleef & Arpels by Laetitia Benat; Britney Spears by Yann Céh

BEST OF THE SEASON
By Katja Rahlwes

PURPLE INTERVIEWS
Michael Lonsdale by Matthieu Orléan; Jeremy Blake by Dike Blair; Olivier Mosset by Séphanie Moisdon

PURPLE FASHION
Leigh Yeager by Antoinette Aurell; Maritime Hotel, New York by Terry Richardson; Purple People by Paolo Roversi; Dragon Boys by Hiromix; Living Room by Marcelo Krasilcic; Biotope by Viviane Sassen; Seth & Dana by Terry Richardson; I'll Be Your Mirror by Anuschka Blommers & Niels Schumm

PURPLE INTERVIEWS
Emmanuelle Mafille with Elein Fleiss; Chloé Delaume with Anna Dubosc

PURPLE STAR
Gabrielle Lazure by Serge Leblon

PURPLE BEAUTY
Vava Ribeiro; Kerry Hallihan; Pierre Bailly

PURPLE INTERVIEWS
Monte Hellmann with Matthieu Orléan; Craig Shumacher with Jeff Rian; Tony Alva with Yan Céh

ATHENS, CITY OF OLYMPUS By Camille Vivier

PURPLE PROSE: THE FUTURE
Reloaded Revolutions by Slavoj Zizek; Programme en Cours by Ferdinand Gouzon; 21st Century Radical Chic by Wolfgang Tillmans; L'artiste futur by François Laruelle; Surabaya, Johnny by Gary Indiana; L'avenir de la Relation by Mehdi Belhaj Kacem

PURPLE INTERIORS
Jardins Chinois by Dominique Gonzalez-Foerster; Sextopia by Olivier Ansellem; Architecture of Sex by Noritoshi Hirakawa; Fassbinder's World by Marina Faust; Paris by Mark Borthwick

PURPLE JOURNAL NUMÉRO ZÉRO WITH PURPLE FASHION 1
Spring/Summer

96 pages
black & white
27.5 x 21 cm
10.8 x 8.3 in

PHOTOGRAPHY
Laetitia Benat; Giasco Bertoli; Mark Borthwick; Christophe Brunnquell; Susan Cianciolo; Anders Edström; Marina Faust Elein Fleiss; Jonathan Hallam; Angela Hill; Takashi Homma; Pierre Leguillon; Kataja Rahlwes; Henry Roy; Sabine Schruender; Robert Stadler; Chikashi Suzuki; Camille Vivier

CAPTIONS
Laetitia Benat; Marina Faust; Elein Fleiss; Agathe Godard; Sébastien Jamain; Pierre Leguillon; Katja Rahlwes; Tiphaine Samoyault; Sabine Schruender

**THE PURPLE
JOURNAL 1**
Summer

96 pages
black & white
full color
27.5 x 21 cm
10.8 x 8.3 in

COVER
Amit Berlowitz,
Angela Hill, Camille
Vivier, Takashi Homma

CONTENTS
Notes on Hope by
Michel Zumpf; Six Sided
Divorce by Jeffrey
Rian; My Name is Elik
Elhanan... My Name
is Guy Elhanan... And
All This Precious Time
Lost for the Division
2 Games by Gérard
Duguet-Grasser; Not far
from Helsinki, in Gulf
of Finland, From Winter
to Spring by Laetitia
Benat; The Fragile
Heritage of François
Augiéras by Alain
Lacroix; Fragments of
a Letter from Belgrade
by Jonathan Boulting;
Under the White Dust
by Cora Maghnaoui; The
Hand on the Face by
Claude Lévêque

**THE PHOTOGRAPHIC
FOLDER**
The Special Paris
supplement

Letter from Malaysia
by Beth Yahp; Eulogy
for Maine-Océan by
Ferdinand Gouzon; The
Idea-Makers of the Left
by Curtis Winter;
I Forgot What We Were
Talking About by Elein
Fleiss and Sébastien
Jamain; Figures of
Fate: Slot Machines...
Voting Machines by
Jeffrey Rian; Portrait
of Suely Rolnik by
Manon de Boer;
The 3 by Christophe
Brunnquell; Notes on
the Cinema by Laetitia
Benat, Elein Fleiss,
Sébastien Jamain,
Tiphaine Samoyault;
Sequence by Sébastien
Jamain; A Whole Pile
of Books by Dominique
Gonzalez-Foerster;
Mini-Reportage by Elein
Fleiss; Seasonal Affects
by Sharon Mesmer;
Cult Object by Gérard
Duguet-Grasser; A
Street by Elein Fleiss

**THE PURPLE
JOURNAL 2**
Fall

107 pages
black & white
full color
27.5 x 21 cm
10.8 x 8.3 in

COVER
Henry Roy and
Takashi Homma

CONTENTS
No Such Thing as
Paranoia by Gary
Indiana; Eight Bridges
on the Yang Tse by
Tiphaine Samoyault;
Tiny Jungles by Fabrizio
Gallanti; To Lack
Without Limits by Mehdi
Belhaj Kacem; Journal
from Laos by Ruben
Dao; In the Shadows
of the Signposts on the
Road by David Berman

**THE PHOTOGRAPHIC
FOLDER**
The Blue Folder:
Kumiko Muraoka, Dust
Optimism (1936-1946)

Anxious Days in
Kinshasa by Henry Roy;
The Secret/Het Geheim
by Alain Lacroix; Here,
Where I Met Faith
Yang by Elein Fleiss;
The Pitcher Goes So
Often to the Water
That Some Fine Day
it Breaks by Gérard
Duguet-Grasser; Four-
by-Foured to Oblivion
by Jeffrey Rian; The
Power-Bar Guy's Widow
by Nick Tosches; Queen
of Hearts by Sébastien
Jamain; Hunting Wolrd,
Land of Assassins by
Michel Zumpf; The 3 by
Christophe Brunnquell;
Notes on the Cinema
by Laetitia Benat,
Ferdinand Gouzon,
Sébastien Jamain,
Federico Nicolao,
Tiphaine Samoyault;
Sequence by Marina
Faust; A Whole Pile of
Books by Dominique
Gonzalez-Foerster;
Mini-Reportage by
Laetitia Benat; Interview
of a Mother by Nakako
Hayashi; Seasonal
Affects by Sharon
Mesmer; Cult Object
by Gérard Duguet-
Grasser; A Street by
Elein Fleiss; Extract
of Correspondence by
Raphaël Nadjari

PURPLE FASHION 2
Fall/Winter 2004/2005

433 pages
full color
27.5 x 21 cm
10.8 x 8.3 in

COVER
Juergen Teller

PURPLE NEWS
Winter Elements by
Bettina Komenda and
Katja Rahlwes; Best of
the Season by Anuschka
Blömmers & Niels
Schumm

**PURPLE INTERVIEWS
ON CINEMA**
Gus Van Sant with
Geoffrey Cruickshank-
Hagenbuckle; Olivier
Assayas with Matthieu
Orléan and Olivier Zahm

**PURPLE FASHION
FALL/WINTER
2004/2005**
Elizabeth Peyton
by Annette Aurell;
Nighthawk by Vava
Ribeiro; Age and
Innocence by Masafumi
Sanaï; 5 O'Clock
Dracula by Terry
Richardson; An English
Garden by Corinne Day;
Julia Stegner by Katja
Rahlwes; All Around
Kim by Mark Borthwick

**PURPLE INTERVIEWS
ON ART**
John Armelder with
Stéphanie Moisdon; Tim
Griffin with Dike Blair

**COLLAGES FOR
PURPLE** By Rita
Ackermann

**INNOCENCE AND
AGE** By Martynka
Wawrzyniak; Portraits
by Nicholas Ghesquière,
a Retrospective; Mark
Borthwick; Dominique
Gonzales Foerster; Ola
Rindal; Fabien Baron;
Juergen Teller; David
Armstrong

BIRDTALK
by Richard Prince

PURPLE BEAUTY
Lavender by Richard
Kern; Secrets &
Success by Camille
Vivier; No Disco by
Jean-François Lepage

**PURPLE
ARCHITECTURE**
Comme des Garçons
in Paris by Daniele
Tedeschi; Rome, Lost
Modernity by Olivier
Amsellem; Mobile
Architecture by Cédrick
Eymenier

A PLAY
By Gary Indiana

PHILOSOPHY
Mille morts et un
ultimatum by Jean-
François Laruelle

Desert by Dominique
Gonzales Foerster;
Yale University by Drew
Jarett; Deep America
by Justine Kurland;
Reservists by Giasco
Bertoli; Beaten Portugal
by Bruno Santos

**LAST PURPLE
INTERVIEWS**
Slavoj Zizek with
Josefina Ayerza; Sparks
with Sébastien Jamain

DRAWINGS
Last Laughs by Alain
Séchas

PURPLE FASHION MEN
Genetic Transmission by
Heinz Peter Knes

SPECIAL PROJECT
In The Studio/New York/
2004 by Christopher
Wool

PURPLE LAST PAGE

**TERRY,
THE TERRY
RICHARDSON
PURPLE BOOK
A SPECIAL EDITION
FOR PURPLE
FASHION 2**
Fall/Winter 2004/2005

black & white
27.5 x 21 cm
10.8 x 8.3 in

**THE PURPLE
JOURNAL 3**
Winter

112 pages
black & white
full color
27.5 x 21 cm
10.8 x 8.3 in

COVER
Elein Fleiss

CONTENTS
October Journal

Antonioni by Gérard
Duguet-Grasser; When I
Was Little in School by
Laetitia Benat; Carrol,
Solitude by Yannick
Haenel; A Heroic Time
in the Passes by Alain
Lacroix; Trees, the
Winter by Tiphaine
Samoyault; Autumn
Fragments by Elein
Fleiss

PHOTOGRAPHIC
Reportage: Meiji Jinku,
Tokyo, Chikashi Suzuki

Nothing Stops the
Brave, In Memory
of Old Dirty Bastard
(1968-2004); Ni queue
ni tête by Laetitia Benat;
Baudrillard's Theorem
by Mehdi Belhaj Kacem

**PHOTOGRAPHIC
FOLDER**
Skywriting
by Marc Dachy

**DOSSIER USA: DAY
AFTER THE ELECTION**

Letter from Belgrade by
Jonathan Boulting; Some
Thoughts on Bobby
Fischer and Chess by
Julien Chollat-Namy;
Meeting Richard Boyer:
Carpenter, Craftsman by
Beth; Residential Rentals
a Chinese City by Ruben
Dao; Portrait of Jan
Mot by Manon de Boer;
Milan Seen by Marina
Faust, Andrea Lissoni,
Carlo Antonelli; A Foot,
a Leg by Ferdinand
Gouzon

PHOTOGRAPHIC FOLDER
The Chronicles; Notes on the Cinema by Nikola Chesnais, Elein Fleiss, Ferdinand Gouzon, Sébastien Jamain; A Whole Pile of Books by Dominique Gonzalez-Foerster; Sequence by Sylvain Fontaine; American Story by Jeffrey Rian; Punch's Secret Diary by Nicola Sornaga; Interview of a Mother by Nakako Hayashi; Seasonal Affects by Sharon Mesmer; Cult Object by Gérard Duguet-Grasser; A Street by Elein Fleiss; Extract of Correspondence by Raphaël Nadjari

THE PURPLE JOURNAL 4
Spring

120 pages
black and white
full color
27.5 x 21 cm
10.8 x 8.3 in

COVER
Chikashi Suzuki

JANUARY JOURNAL
Paris, France: Status Report, 10 Years by Nicolas Mir Chaikin

REPORT
Joinville-le-Pont, Elein Fleiss and Henry Roy; Room With a View (View Without a Room) by Beth Yahp; Photo Report: Cafe Multen, Tokyo by Anders Edström; From Transmission to Transition by Vladimir Sojat; Report: The Other China, The Other Tibet by Ruben Dao; Picasso Without Cherry Blossoms by Sébastien Jamain

DOSSIER
Train Stories by Laetitia Benat, Stéphane Benoit, Manon de Boer, Oscar van den Boogaard, Jonathan Boulting, Elein Fleiss, Federico Nicolao, Jeff Rian, Tiphaine Samoyault; Do Not Skip Class or You Will Go to Jail by Joe Maynard; Venice, Second Year, First Month by Lewis Baltz

FROM ELSEWHERE, HERE... Facts and Photographs

TRAVEL DIARY
Notes from Buenos Aires by Szymon Zaleski; The Life of Jean Boghici; Squalor and The Ineffable Beauty of Passing Time by Gérard Duguet-Grasser; Portrait: Sarah Adler by Amit Berlowitz; He Not Busy Being Born is Busy Dying by Yannick Haenel

**COLLECTION OF GARMENTS OF THE SPRING
THE CHRONICLES**
Notes on the Cinema by Laetitia Benat, Ferdinand Gouzon, Sébastien Jamain, Tiphaine Samoyault; Misunderstandings by Gary Indiana; Dylaniana by Daniel Bismuth; A Whole Pile of Books by Dominique Gonzalez-Foerster; Sequence by Amit Berlowitz; Interview of a Mother by Nakako Hayashi; American Story by Jeffrey Rian; Seasonal Affects by Sharon Mesmer; Cult Object by Gérard Duguet-Grasser; A Street by Elein Fleiss; Extract of Correspondence by Raphaël Nadjari

THE PURPLE JOURNAL 5
Summer

116 pages
black & white
full color
27.5 x 21 cm
10.8 x 8.3 cm

COVER
Amit Berlowitz

CONTENTS
May Journal; And in the Rear Window, We'll See the Night Turning by Gérard Duguet-Grasser

PORTRAIT OF A CITY
Ivry-sur-Seine by Elein Fleiss & Henry Roy

The Pigeon by Kumiko Muraoka; Letter from Belgrade by Jonathan Boulting

REPORT
Gershon and Zila Tamir by Amit Berlowitz; Depraved Perspectives by Matthieu Orléan; The Culinary Revolution in Sichuan by Ruben Dao; Bread and Bounty by Beth Yahp; Opium is the Opium of the People by Tiphaine Samoyault

DOSSIER
Around a Building by Laetitia Benat, Cédrick Eymenier, Jean-Michel Fradkin, Ferdinand Gouzon, Alain Lacroix, Jeffrey Rian, Tiphaine Samoyault

FACTS AND PHOTOGRAPHS
From Elsewhere, Here...

Sparks Alive in the Foreground, the Back Remaining Dark by Nicholas Mir Chaikin; 7474 Promises by David Berman; Meeting with Nami by Eve Couturier; Portrait: Arsinée Khanjian by Amit Berlowitz; Japanese April by Elein Fleiss

FASHION
Collection of Summer Garments

THE CHRONICLES
Notes on the Cinema by Laetitia Benat, Yannick Haenel, Sébastien Jamain, Tiphaine Samoyault, Szymon Zaleski; Sequences by Laetitia Benat; Notes on a Book by Alain Lacroix, Federico Nicolao Dylaniana by Daniel Bismuth; American Story by Jeffrey Rian; Interview of a Mother by Nakako Hayashi; Misunderstandings by Gary Indiana; Seasonal Affects by Sharon Mesmer; Notes on Art by Sébastien Jamain; A Street by Elein Fleiss; Extract of Correspondence by Raphaël Nadjari

THE PURPLE JOURNAL 6
Fall/Winter 2005/2006

137 pages
black & white
full color
27.5 x 21 cm
10.8 x 8.3 in

COVER
Stephen Sprott

CONTENTS
Diary of the Equinox by Gérard Duguet-Grasser; Ten Propositions About Animality by Tiphaine Samoyault; Beloved Haiti by Henry Roy; Presence of Ingrid Thulin by Alain Lacroix; Black Market Cinema by Ruben Dao

PORTRAIT OF A CITY
Bagneux by Elein Fleiss and Henry Roy

Ten Words: Small Winter Lexicon by Martine Aballéa, Dike Blair, Sabisha Friedberg, Boris Lehman, Gaëlle Obiégly, Katja Rahlwes, Karen Volkman, Antek Walzcak, Roger White

REPORT
Japanese Class by Anders Edström; Back to Wanda & Barbara Loden by Manon de Boer; Western Europe or the Progressive Disappearance of Angels by Elein Fleiss

FACTS AND PHOTOGRAPHS
From Elsewhere, Here...

DOSSIER
About a Disaster
Nicholas Mir Chaikin, Marcella Durand, Bonny Finberg, Tabitha Haggerty, Sharon Mesmer, Andy Podell, Nick Tosches, Elizabeth Underwood, Phillip Ward

PORTRAIT
Davida Kroll by Amit Berlowitz; Perfect Murder by Anne-Laure Keib

REPORT
Travel to Ohrid by Katarina Radovic & Jonathan Boulting; Night Landscape by Laetitia Benat

DOSSIER
Concert Memories;
Daniel Bismuth, Michel
Cloup, Eve Couturier,
Bonny Finberg,
Mark Fishman, Marc
Giannesini, Yannick
Haenel, Anne-Laure
Keib, Andrea Lissoni,
Lee Ranaldo, Yayako
Uchida

FASHION
Collection of Winter
Garments

CHRONICLES
Notes on the Cinema
by Laetitia Benat,
Elein Fleiss, Tiphaine
Samoyault; Sequences
by Sébastien Jamain;
Notes on a Book by
Laetitia Benat, Daniel
Bismuth; American
Story by Jeffrey
Rian; Why People
Have a Garden by
Nakako Hayashi;
Misunderstandings by
Gary Indiana; Dylaniana
by Daniel Bismuth;
Seasonal Affects by
Sharon Mesmer; Notes
on Art by Yannick
Haenel; A Street by
Elein Fleiss; Extract
of Correspondence by
Raphaël Nadjari

PURPLE FASHION 3

416 pages
full color
28.3 x 20.7 cm
11.1 x 8.2 in

COVER
Terry Richardson

PURPLE NEWS

BEST OF THE SEASON
By Terry Richardson
and Chloë Sevigny

SUMMER ELEMENTS
2005 By Pierre Even

PURPLE INTERVIEWS
Ashley Bickerton with
Alison M. Gingeras;
Chuck Palahniuk
with Yan Céh; The
McGuffin Institute
with Gary Indiana;
Los Super Elegantes
with Pablo Léon de la
Barra; Eminem with
Yan Céh; Jess Franco
with Matthieu Orléan;
Jonathan Meese with
Christine Macel; Yann
Andréa with Anna
Dubosc

**PURPLE WOMEN
SPRING/SUMMER
2005**
Gracepunk by Anette
Aurell; Goin'out by
Katja Rahlwes; Actrices
& Artists by Camille
Vivier; Little Glitz Girl
by Terry Richardson;
Belgrade by Alex
Antitch; Who's Afraid of
Red, Yellow and Blue by
Giasco Bertoli; Concret
Ginga by Marcelo
Krasilcic; Afternoon by
Vanina Sorrenti; Just
Married by Pierre Even;
Paintings Christophe
Brunnquell

PURPLE BEAUTY
Bijou by Vava Ribeiro;
Uniformity by Kenshu
Shintsubo; Faits Divers,
drawings by Emmanuelle
Mafille; Fifteen by
Martynka Wawrzyniak

**PURPLE MEN SPRING/
SUMMER 2005**
Insiders by Martien
Mulder; Dior Homme
by Gus Van Sant; 853
Kamikaze by Hedi
Slimane; Tokyo, City of
Golf by Takashi Homma

VISUAL ESSAY
Naked by Vanessa
Beecroft; Leave a
Dog Alone by Rita
Ackermann; 1993/2005
by Inez van Lamsweerde
& Vinoodh Matadin;
Purple America by
Andro Wekua

**THE HIPPIE
DRAWINGS,
THE RICHARD PRINCE
PURPLE BOOK
A SPECIAL EDITION
FOR PURPLE
FASHION 3**

black & white,
28.3 x 20.7 cm
11.1 x 8.2 in

PURPLE FASHION 4

416 pages
full color
20.7 x 28.3 cm
11.1 x 8.2 in

COVER
Terry Richardson

PURPLE NEWS
New York by Glenn
O'Brien; Shanghai
by Miltos Manetas;
Mexico by Pablo León
de la Barra; Chicago by
Valérie Shields

**WINTER ELEMENTS
2005/2006**
By Pierre Even

BEST OF THE SEASON
By Terry Richardson

PURPLE INTERVIEWS
John Baldessari with
Hans Ulrich Obrist; Jun
Takahashi with Olivier
Zahm; Mickey Rourke
with Olivier Zahm, Seth
Goldfarb, Alex Botolow
& Pink; Nicolle Meyer
with Olivier Zahm; Rick
Owens with Olivier
Zahm; Ellen Allien with
Yan Céh; Wilhelm Sasnal
with Craig Garrett

PURPLE FASHION
Soft Drag by Anuschka
Blommers & Niels
Schumm; Shootin'
from the Hip by Jork
Weismann; Shannon
Click by Richard Kern;
My Kingdom by Daniel
Jackson; Should I Get
Married? by Martynka
Wawrzyniak; Drugs and
Medicine by Viviane
Sassen

PURPLE MEN
Helden by Philip
Gay; Tim Jefferies by
Stéphane Gautronneau;
Hot Honest by Tobias
Zarius

PURPLE BEAUTY
One Piece, One
Model, One Look by
Katja Rahlwes; Sweet
Summer Sweat by
Bettina Komenda; New
Generation Hollywood
by Vava Ribeiro;
Pierre Hardy by Harri
Peccinotti; Paradise
Found by Katerina Jebb;
Versailles in June by
Laetitia Benat

VISUAL ESSAY
Half the Sky by Miltos
Manetas; The Feast
of the Beast by Rita
Ackermann; Brooke
Shields by Richard
Prince; Untitled 1999
by Stefano Pilati;
Kristen McMenany by
Juergen Teller

**INTERZONE,
THE HEDI SLIMANE
PURPLE BOOK
A SPECIAL EDITION
FOR PURPLE
FASHION 4**

black & white
28.3 x 20.7 cm
11.1 x 8.2 in

**THE PURPLE
JOURNAL 7**
Spring

112 pages
black & white
full color
27.5 x 21 cm
10.8 x 8.3 in

COVER
Laetitia Benat

CONTENTS
Dossier France in the
Conversation by
Yannis Arzimanoglou,
Marina Faust, Jonathan
Hallam, Mariko Inoue,
Kumiko Muraoka, Katja
Rahlwes, Szymon
Zaleski

**FACTS AND
PHOTOGRAPHS**
From Elsewhere, Here...

LETTERS FROM
Pescara by Gérard
Duguet-Grasser;
New York by Nick
Tosches; Amsterdam
by Henry Roy; Burano
by Federico Nicolao;
Austin by Elizabeth
Underwood; Reykjavik
by Paul Lydon; Belgrade
by Jonathan Boulting

VIEWS FROM
New York by Lila
Heller; Hong Kong by
Elein Fleiss; Kirkenes
by Banu Cennetoglu;
Shanghai by Vikram
Kansara

CITIES AROUND PARIS
Alfortville by Elein
Fleiss & Henry Roy

**TOPOGRAPHY
OF A CITY**
The Turin Chronicles by
Laetitia Benat, Cédrick
Eymenier, Elein Fleiss,
Yannick Haenel, Jean-
Jacques Palix, Henry
Roy, Tiphaine Samoyault

PURPLE GALLERY #1
Henry Roy

FASHION
Collection of Garments
for Spring/Summer
2006

PORTRAIT
Hiam Abbass by Amit
Berlowitz

THE CHRONICLES
Losing by Gaelle
Obiégly; Architecture
by Arnoldo Rivkin;
American Story by
Jeffrey Rian; Notes
on the Cinema by
Eve Couturier, Gaelle
Obiégly, Pierre
Weiss; Notes on Art
by Andrea Lissoni;
Misunderstandings by
Gary Indiana; Dylaniana
by Daniel Bismuth;
Notes on a Book by
Béatrice Leca, Daniel
Bismuth; Seasonal
Affects by Sharon
Mesmer; Why People
Have a Garden by
Nakako Hayashi; Extract
of Correspondence
by Raphaël Nadjari; A
Street by Elein Fleiss

**THE PURPLE
JOURNAL 8**
Summer

109 pages
black & white
color
27.5 x 21 cm
10.8 x 8.3 in

COVER
Henry Roy

CONTENTS
Memories Classified
According Their Degree
of Brightness by
Tiphaine Samoyault;
Bukowski or the CPE
by Henry Roy; Views
of Sao Paulo by Elein
Fleiss; Collages,
2006 by Christophe
Brunnquell; Days of
Strike in Saint-Denis
by Tiphaine Samoyault;
My Life as a Student,
Kosuke Tanizaki by
Elein Fleiss; New York
Demonstrations by Alex
Antitch; Lower East
Side Transfer by Vikram
Kansara

DOSSIER
France in the
Conversation

PHOTOGRAPHS
From Elsewhere, Here...

LETTER FROM
Belgrade by Jonathan
Boulting

PURPLE GALLERY #2
Amit Berlowitz

CITIES AROUND PARIS
Clichy-la-Garenne by
Elein Fleiss and
Henry Roy

LETTER FROM
Brussels by Szymon
Zaleski; Letter from
Vienna by Gaelle
Obiégly; Views from
Rio de Janeiro by Elein
Fleiss; Bunraku, the
Art of Ningyo-Joruri by
Marc Dachy; Emmanuel
Boos, Ceramic Artist
by Laetitia Benat; Dare
Wright by Danièle
Gibrat; Views from
Istanbul by Banu
Cennetoglu

FASHION
Collection of Garments
for Spring/Summer
2006

THE CHRONICLES
Seasonal Affects
by Sharon Mesmer;
Misunderstandings
by Gary Indiana; A
Street by Elein Fleiss;
Notes on the Cinema
by Elein Fleiss, Gaelle
Obiégly, Pierre Weiss;
Dylaniana by Daniel
Bismuth; Loosing by
Gaelle Obiégly; Notes
on a Book by Bonny
Finberg; Notes on
Architecture by Arnoldo
Rivkin; Intstants by
Alexandra Koubichkine;
New Orleans Gypsy by
Elizabeth Underwood;
Accessible Happiness by
Gérard Duguet-Grasser;
Why People Have a
Garden by Nakako
Hayashi; Notes on Art
by Dike Blair

**THE PURPLE
JOURNAL 9**
Summer

109 pages
black & white
full color
27.5 x 21 cm
10.8 x 8.3 in

COVER
Laetitia Benat

Hour Arithmetic Kumiko
Muraoka; The Typical
Trick by Sébastien
Jamain; Vacation
Postcards by Tiphaine
Samoyault; The Future
by Gaelle Obiégly;
Letter from Sainte Anne
by Elisabeth Obadia;
Portrait, Lizzi Bougatsos
by Laetitia Benat

**FRANCE IN THE
CONVERSATION**
Interview with Xian
Zhen Lui

CITIES AROUND PARIS
Boulogne-Billancourt by
Elein Fleiss and
Henry Roy

The Refuge of Ueno
by Mariko Inoue

DOCUMENTS
Mario Savio, Berkeley,
1964 with Introduction
by Gary Indiana; The
University of Buenos
Aires by Florencia
Alvarez & Andres
Lehmann

**ELEMENTAL
REVELATIONS**
By Martine Aballéa,
Geoffrey Cruickshank-
Hagenbuckle, Marina
Faust, Mark Fishman,
Henry Roy, Tiphaine
Samoyault, Szymon
Zaleski

PURPLE GALLERY #3
Laetitia Benat

George van Dam,
Violonist by Elein
Fleiss; Dialogue with
Modernism by Sophie
Bueno-Boutellier, Niels
Trannois, Jean-Michel
Wicker; Tomb of Moïse
Franco by Daniel Franco

PHOTOGRAPHS
From Elsewhere, Here...

DOCUMENTS
Letters from Beirut by
Hanady Salman, Rasha
Salti, Zena el-Khalil
Gush Shalom Messages;
Europe Slowly Poisened
by Daniel Franco

FASHION
Collections of Garments
for Fall and Winter;
Garments for Fall and
Winter by Jonathan
Hallam

THE CHRONICLES
Accessible Happiness by
Gérard Duguet-Grasser;
Seasonal Affects
by Sharon Mesmer;
The Most Beautiful
Film in the World
by Yannick Haenel;
Misunderstandings by
Gary Indiana; Dylaniana
by Daniel Bismuth; Why
People Have a Garden
by Nakako Hayashi;
Notes on Architecture
by Arnoldo Rivkin;
Instants by Alexandra
Koubichkine; Notes on
Art by Jeffrey Rian;
Losing Gaelle by Obiégly
A Street by Elein Fleiss

PURPLE FASHION MAGAZINE 5
Spring/Summer

432 pages
full color
30 x 23 cm
11.8 x 9 in

COVER
Inez van Lamsweerde & Vinoodh Matadin

PURPLE NEWS
Alicudi by Paola Pivi; Isle of Vieques by Glenn O'Brien; Ile d'Yeu by Catherine Despont; A Private Island by Jeff Rian; Shelter Island, New York by Valerie Shields; Jamaica by Massimo Torrigiani

SUMMER ELEMENTS
Shoes and Lingerie by Vanina Sorrenti

BEST OF THE SEASON
By Terry Richardson and Stéphane Feugère

PURPLE INTERVIEWS
John Galliano with Olivier Zahm; Haider Ackermann with Olivier Zahm and Samuel Dira; Glenn O'Brien with Olivier Zahm; Ingrid Caven with Olivier Zahm; Andreas Angelidakis with Miltos Manetas; Miranda July with Hans Ulrich Obrist; Raphaël Nadjari with Ariel Wizman; Scout Niblett, Andy Warhol's Questions with Yan Céh

PURPLE STORIES
Samedi the Deafness by Jesse Ball; Detroit by Payam Sharifi

PURPLE FASHION WOMEN
Carine Roitfeld by Inez van Lamsweerde & Vinoodh Matadin; The Private Case by Terry Richardson and Richard Prince; Summertime Blues by Johnathan Hallam; Portrait of the Artist as a Young Man by Alexei Hay; Yves Saint Laurent by Stefano Pilati and Juergen Teller; Bless Homes First Retrospective; Black Beauty by Désiree Heiss and Jork Weismann; Nothing But Dresses by Katja Rahlwes; Gender Bender by Vava Ribeiro; Chloë Sevigny by Inez van Lamsweerde & Vinoodh Matadin

PURPLE FASHION MEN
Peter Saville's Estate by Donald Christie; Men's Standards Revisited by Philippe Gay, Juergen Teller, Bettina Komenada, Stéphane Feugère; Gotham City by Terry Richardson

PURPLE TRAVEL
Villa La Cañada by Todd Cole; Privacy by Le Corbusier by Pierre Even, Riviera Villas by Olivier Ansellem; Villa Noailles by Naoki Takizawa

PURPLE BEAUTY
Casque d'Or by Anuschka Blommers and Niels Schumm

VISUAL ESSAYS
Bird Kisses by Aya Takano; The Wrong Gallery; The American Upper Class by Hugo Tillman; Roman Photo by Richard Kern

A MEMORIAL TRIBUTE TO BOB RICHARDSON

PURPLE LAST PAGE
Marilyn Manson by Christophe Brunnquell

ED IN JAPAN, THE JUERGEN TELLER PURPLE BOOK A SPECIAL EDITION FOR PURPLE FASHION MAGAZINE 5

black & white
28.3 x 20.7 cm
11.1 x 8.2 in

PURPLE FASHION MAGAZINE 6
Fall/Winter

432 pages
full color
30 x 23 cm
11.8 x 9.0 in

COVER
Terry Richardson

FASHION REPORT
Paris Shows by Stéphane Feugère

PURPLE NEWS
France by Jeff Rian; America by Catherine Despont; Japan by David Gordon; Russia by Payam Sharifi; Senegal by Glenn O'Brien; Panama by J.G. Ballard and Richard Prince

WINTER ELEMENTS 2006/2007
by Pierre Even

BEST OF THE SEASON
Fall/Winter 2006/2007 by Terry Richardson

PURPLE INTERVIEWS
Charlotte Gainsbourg with Olivier Zahm; Riccardo Tisci with Olivier Zahm; Gardar Eide Einarsson with Bob Nickas; Chris Kraus with Gary Indiana; Proenza Schouler with Olivier Zahm; Charlotte Marionneau with Yan Céh; Christopher Wool with Glenn O'Brien; Mark Parker with Carlo Antonelli; Leelee Sobieski with Olivier Zahm; M. Blash with Olivier Zahm

PURPLE FASHION WOMEN
Camille Bidault Waddington by Horst Diekgerdes; Infrared Dreams by Alexei Hay; Helena Christensen by Inez van Lamsweerde and Vinoodh Matadin; The Birds by Katja Rahlwes; The Genealogy of Morals by Serge Leblon; Housewear by Liz Collins; Sport Couture by Desiree Heiss and Jork Weismann; Role Reversal by Vava Ribeiro

PURPLE FASHION MEN
Marc Jacobs by Juergen Teller; Pete Doherty by Hedi Slimane; Yves Saint Laurent Cruise by Nathaniel Goldberg

PURPLE STORIES
By David Gordon

PURPLE TRAVEL
Air by Heinz Peter Knes

NEW YORK DOLLS
By Terry Richardson

PURPLE BEAUTY
Veiled by Katsuya Kamo; Dusty Pink by Olivier Zahm

VISUAL ESSAY
She Smiles For The Camera by Christopher Wool

GOOD MORNING NEW YORK, THE RITA ACKERMANN PURPLE BOOK A SPECIAL EDITION FOR PURPLE FASHION MAGAZINE 6

black & white
28.3 x 20.7 cm
11.1 x 8.2 in

TO BE CONTINUED

FIRST PUBLISHED IN THE UNITED STATES OF AMERICA IN 2008
BY RIZZOLI INTERNATIONAL PUBLICATIONS, INC.
300 Park Avenue South, New York, NY 10010
www.rizzoliusa.com

CONCEPT
Olivier Zahm

EDITOR
Martynka Wawrzyniak

ASSOCIATE EDITOR
Jordan Hruska

PROJECT COORDINATOR
Chris Steighner

PHOTO EDITING
Christophe Brunnquell and Elein Fleiss

TEXTS
Bruce Benderson, Dike Blair, Elein Fleiss, Kim Gordon, Jordan Hruska, Gary Indiana,
Sébastien Jamain, Mehdi Belhaj Kacem, Jutta Koether, Bob Nickas, Gaëlle Obiégly,
Glenn O'Brien, Jeff Rian, Stéphanie Moisdon, Éric Troncy and Olivier Zahm.

TRANSLATIONS
Molly Stevens

ILLUSTRATIONS
Christophe Brunnquell

STILL PHOTOGRAPHY
Andrea Thompson

INSIDE JACKET PHOTOGRAPHY
Camille Roman

EDITED, ART DIRECTED and DESIGNED at M/M (PARIS)

2008 2009 2010 2011 / 10 9 8 7 6 5 4 3 2 1

Distributed in the U.S. trade by Random House, New York
Printed in China

ISBN-10: 0-8478-3020-9
ISBN-13: 978-0-8478-3020-6

Library of Congress Catalog Control Number: 2007942625